Criminal Justice
Recent Scholarship

Edited by
Marilyn McShane and Frank P. Williams III

A Series from LFB Scholarly

Genes and Abuse as Causes of Offending

Jamie Vaske

LFB Scholarly Publishing LLC
El Paso 2011

Library of Congress Cataloging-in-Publication Data

Vaske, Jamie, 1981-
  Genes and abuse as causes of offending / Jamie Vaske.
    p. cm.
  Includes bibliographical references and index.
  ISBN 978-1-59332-458-2 (hardcover : alk. paper)
  1. Criminal behavior. 2. Substance abuse. 3. Victims of crimes--
Psychological aspects. I. Title.
  HV6080.V28 2011
  364.2--dc22
                                        2011011078

ISBN 978-1-59332-458-2

Printed on acid-free 250-year-life paper.

Manufactured in the United States of America.

Table of Contents

v

List of Tables

List of Figures

Acknowledgements

I dedicate this book to my parents, to my family and friends, and to the University of Cincinnati School of Criminal Justice faculty and students. This work would not have been possible without your dedication, knowledge, and support. I thank Drs. Jeffrey T. Ward, John Wooldredge, Michael Benson and Constance Chapple for their comments on this study. I would like to give a special thank you to Dr. John Paul Wright for his unwaivering guidance and mentorship. Finally, I would like to acknowledge the scholars and practitioners who devote their lives to investigating the complexities of human development, for their work provides insights into who we are as humans and how we behave.

CHAPTER ONE
Introduction

Childhood and adolescent victimization have been linked to higher levels of criminal behavior. For instance, studies have found that childhood abuse is associated with antisocial behavior during early adolescence, delinquency, substance abuse, and criminal arrest in adulthood (Hussey, Chang, & Kotch, 2006; Stouthamer-Loeber, Loeber, Homish, & Wei, 2001; Widom, 1989a). Other forms of victimization, such as adolescent violent victimization and intimate partner violence, are also related to criminal behavior and substance use during adolescence and adulthood (Roberts, Klein, & Fisher, 2003; Singer, 1986). The positive relationship between offending and childhood and adolescent victimization has been reported across studies that use officially reported measures of abuse (Widom, 1989a), self-reported measures of abuse (DeHart, 2004), data from offender samples (Kingree, Phan, & Thompson 2003), data from general population samples (Fitzgerald, 2002), and official and self-reported measures of offending (Smith & Thornberry, 1995). Thus, victimization appears to be a robust correlate of criminal behavior.

Criminological research has shown that victimization plays an important role in the etiology of offending, especially among females. Yet, there are at least four caveats that need to be considered when examining this hypothesis. First, the relationship between victimization and offending may be contingent upon the timing and context of abuse (Kruttschnitt & MacMillian, 2006). For instance, Ireland, Smith, and Thornberry's (2002) analysis of youths from the Rochester Youth Development Study revealed that childhood maltreatment was not significantly related to drug use and delinquency during adolescence. Their results, however, revealed that adolescent maltreatment was positively related to adolescent drug use, general delinquency, and violent crime. Other studies have reported that the context of abuse (i.e., parent vs. partner) may condition the effects of victimization on antisocial outcomes, such as psychological distress and criminal behavior (Lang, Stein, Kennedy, & Foy, 2004). In light of this evidence, it is important to simultaneously evaluate the effects of childhood and adolescent victimization on various types of criminal behavior.

Second, research has shown that victimization is not randomly distributed across individuals, and that certain individuals are more likely to be victimized than other individuals (Farrell & Pease, 1993). That is, an individual's probability of victimization may be a function of his or her personality traits and behavior (Hindelang, Gottfredson, & Garofalo, 1978; Miethe, Stafford, & Long, 1987). For instance, individuals who exhibit greater antisocial personality traits are more likely to be victimized than individuals who do not exhibit these traits (Schreck, 1999). The origin of antisocial traits is a debatable issue, but twin studies have shown that a substantial percentage of variation in antisocial personality traits is attributable to genetic factors (Plomin, 1990). In addition, a recent twin study revealed that genetic factors explained approximately 25 percent of the variation in intimate partner violence (Hines & Saudino, 2004). In light of these lines of evidence, it may be expected that individuals' probability of victimization may be related to genetic factors. That is, individuals who have a genetic predisposition towards antisocial personality traits may evoke negative reactions from others or actively select themselves into high risk situations that increase their risk of victimization. This is referred to as an active or evocative gene-environment correlation.

Third, studies have shown that a substantial percentage of abused and victimized youths do not engage in criminal behavior (Cicchetti, Rogosch, & Sturge-Apple, 1993). Widom's (1989a, 1989b) analyses of 667 abused and 667 non-abused children revealed that approximately 25 percent of abused youths were arrested during adolescence or adulthood. Other studies report similar figures (Kurtz, Kurtz, & Jarvis, 1991; Werner & Smith, 1989). This suggests that some additional factors are needed to explain why some abused males and females engage in crime, while others do not. Traditionally, criminologists have examined whether sociological and psychological factors may explain why some abused youths engage in crime and others do not (Aceves & Cookston, 2007). There is, however, some evidence that genetic factors may explain variation in individuals' responses to victimization (Caspi et al., 2002; Scheid et al., 2007). For instance, Jaffee et al. (2005) found that the effects of peer victimization on antisocial behavior were strongest for females who were in the highest genetic risk category. Beaver's (2008a) analyses showed that males who carried dopaminergic genetic polymorphisms were more sensitive to the criminogenic effects of childhood sexual abuse than males who did not carry the genetic polymorphisms. In sum, results from the behavioral genetics literature suggest that differences in genetic polymorphisms may help explain resilience to victimization *within* genders through a gene X environment interaction.

Finally, research suggests that gender conditions the effects of victimization and gene X victimization interactions on antisocial behavior. Studies have shown that females are more sensitive to the effects of victimization (English, Widom, & Brandford, 2002; Rivera & Widom, 1990; Widom, 1989a), yet other studies have shown that males are more sensitive to the effects of stressful life events, such as victimization (McGloin & Widom, 2001; Werner & Smith, 1989). A similar pattern of results is found in the literature that examines whether genetic factors interact with victimization to predict antisocial behavior. Two studies have found that there are no gender differences in the gene X abuse interactions on antisocial behavior (Jaffee et al., 2005; Widom & Brzustowicz, 2006), but one study has only found a significant interaction for boys (Beaver, 2008a) and one study has only found a significant interaction for girls (Brendgen, Boivin, Vitaro, Girard, Dionne, & Pérusse, 2008). The evidence is mixed on whether males or females are more sensitive to the effects of victimization and gene X victimization, but there is a general consensus that gender differences in the effects of victimization and gene X victimization interactions exist.

Gender differences in resilience may partially be a function of gender differences in genetic expression, or some other gender specific process. For instance, a male and a female may both have the same genetic polymorphism and they may both experience the same level of violent victimization. However, the female's genetic polymorphism may be expressed at a higher rate within the brain than the male's genetic polymorphism, due to higher levels of estrogen and progesterone. Subsequently, this higher level of genetic expression may increase females' sensitivity to victimization. Thus, gender differences in the expression of genetic polymorphisms may explain differences in resiliency to victimization *between* genders (gender X gene X environment interaction).

Statement of the Problem

Few researchers have examined the interplay of genetic factors and variables traditionally found in victimization literature from a criminological point of view. Genetic factors and genetically influenced processes (i.e., low self-control) may be related to higher levels of victimization (rGE) (Hines & Saudino, 2004; Wierzbicki, 1989). In addition, studies have shown that genetic factors moderate the effects of victimization on criminal behavior (gene X environment interaction) (Caspi et al., 2002; Ducci et al., 2007; Huizinga et al., 2006). Yet, many of these studies did not investigate whether these effects are invariant across gender. This is surprising in light of evidence that suggests males and females respond differently to environmental stressors (Silberg et al., 1999), and that genetic expression differs across genders (Nguyen & Disteche, 2006; Welle, Tawil, & Thornton, 2008). The current investigation will extend upon this growing literature base by exploring the roles that genetic and environmental factors may play in criminal behavior and substance abuse for males and females.

The current study will examine two types of gene-environment relationships that are related to criminal behavior and substance use for males and females. First, it will investigate whether five genetic polymorphisms (DAT1, DRD2, DRD4, 5HTTLPR, and MAOA) are indirectly related to criminal behavior and to alcohol/drug use through different types of victimization (genetic polymorphism → victimization → criminal behavior). This indirect effect via environmental variables is considered a gene-environment correlation (rGE). Second, the current investigation will examine whether the five genetic polymorphisms moderate the effects of different types of victimization on criminal behavior and alcohol/drug use (GxE). These conditioning or moderating effects are referred to as gene-environment interactions (GxE). All analyses will be separated by gender.

This study explores the following research questions:

1. Do genetic polymorphisms (DAT1, DRD2, DRD4, 5HTTLPR, and MAOA) increase the likelihood that an individual will experience childhood neglect, childhood physical abuse, adolescent violent victimization, and adolescent intimate partner violence during adolescence (gene-environment correlation)?
2. Do these gene-environment correlations vary by gender?
3. Do genetic polymorphisms (DAT1, DRD2, DRD4, 5HTTLPR, and MAOA) increase individuals' sensitivity to the criminogenic effects of childhood sexual victimization, childhood neglect, childhood physical abuse, adolescent violent victimization, and adolescent intimate partner violence (gene X environment interaction)?
4. Do the moderating effects of the dopaminergic, serotonergic, and monoamine oxidase A polymorphisms vary by gender (gender X gene X environment interaction)?

CHAPTER TWO

The Role of Victimization in Criminal Behavior, Alcohol Abuse, and Substance Use for Males and Females

Introduction

Individuals who are victims of childhood abuse, childhood neglect, violent victimization, or intimate partner violence are at an increased risk of displaying antisocial behaviors. It is likely that victimization is linked to antisocial behavior through a series of neuropsychological/genetic, cognitive, and sociological processes. For instance, individuals who are abused in childhood or adolescence may experience a cascade of changes in genetic expression, HPA axis activity, neurotransmitter activity, and brain structure and function. As a result, abused individuals may display cognitive and psychological problems ranging from depression to antisocial personality disorder (APD). Mental disorders, such as depression or APD, often include a range of cognitive distortions that may cause victims to misperceive events and circumstances, such as discounting positive aspects of things or being overly suspicious of others. These mental disorders can take a toll on one's social relationships, and victims may feel rejected or isolated from prosocial others. In addition, victims' cognitive and psychological problems may cause them to act out in impulsive or erratic ways, such as abusing drugs, getting into fights, or being promiscuous. These behaviors may further reinforce the neuropsychological and cognitive changes that were triggered by a victimization experience; thus creating stability and continuity in maladaptive or antisocial behaviors. This chapter will review the literature on victimization and antisocial behaviors. The first section will discuss the empirical research linking childhood abuse & neglect, intimate partner violence, and violent victimization to criminal behavior and substance abuse. This section will also review the literature that shows that cognitive and sociological risk factors may mediate the effects of victimization on antisocial behavior. The second section will discuss the neuropsychological changes that may occur in response to victimization. These neuropsychological changes may underlie the relationships between victimization, cognitive distortions, and antisocial behavior.

Childhood and Adolescent Abuse and Neglect
A large number of studies have examined whether abuse or neglect have a direct, independent effect on antisocial behavior. The evidence from both prospective and retrospective studies shows that childhood abuse and neglect have a significant effect on offending and substance use. For instance, Widom and her colleagues have shown that abuse and neglect are significantly related to both violent and nonviolent criminal behavior during adolescence and adulthood. Using data from of 908 victims of physical/sexual abuse and 667 matched controls, these analyses revealed that youths who were abused were more likely to be arrested as a juvenile and as an adult, especially for violent crimes (Widom, 1989b; Maxfield & Widom, 1996). Widom and Maxfield (2001) reported that childhood abuse increased the likelihood of juvenile arrest by 59 percent and increased likelihood of adult arrest by 28 percent. The prevalence and frequency of arrest during adulthood was also significantly higher among the abused youths compared to the matched controls (Widom, 1989a). Rivera and Widom (1990) found that the age of onset for delinquent behavior was significantly earlier for abused youths. Finally, abused and neglected youths were more likely to be comorbid for non-violent arrests and substance abuse than non-abused controls (Widom & White, 1997).

Widom and colleagues have also found that childhood neglect and abuse are related a variety of alcohol and substance use behaviors. For instance, Widom, Schuk, and White (2006) found that abused and neglected youths were more likely to exhibit alcohol and drug use problems in mid-adulthood (average age 40). The authors also found that abused and neglected females were more likely to use illicit substances within the past year, especially marijuana. It is important to note that prior research from Widom and colleagues found that there was no significant difference between abused youths and non-abused youths in the prevalence of drug use in early adulthood (average age 29) (Widom, Weiler, & Cottler, 1999), especially for males (Widom & White, 1997); thus, suggesting that effect of abuse on substance use may not emerge until mid-adulthood for males. Other studies of young and middle aged adults, however, have found that childhood abuse is related to adulthood substance abuse (Wilsnack, Vogeltanz, Klassen, & Harris, 1997).

Additional prospective and matched control studies have also reported a link between childhood abuse and later offending. Zingraff and colleagues (1993) compared the delinquency rates of abused and non-abused youths and found that abused youths had more delinquency petitions to the court (especially for general and status offenses) than non-abused youths. Smith and Thornberry's (1995) analysis of 3,372 youths from the Rochester Youth Development Study found that childhood maltreatment was related to serious self-reported and officially reported delinquency, but maltreatment was not related to minor delinquency. Ireland et al.'s (2002) study of youths from the Rochester Youth Development Study revealed that youths who experienced maltreatment during childhood and adolescence were more likely to exhibit chronic delinquency problems, compared to youths who experienced maltreatment only during childhood or adolescence. Data from the Pittsburgh Youth Study revealed that maltreated boys were more likely to exhibit authority conflict behaviors (i.e., defiant behavior, truancy, running away) and overt behavioral problems (i.e., aggression, physical fighting) (Stouthamer-Loeber et al., 2001). English et al.'s (2002) analysis of 877 abused youths and matched controls found that abused and neglect youths were 4.8 times more likely to have a juvenile arrest, and 2 times more likely to have been arrested as an adult. Siegel and Williams's (2003) comparison of sexually abused youths and matched controls also revealed that childhood sexual abuse was significantly related to offending during juvenile and adulthood, especially violent offending. Finally, Lansford and colleague's (2007) analysis of approximately 600 youths from the Child Development Project revealed that physically abused youths, on average, had higher levels of official and self-reported arrests, officially reported violent offenses, officially reported non-violent offenses, and officially reported status offenses.

Studies that use other methodologies (i.e., retrospective abuse measure, case control, meta-analysis) also show a link between childhood abuse and later antisocial behavior (Kunitz, Levy, McCloskey, & Gabriel, 1998; Widom & Hiller-Sturmhöfel, 2001; Simpson & Miller, 2002). Longitudinal studies that use a retrospective measure of childhood abuse have found evidence of these relationships (Lemmon, 1999; Kendler, Bulik, Silberg, Hettema, Myers, & Prescott, 2000; Herrera & McCloskey, 2003; Lansford, Malone, Stevens, Dodge, Bates, & Pettit, 2006). For instance, Hussey et al.'s (2006) analysis of data from the core wave III Add Health sample revealed that childhood maltreatment was significantly related to alcohol use, marijuana use, and violent offending in adolescence. Results from the Adverse Childhood Experiences Study also show that abused and neglected individuals are more likely to have an early onset of drug use and they are more likely to use drugs over their lifetime (Dube, Williamson, Thompson, Felitti, & Anda, 2004). Case control studies, such as Browne et al.'s (1999) analyses, have also reported that the prevalence of abuse and neglect is exceptionally high among offenders and substance abusers, especially female offenders and female substance abusers (Kingree, Phan, & Thompson, 2003; Belknap & Holsinger, 2006; Messina & Grella, 2006). Dembo et al.'s (1990) analysis of detained juveniles revealed that physical abuse was associated with adolescent cocaine use, and childhood sexual abuse was significantly related to marijuana use in adolescence. Finally, Hubbard and Pratt's (2002) meta-analysis of 97 effect sizes showed that physical and sexual abuse was a significant predictor of female delinquency. Thus, findings from studies that vary in sample composition, sample design, and research design converge to show that abuse and neglect may increase one's risk of offending during adolescence and adulthood.

Despite the substantial amount of evidence that abuse/neglect increases the likelihood of offending, studies have shown that the effect of abuse/neglect may vary by type of maltreatment and also by gender (Dembo et al., 1990; Maxfield & Widom, 1996; Cullerton-Sen, Cassidy, Murray-Close, Cicchetti, Crick, & Rogosch, 2008). Widom and Ames (1994) found that neglect was significantly related to adolescent and adult offending, but sexual abuse and physical abuse were not related to offending. Kingree et al.'s (2003) analysis of 272 incarcerated youths also revealed that recidivism was related to emotional and physical neglect, but recidivism was not related to physical abuse, sexual abuse, or emotional abuse. Thus, it appears as if neglect may have a stronger effect on offending than various types of abuse.

There is also some evidence that females are more sensitive to the criminogenic effects of abuse and neglect than males (Widom, 1989a; Ireland & Widom, 1994; Widom & White, 1997; Lansford, Miller-Johnson, Berlin, Dodge, Bates, & Pettit, 2007). For instance, Cullerton-Sen et al.'s (2008) analysis of 211 maltreated youth and 199 non-maltreated youth revealed that sexual abuse was associated with higher levels of relational aggression for females, but sexual abuse was not associated with males' relational aggression. Further, Widom and colleagues reported that abuse significantly increased females' risk of engaging in violent offenses during adolescence and marijuana use in mid-adulthood, but abuse did not influence males' risk of violent juvenile offending or adult marijuana use (Rivera & Widom, 1990; Widom & Maxfield, 2001; Widom et al., 2006). English et al. (2002) found that abused females were more at risk for violent offending during adolescence and adulthood than abused males. Finally, results from correctional populations have shown that delinquent girls were more likely cite abuse and neglect as reasons for engaging in crime than delinquent boys (Belknap & Holsinger, 2006). These studies suggest that childhood abuse and neglect should have a stronger effect on females' offending and substance use than on male offending and substance use. A growing body of research, however, suggests that males are more sensitive to the effects of childhood abuse and neglect than females (McGloin & Widom, 2001). While it remains unclear whether males or females are more sensitive to the criminogenic effects of victimization, it appears that there are gender differences in the effects of victimization on antisocial behavior.

Pathways linking abuse to offending

Aside from the direct effects of abuse on offending, researchers have argued that abuse may indirectly lead to offending via running away, substance use, and/or poor mental health (Chesney-Lind, 1986; Widom & Hiller-Sturmhöfel, 2001). Many of the early pathways put forth in the literature emerged from ethnographic studies of female delinquents or female offenders (Daly, 1994), while the more recent pathways in the literature emerge from quantitative studies of general population or matched comparison samples (Widom et al., 2006). These various types of studies have helped researchers answer the question "*Why* does abuse increase the risk of antisocial behavior?" or "What is the mediating mechanism linking abuse to antisocial behavior?" Further, many of these studies have found that the pathways linking abuse to antisocial behavior significantly differ for males and females (Goldstein, Flett, & Wekerle, 2010); thus, the reasons why abuse increases the risk of offending may vary across gender.

Chesney-Lind's pathway linking childhood abuse to offending

Chesney-Lind and colleagues have reviewed the life histories of abused females and put forth a model that links childhood and adolescent abuse to delinquency (Chesney-Lind, 1986). This pathway model hypothesizes that females who are abused or neglected by a parent or caregiver will runaway from home to escape such negative treatment. Once girls run away from home, they are often forced (by their circumstances) to engage in illegal behaviors to survive on the street (DeHart, 2004). These coping/survival strategies are shaped by their gender. For instance, girls may be more likely to trade sexual favors for money, lodging, or other goods to aid in their survival, while boys may be more likely to engage in robbery to survive (Chesney-Lind & Shelden, 1998). Entrance into a street lifestyle may then encourage girls' to engage in other types of delinquent behavior, such as substance abuse and robbery (Giordano, Deines, & Cernkovich, 2006).

While scholars frequently couch the relationship between childhood abuse and delinquency in Chesney-Lind's pathways model, few researchers have empirically examined this model. Studies from Widom and colleagues are some of the few studies that have fully tested this pathway into offending. Widom and Ames (1994) analysis of a matched pairs sample of 908 abused and 667 nonabused youths showed that abused or neglected children were more likely to run away than youths who were not abused or neglected. Further, childhood sexual abuse and childhood neglect were significantly associated with arrest for prostitution during adulthood. Their results, however, failed to find that running away during adolescence predicted adulthood prostitution; thus, running away did not mediate the effects of abuse and neglect on prostitution.

Kaufman and Widom's (1999) analysis of the matched pairs sample revealed that running away did not mediate the effects of childhood abuse on juvenile delinquency. More specifically, they found that childhood abuse/neglect had a significant positive effect on whether a juvenile had been arrested during adolescence. This relationship remained virtually unchanged when measures of running away (run away before age 18, run away overnight before age 15, run away more than once before age 15, and arrest for running away) were entered into the equation. The measures of running away had independent effects on the prevalence of juvenile arrest. Thus, childhood abuse/neglect and running away had independent effects on delinquency, but running away did not mediate the relationship between abuse/neglect and dependency.

Finally, using the matched pairs sample from their previous works, Wilson and Widom (2010) examined whether childhood abuse and neglect indirectly increased the risk of adulthood prostitution via early sexual initiation, running away, juvenile crime, and school problems. Their structural equation models showed that childhood physical abuse, sexual abuse, and neglect were associated with earlier initiation in sexual behaviors, a greater likelihood of running away, higher levels of juvenile crime, and higher levels of school problems. However, running away was not significantly associated with prostitution, and the indirect effect involving running away was not statistically significant. These results suggest that running away does not mediate the effects of abuse and neglect on adulthood prostitution; thus, there must be additional reasons why abused and neglected youths are at an increased risk of prostitution.   Other studies have provided partial tests of the pathway model. Miller's (1986) ethnography of 64 female street hustlers revealed that a subgroup of females responded to sexual abuse by running away and using drugs or alcohol.   Her analyses also showed that Hispanic females and Caucasian females were more likely to run away as a way to escape sexual abuse than African American females. Kurtz et al.'s (1991) comparison of abused and non-abused runaways also found that a subgroup of youths (27.7%) ran away in response to experiencing abuse at home.   These results suggest that abused youths are more likely to runaway and more likely to engage in various types of criminal behavior during adulthood (Chesney-Lind & Sheldon, 1998; Gilfus, 1992).

Daly's pathways linking childhood abuse to offending

Daly (1994) analyzed data from 40 female felony offenders and 40 male felony offenders to examine their pathways into felony court. Using information from presentence investigation reports, she was able to identify five types of female felony offenders and four types of male felony offenders.   Each of these offender types had different pathways into felony court.   Childhood abuse and neglect characterized two of the pathways for females and one of the pathways for males.   For females, reports of childhood abuse and neglect were associated with the "street woman" and the "harmed and harming woman."   The street woman's pathway into offending begins by: (a) being abused and subsequently running away to escape abuse; and/or (b) becoming enticed with the criminal lifestyle, and running away to emerse herself into the street life. These women often developed drug addictions and were involved in a wide range of criminal behaviors, including prostitution, stealing, and selling and using drugs.   Harmed and harming women also experienced childhood abuse and neglect, but their abuse experiences often led to severe behavioral problems and violent behavior.   As these girls got older, they often engaged in serious violent behaviors when under the influence of alcohol.

For harmed and harming males, childhood abuse and neglect often led to a "life without purpose" (Daly, 1994, p. 72).   Many of the harmed and harming males did not take an active interest in school or work, and ultimately drifted from one hustle to another. This trajectory for males is different than the pathway for harmed and harming women. For harmed and harming women, their abuse led to the development of violent behavior, especially when they consumed alcohol or drugs. Harmed and harming men, on the other hand, did not routinely engage in alcohol related violent behavior. The defining characteristic of the male harmed and harming trajectory was the co-occurrence of a lack of purpose and substance abuse.

Subsequent researchers have also identified the street woman and harmed and harming woman in their samples. For instance, Reisig et al.'s (2006) analysis of 248 women under community supervision found that eight percent were classified as "street women" and 17 percent were classified as "harmed and harming women." Simpson and colleagues (2006) examined life history data from 351 female offenders who were in jail. The authors found that a group of female offenders fit descriptions of the street women and harmed and harming women subtypes. The women fitting the description of the street woman had more lifetime arrests, lifetime jail terms, lifetime prison terms, and lifetime felony convictions. For the harmed and harming women subtype, these female offenders exhibited higher levels of childhood physical abuse, childhood sexual abuse, using violence against a violent partner, having a romantic partner who engages in crime, experienced intimate partner violence, and had a high school diploma or GED. Finally, Salsbury and VanVoorhis (2009) found evidence of a harmed and harming pathway in their analysis of 300 female probationers. Their analyses revealed that childhood abuse and neglect increased the risk of mental illness, and mental illness was associated with higher levels of substance use. Substance use, in turn, was significantly associated with a greater likelihood of being admitted to prison. This pathway (abuse → mental illness → substance use → prison admission) follows the harmed and harming women pathway. In sum, research has shown that abuse may indirectly lead to criminal behavior via substance abuse and a history of emotional and behavioral problems.

Alternative pathways from abuse to offending and substance abuse

In addition to Chesney-Lind's and Daly's pathways, a number of researchers have put forth alternative hypotheses for why child maltreatment may lead to higher levels of criminal behavior and substance abuse. These hypotheses have been grounded in social learning theory, social control theory, general strain theory, the developmental damage view model, social information processing perspectives, attachment theory, ecodevelopment theory, and various other perspectives. Table 2.1 displays the various alternative pathways that have been put forth in the literature. As shown in the table, childhood abuse and neglect have a wide range of psychological, social, and behavioral consequences. These negative consequences begin in early childhood and extend into mid-adulthood. Thus, childhood maltreatment may directly and indirectly lead to greater criminal behavior and substance use across the life-course.

Intimate Partner Violence

Researchers have noted that a disproportionate percentage of female offenders report that they have been abused by a partner. For instance, Snell and Morton's (1994) analysis of data from 13,986 inmates in state prisons nationwide found that 30 percent of the incarcerated women reported they had been abused by a spouse or ex-spouse, compared to 1 percent of incarcerated males. Also, 27.6 percent of incarcerated females said they were abused by a boyfriend/girlfriend, and only 2 percent of males reported they were abused by a boyfriend/girlfriend. Gilfus (1992) reported that 16 out of 20 incarcerated females in her sample reported that they had been battered by a spouse or partner in their life history interviews. Browne, Miller, & Maguin's (1999) analysis of 150 incarcerated women revealed that 75 percent of the females had been physically abused by an intimate partner in adulthood. Other researchers have more closely examined the role of intimate partner violence in female offenders' lives. DeHart (2004) conducted interviews with 60 incarcerated females in a maximum security prison. She found that victimization was directly and indirectly related to women's offending. Females reported that they would engage in violence as a means to retaliate against their abuser and/or to end their abuse. Also, the female offenders reported that they would have to miss work due to their beatings, or that their partner threatened them with violence if they did not quit a certain job. As a result, women would engage in illegitimate activities to provide money and goods to the household.

While studies of adult female offenders have highlighted the role of intimate partner violence in females' offending (Daly, 1994; DeHart, 2004), other scholars have used data from general population studies to show a link between adolescent intimate partner violence and females' antisocial behavior. Silverman and colleagues (2001) analyzed data from female high school students from the Massachusetts Youth Risk Behavior Survey and found that approximately 20 percent of adolescent females reported that they had been sexually and/or physically abused by a romantic partner. Also, females who were physically and/or sexually abused by a romantic partner had an increased risk of heavy smoking, binge drinking, driving and drinking alcohol, and using cocaine. Data from the National Longitudinal Study of Adolescent Health also revealed that approximately 20 percent of adolescent males and females reported that they were verbally and physically abused by an intimate partner within the past year. Similar to previous studies, the authors found that adolescent intimate partner violence was associated with higher levels of delinquency, substance use, violent behavior, and depression among males and females (Roberts & Klein, 2003; Roberts, Klein, & Fisher, 2003). Roberts and Klein (2003) also reported that adolescent intimate partner violence had a stronger effect on substance use for females than males. Other studies have also shown that adolescent intimate partner violence has a stronger effect on females' substance use than males (Eaton, Davis, Barrios, Brener, & Noonan, 2007).

In sum, adolescent intimate partner violence is quite prevalent among United States teens. Approximately 20 percent report that they have experienced some form of abuse at the hands of an intimate partner. Also, these studies show that adolescent intimate partner violence may be associated with higher levels of offending, especially for females. Thus it is expected that adolescent intimate partner violence should increase the risk of criminal behavior and substance use, and that the associations between intimate partner violence and antisocial behavior may be significantly stronger for females than males.

Table 2.1. Alternative pathways linking abuse to criminal behavior and substance abuse

Author(s) & Year	Sample	Pathway
Dembo et al. (1989)	145& 398 juvenile detainees	Physical abuse → self derogation → illicit drug use Sexual abuse → self derogation → illicit drug use
Dembo et al. (1990)	398 juvenile detainees	Physical abuse → self derogation → marijuana use
Dodge et al. (1995)	584 kindergarteners	Phys. abuse → poor social inform. skills→ anti. beh.
Weiler & Widom (1996)	652 abused youths, 489 non-abused youths	Child abuse & neglect → psychopathy → violent beh. & arrests for violence
Brenzina (1998)	2,213 10th grade males	Maltreatment → lack of commitment to school → delinquency Maltreatment → deviant beliefs → delinquency Maltreatment → anger → delinquency

Table 2.1. Alternative pathways linking abuse to criminal behavior and substance abuse cont.

Author(s) & Year	Sample	Pathway
Kunitz et al. (1998)	352 adults in tx prgm 434 alc depend adults 300 non-alc. depend.	Physical abuse → conduct disorder → alcohol dependence
Schuck & Widom (2001)	466 abused females 333 non-abused	Child abuse & neglect → using drugs or alc → alc. symptoms
Simpsosn & Miller (2002)	126 empirical articles	Child abuse → Axis I disorders → substance abuse
DeHart (2004)	60 incarcerated females	Child abuse → psychological functioning → crime & substance abuse Child abuse → aggression → crime & substance use Child abuse → disruption in family/peer networks → crime & substance abuse Child abuse → running away → crime & subst. use Child abuse → school performance → antis. beh.

Table 2.1. Alternative pathways linking abuse to criminal behavior and substance abuse cont.

Author(s) & Year	Sample	Pathway
Grayson & Nolen-Hoeksema (2005)	697 women	Child sex abuse → distress → using alc. to cope → alcohol related problems Child sex abuse → using alc. to ↑ positive emotions → alcohol related problems
Stuewig & McCloskey (2005)	363 mothers	Maltreatment → parental rejection → lack of guilt proneness → delinquency Maltreatment → lack of parental warmth → lack of guilt prone.→ delinquency

Table 2.1. Alternative pathways linking abuse to criminal behavior and substance abuse cont.

Author(s) & Year	Sample	Pathway
Widom et al. (2006)	676 abused youths, 520 matched controls (avg. age 28.7 yrs)	Child abuse & neglect → alcohol symptoms → violent arrests (females) Child abuse & neglect → early aggression → violent arrests (males)
Salzinger et al. (2007)	100 abused youths, 100 matched controls	Child physical abuse → poor parental attachment → violent delinquency Child physical abuse → adol. verbal & physical abuse → violent delinquency
Teague et al. (2008)	480 male & female adult offenders	Child abuse → lower maternal support → general criminal behavior

Table 2.1. Alternative pathways linking abuse to criminal behavior and substance abuse cont.

Author(s) & Year	Sample	Pathway
White & Widom (2008)	582 abused & non-abused females (avg. age 40)	Child abuse & neglect → PTSD → illicit substance use & problems Child abuse & neglect → stressful life events → illicit substan. use & problems Child abuse & neglect → delinquent behavior → illicit substan. use & problems
Goldstein et al. (2010)	218 college students	Child abuse → using alc. to ↑ positive emotions → alcohol problems (males) Child neglect → coping w/anxiety → alcohol consumption (males) Child neglect → coping w/depression → alcohol consumption (males) Child abuse → coping w/depression → alcohol consequences (females)
Wilson & Widom (2010)	676 abused adults 520 matched controls	Child abuse & neglect → early sexual initiation → prostitution

Violent Victimization

Studies have found that other forms of victimization, such as violent victimization during adolescence, is also related to offending (Singer, 1986; Fitzgerald, 2002). The context surrounding adolescent violent victimization, however, may be very different from the context surrounding abuse and neglect. Adolescent females may be violently victimized by peers or a stranger, while the perpetrators of child abuse are usually the parents or caretaker. In addition, adolescent females may play a more active role in their violent victimization, compared to their role in childhood abuse and neglect. Baskin and Sommers (1993) provide a detailed description of the context surrounding adolescent females' violent victimization. Their analysis of life history interviews with 170 female felony offenders revealed that a criminal lifestyle increased their risk of being robbed or physically assaulted. For instance, one participant described how she was selling drugs and hanging out with one of her male customers, when he started to hallucinate from the PCP. He grabbed a knife and tried to stab her, but she ended up getting the knife away from him and killing him. Additional female offenders reported similar experiences. The authors concluded that the females were "frequently thrust in violence-prone situations in which the victim enters as an active participant, shares the actor's role, and becomes functionally responsible for it" (pg. 123). This suggests that there is an intricate interplay between violent victimization and offending in adolescence.

Additional studies have also noted that males and females have a greater risk of victimization if they engage in a deviant lifestyle (Sampson & Lauritsen, 1990, 1993). For instance, Shreck and colleagues (2002) found that individuals who were low in self-control were more likely to have weak bonds to conventional others, more likely to associate with delinquent peers, and more likely to engage in crime. In turn, these factors (weak social bonds, delinquent peers, and delinquency) increased youths' risk of victimization. Shaffer and Ruback's (2002) analysis of 5,003 youths from the Add Health sample revealed that juveniles who were engaging in violent crime were 5.3 times more likely to be victimized than youths who were not engaging in violent crime. The authors also asserted that violent victimization in wave I increased the odds that a youth would engage in violent crime in wave II. Other studies have also reported a reciprocal effect between violent victimization and offending (Lauritsen, Sampson, & Laub, 1991).

Finally, there is some evidence that violent victimization has a stronger effect on females' delinquent behavior than males' behavior (Bloom, Owen, & Covington, 2006). Fitzgerald's (2002) analysis of 4,296 youths from the National Longitudinal Survey of Children and Youth revealed that gender interacted with adolescent violent victimization to predict higher levels of property and violent crime. This study shows that females may be more sensitive to the criminogenic effects of adolescent violent victimization than males. Other studies, however, have found that males' who are violently victimized are more likely to engage in serious delinquent behaviors than female victims (Fagan, Piper, & Cheng, 1987). Scholars have noted that there is not enough evidence one way or another to suggest that the effect of victimization on offending varies by gender (Macmillian, 2001).

Summary

In sum, research has shown that individuals who experience childhood maltreatment, intimate partner violence, and/or violent victimization are at-risk for criminal behavior, alcohol abuse, and drug abuse in adolescence and adulthood. Furthermore, victimization may set off a cascade of negative consequences (i.e., depression, childhood behavioral problems, running away) that further exacerbate their risk for antisocial behavior across the life course. The pervasive negative consequences of victimization may seem to embed victims into a risky lifestyle that is characterized by drug use, risky sexual behaviors, psychological problems, and antisocial behavior. A possible explanation for the pervasiveness of the negative consequences is that a person's victimization experience may result in physiological and neuropsychological changes within the body. Since many of our organs and systems are responsible for multiple processes and circuits within the body, it can be expected that changes within one of our bodily systems may be expressed in a variety of ways. For instance, studies have shown that victimization experiences are associated with a reduction in brain volume in the prefrontal cortex. The prefrontal cortex is active during times of planning, regulation, knowledge integration, physical movement, oral or written communication, memory, and various other tasks (Fuster, 2001). Thus, problems or deficits within the prefrontal cortex may result in issues in any or all of these functions. Further, as discussed below, childhood abuse and neglect may set off a "cascade" of inter-related neurobiological consequences (Teicher, Andersen, Polcari, Anderson, Navalta, & Kim, 2003), that may coalesce into a propensity for maladaptive behaviors.

Genetic and Neurobiological Consequences of Victimization & Neglect

Victimization may increase the risk of antisocial behavior because victimization sets in motion a series of physiological, neurobiological, and molecular changes within the body. These changes ultimately create a situation where the central nervous system has too much arousal and too little inhibition. Animal and human studies have shown that childhood maltreatment may lead to: (1) an overactivation and oversensitivity of the hypothalamic-pituitary-adrenal axis; (2) reduced volume in the hippocampus, prefrontal cortex, and corpus callosum; (3) unpredictable activity in the amygdala; (4) higher basal and tonic levels of dopamine; and (5) lower concentrations of serotonin. The functional implications of these consequences may include depression, anxiety, hypersensitivity to stressors, reduced behavioral inhibition, unchecked negative emotions, hyperactivity, and a greater sensitivity to the pharmacological effects of drugs.

Research has shown that these 'detrimental' changes often co-occur in multiple systems and that a change in one component will often influence the functioning of one another (Meaney, Brake, & Gratton, 2002; Teicher et al., 2003; Pruessner, Champagne, Meaney, & Dagher, 2004); thus, these individual components are most likely part of a larger neurobiological circuit that influence various maladaptive behaviors (Schepis, Adinoff, & Rao, 2008). For instance, stress in childhood may lead to increased dopamine activity in the nucleus accumbens and amygdala in adulthood (Andersen, Lyss, Dumont, & Teicher, 1999). Higher dopamine activity in the nucleus accumbens has been linked to higher levels of drug use. The high level of dopamine in the nucleus accumbens may exacerbated by four additional consequences of abuse and neglect: (1) a lower volume of the prefrontal cortex (which regulates activity in the nucleus accumbens, and may inhibit the projection of dompaine from the amygdala to the nucleus accumbens) (Andersen, Tomada, Vincow, Valente, Polcari, & Teicher, 2008); (2) lower serotonin activity in the nucleus accumbens and amygdala (which inhibits activity in the nucleus accumbens and amygdala) (Andersen et al., 1999); (3) a lower density of GABA and benzodiazepine receptors in the amygdala (which inhibit amygdala activity, and prevent the stimulation of the nucleus accumbens) (Caldji, Francis, Sharma, Plotsky, & Meaney, 2000; Teicher et al., 2003); and (4) higher basal levels of glucocorticoids, which can increase one's sensitivity to the pleasurable effects of drugs (Deroche, Marinelli, Maccari, Le Moal, Simon, & Piazza, 1995). Thus, stress produces a myrid of neurobiological consequences, and these neurobiological consequences work together to produce an alternative path of development that may be characterized by negative emotionality, aggression, and substance use.

Effect of victimization and neglect on activity in the HPA axis, brain activity, dopaminergic system, and serotonergic system

The hypothalamic-pituitary-adrenal axis is one of the primary systems that are activated during times of stress. When an individual is exposed to even a small amount of stress, this sets in motion a series of events that helps one deal with stress (i.e., fight or flight) and then regain composure after the stressor has diminished. Exposure to stress triggers the release of corticotropin releasing hormone (CRH) in the amygdala and paraventricular nucleus (PVN) of the hypothalamus. CRH, along with a neuropeptide called vasopressin, stimulate the release of adrenocorticotropic hormone (ACTH) in the anterior pituitary (Figure 2.1). Activation of the amygdala and release of CRH and ACTH creates a feeling of alertness and arousal. If these processes continued to be activated, a person would be in a constant state of arousal or hypersensitivity to external stimuli. Luckily, the body has developed a system to regulate the activation of the amygdala, CRH, and ACTH. Once ACTH is secreted, it signals the adrenal glands to produce and release glucocorticoids, such as cortisol (in humans) or corticosterone (in mice). Glucocorticoids are part of a negative feedback loop which inhibits HPA axis activity and the hippocampus; thus, "shutting down" the release of CRH and ACTH, and bringing the HPA axis back into equilibrium. If there is a dysfunction in the glucocorticoid process, then an individual may remain in a state of excitability, and it may seem as if they are "on edge" or hypersensitive to minor stressors.

Figure 2.1. Illustration of HPA axis

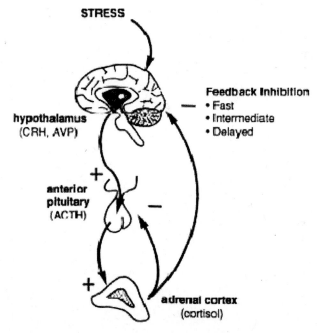

http://www.cns.med.ucla.edu/Images/HPAAxis.GIF

Animal and human studies have shown that childhood abuse and maltreatment influence the functioning of the HPA axis (Champagne & Curley, 2009; Holmes, le Guisquet, Vogel, Millstein, Leman, & Belzung, 2005). Dysfunctions within the HPA axis may be related to depression (i.e., avoidance behaviors), trouble concentrating, and substance abuse (i.e., anhedonia) (Catena et al., 2007; Ehlert, Gaab, & Heinrichs, 2001). Studies show that neglect and abuse leads to higher levels of corticotropin releasing hormone (CRH) in the paraventricular nucleus (PVN), high levels of CRH mRNA in the hypothalamus, high plasma levels of adrenocorticotropic hormone (ACTH), higher baseline levels of cortisol (Cicchetti & Rogosch, 2001), lower negative feedback sensitivity to glucocorticoids (such as cortisol), and lower glucocorticoid receptor density in the hippocampus and frontal cortex (Meaney, 2001; Zhang, Grady, Tsapakis, Andersen, Tarazi, & Baldessarini, 2004a). Abused and maltreated offspring also have a lower density and binding potential of $GABA_A$ and benzodiazepine receptors (Teicher et al., 2003; Zhang et al., 2004a).

These findings suggest that abused and neglected individuals may be more likely to experience feelings of anxiety or arousal (i.e., higher CRH, increased sympathetic nervous system activity), and they do not "calm down" as efficiently or to the same degree as non-abused individuals (i.e., less negative feedback sensitivity, lower density of $GABA_A$ and benzodiazepine receptors). In addition to the higher baseline levels of CRH and cortisol, maltreated individuals are also more likely to have larger increases in these chemicals in response to stress in adolescence and adulthood than individuals who are not maltreated (Tarullo & Gunnar, 2006). Thus, maltreated individuals may exhibit higher levels of anxiety and arousal in general, and they may experience abnormally high levels of arousal when they are presented with a stressful situation.

Hyperactivation of the HPA axis may also impact other structures and systems within the brain. For instance, hyperactivation of the HPA axis may prevent neurogenesis and synaptogenesis, prevent glial cell division and inhibit myelination, increase necrosis of hippocampal neurons, and lead to errors in synaptic pruning (Andersen & Teicher, 2009; Teicher, Tomoda, & Andersen, 2006). These findings suggest that hyperactivation of the HPA axis prevents the growth of neurons and synapses, it interferes with processes that increase efficiency of information transfer, and it increases cell death within the hippocampus. Hyperactivity in the HPA axis may also influence neurotransmitter systems (Meaney et al., 2002). Pruessner et al. (2004) found a significant positive relationship between baseline cortisol levels and the release of dopamine in the ventral striatum. Together, these findings suggest that maltreatment may influence HPA axis functioning, and in turn HPA axis dysfunctions lead to changes in neurotransmitters and changes the growth of brain cells. Childhood abuse and adolescent victimization may influence the dendrite and synaptic density of multiple brain structures, including the hippocampus and prefrontal cortex. Studies have shown that the volume of the hippocampus, corpus callosum, prefrontal cortex, amygdala, and cerebellar vermis are reduced among individuals who experience childhood abuse or adolescent victimization (Teicher et al., 2003). As a result of these structural deficits, maltreated individuals may exhibit memory problems, have underdeveloped verbal and language skills, and have trouble regulating their emotions and behavior. Researchers have also discovered that structural and functional deficits may vary by timing of abuse. Andersen and Teicher (2009) provide evidence that victimization during childhood is linked to structural deficits in the hippocampus during adulthood, while victimization during adolescence has an immediate and long lasting effect on the prefrontal cortex (Leussis & Andersen, 2008). For instance, path analyses of results from MRI scans revealed that the volume of the hippocampus was significantly lower among women who experienced childhood sexual abuse during the ages of three to five (Andersen et al., 2008). The volume of the frontal cortex was significantly lower among women who experienced childhood sexual abuse between age 14 and 16.

In addition to the effects on brain structure, numerous studies have shown that childhood maltreatment and stress influence activity in the neurotransmitter systems (Andersen et al., 1999; Maestripieri, 2005). Childhood and adolescent maltreatment has been linked to higher levels of dopamine concentrations and release in the ventral striatum (i.e., nucleus accumbens), dorsal striatum, amygdala, and prefrontal cortex (Andersen & Teicher, 2009; Jones, Hernandez, Kendall, Marsden, & Robbins, 1992; Matthews, Dalley, Matthews, Tsai, & Robbins, 2001). For instance, Pruessner et al.'s (2004) analysis of 120 healthy college students found that students who reported poor parental supervision and poor parental warmth had higher concentrations of dopamine in the ventral striatum in response to a stressful task than students who reported an affectionate relationship with their parents. The higher levels of dopamine activity in the striatum, especially in the nucleus accumbens, may be a result of hyperactivity in the HPA axis (i.e., higher levels of glucocorticoids such as cortisol). The administration of glucocorticoids to animals has shown to increase dopamine activity in the nucleus accumbens (Meaney et al., 2002). Thus, childhood maltreatment influences multiple systems within the brain, and these systems work together to influence cognition and behavior.

Studies have also shown that maltreatment is related to lower levels of serotonin activity (Champagne & Curley, 2008; Maestripieri, 2005; Maestripieri, McCormack, Lindell, Higley, & Sanchez, 2006; Shannon et al., 2005). Ichise and colleagues (2006) found that rhesus monkeys that experienced maternal separation had lower levels of serotonin transporter binding in the raphe, thalamus, ventral striatum, amygdala, hippocampus, anterior cingulated gyrus, and hypothalamus. In addition, monkeys that experienced maternal separation had CSF 5HIAA concentrations that were approximately 17 percent lower than 5HIAA concentrations in non-separated monkeys. Other studies have also shown that serotonin levels are lower in the nucleus accumbens and prefrontal cortex among subjects experiencing neglect or separation (Jones et al., 1992; Matthews et al., 2001). These studies, in addition to studies showing higher levels of dopamine, suggest that maltreated children may exhibit aggressive behaviors because they have both a higher level of an excitatory neurotransmitter (i.e., dopamine) and a lower level of an inhibitory neurotransmitter (i.e., serotonin) in the same brain structures (i.e., ventral striatum and frontal cortex) (Teicher et al., 2003). Thus, maltreated individuals may engage in aggressive and hyperactive behaviors because they have too much arousal (i.e., high dopamine activity, hyperactive HPA axis) and too little inhibition (i.e., low serotonin, deficits in the hippocampus and prefrontal cortex, low GABA processing).

Individuals who experience maltreatment may engage in aggressive and hyperactive behaviors, but they may also be more likely to abuse substances, especially substances that primarily stimulate the dopaminergic system (i.e., cocaine, methamphetamine). It is hypothesized that the heightened level of dopamine activity for maltreated individuals creates a situation where they experience little to no pleasure from normally pleasurable events, such as eating food or having sex (Andersen & Teicher, 2009). This state of anhedonia increases the likelihood that maltreated individuals will seek out drugs and alcohol to overcome this state. Drugs and alcohol stimulate the dopaminergic system and cause large doses of dopamine to be released into the nucleus accumbens. While abused individuals are less sensitive to every day pleasures, they may be more sensitive to the dopaminergic effects of drugs (Holmes et al., 2005; Meaney et al., 2002). For instance, offspring that were isolated from their mothers had larger doses of dopamine released in the nucleus accumbens when given doses of amphetamine than offspring who were not isolated (Jones et al., 1992). Marco and colleagues (2008) found that maternally deprived offspring were more sensitive to the mood altering effects of cannabinoids than offspring that were not deprived of their mother's presence and affection. Other studies have also shown that individuals with unusually high baseline levels of dopamine activity are more sensitive to the dopaminergic effects of psychotropic and illegal drugs (Dagher & Robbins, 2009).

Epigenetic effects of victimization

In addition to influencing the amount of activity in neuropsychological systems, victimization can have long term effects on the expression of genes. That is, victimization can 'turn off' or 'turn on' genes within the body. Victimization may change genetic expression through histone acetylation and methylation. Histone acetylation permits the expression of a genetic sequence, while methylation silences a genetic marker. These processes regulate gene expression by influencing key structures in genes and chromosomes.

Before discussing the acetylation of histones, it is first necessary to understand what histones are and their functions in genetic expression. Histones are positively charged DNA binding proteins that help package DNA into a cell, and which regulate transcriptional factors' access to DNA sequences. DNA is very long and it must be packaged into a cell in an efficient manner. In order to accomplish this, negatively charged DNA tightly wraps around the positively charged histones in a thread and spool fashion (Figure 2.2). This tight wrapping of the DNA around a histone prevents transcriptional factors from accessing the beginning of a gene (i.e., the transcription initiation site), and effectively prevents the DNA sequence from being expressed. However, acetylation can occur where an acetyl group is attached to the tail of the histone. Acetylation makes the histone more negatively charged and it loosens the wrapping of the DNA from the histone. This loosening of the DNA allows transcriptional factors to access the DNA sequence, and the DNA sequence can then be transcribed and expressed. If deacetylation occurs (i.e., removal of the acetyl group), then DNA will wrap tightly around the histone and genetic expression will be reduced.

What is a glucocorticoid receptor and why is it important?
Our bodily structures communicate through chemical and electrical signals. For instance, neurons communicate with each other by sending chemical 'messages' from one neuron to another neuron. The receiving neuron has a structure, called a receptor, which receives the chemical 'message.' Thus, glucocorticoid receptors are important because they provide a docking station for glucocorticoid hormones, so that the glucocorticoid can tell neurons to downregulate neurons in the HPA axis and hippocampus. Downregulation of the HPA axis and hippocampus leads to reduced feelings of stress and greater control over one's feelings and behavior. Failure to downregulate these systems results in hypersensitivity to stress and impulsive behaviors.

Methylation occurs when a methyl group is attached to the 'beginning' of a genetic sequence, typically in a region called a promoter. More specifically, the promoter region is a section of the gene that begins the expression of a gene. The promoter often has a genetic sequence referred to as a CpG island. A CpG island is a cytosine base followed by a guanine base, and the two are held together by a phosphodiester bond. Methyl groups attach to this CpG island or dinucleotide, and 'shut off' the gene by preventing transcriptional factors from initiating the copying of DNA (see Chapter 3 for description of transcription). Since the DNA sequence cannot be copied, it cannot be 'read' and it will not result in a specified protein.

Studies have shown that maternal behavior can trigger methylation and acetylation of the glucocorticoid receptor gene, and that these epigenetic changes can result in changes in the density of glucocorticoid receptors in the hippocampus (Liu et al., 1997; Weaver et al., 2004; McGowan et al., 2009). For instance, Weaver et al.'s (2004) analysis of rats revealed that a CpG dinucleotide in the promoter region of the glucocorticoid receptor (GR) gene was methylated among offspring of low licking/grooming (i.e., low intimate contact) mothers, but not among offspring of high licking/grooming mothers. Their results also revealed that offspring of low licking/grooming mothers had less histone acetylation in the promoter region of the GR gene and less binding of transcription factors to the promoter region. Thus, Weaver and colleagues (2004, 2007) found that low intimate mother-offspring contact resulted in processes that blocked access to the gene (i.e., deacetylation) and 'shut off' the gene (i.e., methylation), which resulted in less GR gene mRNA and fewer glucocorticoid receptors. The implication is that offspring who do not experience quality mother-offspring contact may have a weak negative feedback sensitivity to glucocorticoids (i.e., cortisol), and as a result, may be more sensitive to stressful or negative events.

Weaver and other researchers have also investigated the mechanisms underlying these relationships. Before discussing the mechanisms underlying the relationship of maternal contact and gene expression, it is important to describe the specific site that is methylated on the GR receptor gene. The GR receptor gene, similar to other genes, has a promoter region. A promoter region is a section at the beginning of a genetic polymorphism, in which transcription factors attach to the region and then begin to replicate the DNA instructions (in hopes of producing a certain protein). Within the promoter region of the GR receptor gene, there is a section referred to as exon 1_7 (in mice) or NR3C1 (in humans) and it has a binding site for a transcription factor called nerve growth factor induced protein A (NGFI-A) (Figure 2.4). When NGFI-A binds to its response element, this initiates expression of the glucocorticoid receptor gene, which increases glucocorticoid activity within the hippocampus and HPA axis. Thus, methylation of the CpG island in the NGFI-A response element on the

GR receptor polymorphism will reduce the expression of glucocorticoid receptors within the brain.

Figure 2.2. Illustration of histones

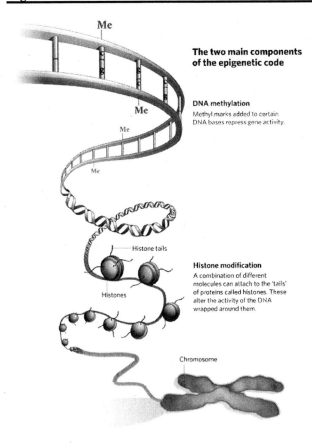

The two main components of the epigenetic code

DNA methylation
Methyl marks added to certain DNA bases repress gene activity.

Histone tails

Histones

Histone modification
A combination of different molecules can attach to the 'tails' of proteins called histones. These alter the activity of the DNA wrapped around them.

Chromosome

Qui, J. (2006). Epigenetics: Unfinished symphony. *Nature, 441*, 143-145.

Figure 2.3. Illustration of the site on the GR gene that is susceptible to methylation

Glucocorticoid receptor gene

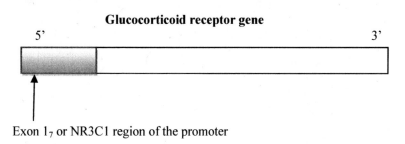

Exon 1₇ or NR3C1 region of the promoter

Exon 1₇ or NR3C1 region of the promoter

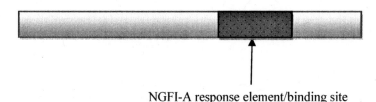

NGFI-A response element/binding site

NGFI-A response element/binding site

5' CpG dinucleotide

The mechanisms underlying the relationship between maternal behavior and the expression of the GR gene may include thyroid hormones, the serotonin system, signal transduction (i.e., cAMP, protein kinase A), and nerve growth factor induced protein A (Figure 2.4) (Szyf, Weaver, Champagne, Diorio, & Meaney, 2005). Animal studies have shown that positive maternal behavior increases thyroid hormone (i.e., triiodothyronine) levels. In turn, increases in thyroid hormones increase serotonin activity in the hippocampus (Smythe, Rowe, & Meaney, 1994). The increase in serotonin activity corresponds to an increase in the NGFI-A via higher levels of cAMP and cAMP protein kinase A activity (Meaney et al., 2000). Finally, higher NGFI-A levels (along with other transcriptional factors, such as CREB and CBP) will lead to greater expression of the glucocorticoid receptor gene and a greater density of glucocorticoid receptors, especially when the NGFI-A response element is not methylated and the histones are acetylated. If the NGFI-A response element is methylated or deacetylated, NGFI-A will not bind to the GR promoter and there may be fewer glucocorticoid receptors in the hippocampus (Weaver et al., 2007).

While research has predominantly emphasized the epigenetic alterations in the GR gene, scholars have begun to show that maternal behavior may influence the expression of other genetic variants. For instance, Champagne and colleague's (2006) analysis of mice revealed that offspring of low licking/grooming mothers had a decreased expression of estrogen receptor-α gene in the medial preoptic area of the hypothalamus, compared to offspring of high licking/grooming mothers. These differences in expression were the result of methylation of the ERα promoter among offspring of low licking/grooming mothers. Further, Weaver and colleagues (2006) found that 253 transcripts were upregulated and 50 transcripts were downregulated in the hippocampus in offspring of high licking/grooming mothers, compared to offspring of low licking/grooming mother. A recent study found that early life stress lead to hypomethylation of five CpG islands on the arginine vasopressin gene (AVG) in the paraventricular nulecus of the hypothalamus, which resulted in higher levels of AVG mRNA (i.e., greater expression of the AVG) (Murgatroyd et al., 2009). Overexpression of AVG may lead to an oversecretion of ACTH. The results of these studies show that maternal behavior may influence the expression of numerous genes within the hippocampus and hypothalamus, and that these epigenetic effects may last well into adulthood.

Figure 2.4. Diagram of the processes linking maternal behavior to glucocorticoid receptor expression

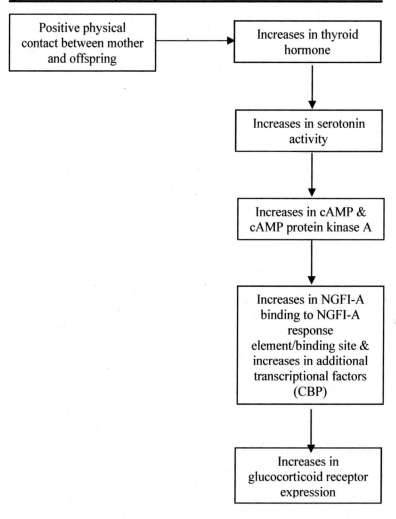

Gender differences in the neurobiological consequences of victimization and neglect

Gender differences in the psychological and sociological consequences, may arise due to gender differences in neurobiological changes resulting from victimization or neglect experiences. More specifically, gender differences in the effects of victimization on HPA axis activity, brain structure and function, and neurotransmitter systems may help explain why some psychological and sociological consequences of victimization are more prevalent or exacerbated among one gender. For instance, males who are exposed to social stress (i.e., victimization) may be less likely to display symptoms of anxiety (than females) because they have greater concentrations of tyrosine hydroxylase after stress than females (Leussis & Andersen, 2008).

Similar to criminological research (McGloin & Widom, 2001), developmental research has found that males may be more sensitive to the neuropsychological consequences of neglect and victimization than females (Llorente et al., 2008; McCormick, 2010). Animal studies have revealed that male rats who are deprived of their mother or who are exposed to stressful conditions have greater neuronal activity in the paraventricular nucleus (PVN) of the hypothalamus, higher basal levels of ACTH, and lower levels of glucocorticoid receptor mRNA in the PVN (Avishai-Eliner, Hatalski, Tabachnik, Eghbal-Ahmadi, & Baram, 1999; Genest, Gulemetova, Laforest, Drolet, & Kinkead, 2004); thus, males who are neglected or victimized may be more likely to have a hyperaroused HPA axis than victimized females. In addition to HPA axis alterations, victimization and neglect may have more detrimental effects on brain structure for males than females. Maltreated males have greater reductions in volume of the corpus callosum and prefrontal cortex (PFC) than maltreated females (DeBellis & Keshavan, 2003; Teicher et al., 2003; Teicher et al., 2006). Further, males who experience repeated stress have greater reductions in myelin proteins in the prefrontal cortex than stressed females (Leussis & Andersen, 2008). Neglected and victimized males, therefore, may have less volume in key regulatory structures (i.e., PFC) and less efficient processing of inhibitory messages (i.e., decreased myelin protein in PFC). Finally, Matthews and colleagues (2001) found that maternally separated males had lower levels of serotonin activity in the medial prefrontal cortex, but maltreated females did not experience any changes in serotonin activity. These findings indicate that neglect and victimization may cause males to 'deviate from the norm' more so than females; thus, males may be more sensitive to the effects of victimization and abuse than females, and this is expressed in biological, psychological, and sociological ways.

If males are more sensitive to the neuropsychological consequences of victimization and neglect, it may be hypothesized that victimized males will exhibit problems related to hyperactivity in the HPA axis, low concentrations of serotonin, and reduced volume in regulatory brain structures more so than victimized females. Victimized males, for example, may have greater hyperactivity in the HPA axis (i.e., higher CRH, ACTH, cortisol) than victimized females. As a result, victimized males may exhibit higher levels of negative emotionality and greater problems with self-control than victimized females. Similarly, victimized males may have more behavioral inhibition problems than victimized females since victimized males may have lower levels of serotonin than victimized females. Finally, studies have shown that neglected and victimized males often have more structural and functional problems in the prefrontal cortex than neglected females, and as such victimized males may engage in more impulsive and risky behaviors than victimized females.

While a number of studies reveal that males are more sensitive to the effects of victimization and neglect, it is important to note that some research also shows that: (1) females are more sensitive to the neurobiological effects of victimization, or (2) the neurobiological consequences are different for males and females. For instance, studies indicate that maternal separation has a stronger impact on HPA axis functioning and greater impact on the volume of the hippocampus among females than males (Desbonnet, Garrett, Daly, McDermott, & Dinan, 2008; Oomen et al., 2009; Renard, Rivarola, & Suárez, 2007). If victimization causes greater reductions in the hippocampus and greater hyperactivity in HPA axis for females (relative to males), it would be expected that victimized females would exhibit more learning disabilities and greater depression than victimized males. Other research suggests that victimization does not have a stronger effect on biological functioning for males and females, but that the neurobiological consequences differ for males and females. McCormick (2010) suggested that stress may have an immediate impact on males' HPA axis activity, while the effects of stress on females' HPA axis activity are not seen until late adolescence and adulthood. Leussis and Andersen (2008), however, found that females initially exhibited greater sensitivity to stress, but that the effects quickly faded. For males, the effects of stress were long lasting. Thus, it is not clear whether there are gender differences in the timing of consequences. Other studies have found that stress may differentially impact the functioning of different brain regions and neurotransmitters (Matthews et al., 2001). For instance, Avishai-Eliner et al. (1999) found that glucocorticoid receptor mRNA was decreased in the hypothalamus of maternally separated males, while GR mRNA was higher in the amygdala for females. The research suggests, therefore, that gender does appear to moderate the effects of victimization on neurobiological systems, but it is not currently known how gender conditions these effects.

Take home messages
- Individuals who experience childhood abuse, intimate partner violence, and/or violent victimization are more likely to engage in crime and abuse substances than individuals who are not victims of childhood abuse, intimate partner violence, or violent victimization.
- Victims may be at an increased risk of offending and abusing substances because they experience changes in genetic expression, HPA axis, brain structure and function, and neurotransmitter activity. More specifically, victimization may lead to methylation and histone deacetylation of various genetic variants (i.e., glucocorticoid receptor gene promoter); HPA axis hyper- or hypo-activity; decreased white and gray matter volume in the hippocampus, prefrontal cortex, or corpus callosum; and high basal and tonic levels of dopamine, coupled with low levels of serotonin. These changes may lead to hyperactivity, hyper-sensitivity to stress, and a lack of inhibitory mechanisms, which may place an individual at-risk for antisocial behavior.

- There are gender differences in: (a) the effects of victimization on criminal behavior and substance use, and (b) the effects of victimization on neuropsychological functioning. A large body of literature shows that the effects of victimization on behavior and neuropsychological changes are stronger for males, but there is also some research showing no gender differences or stronger effects for females.

CHAPTER THREE

Introduction to Genetics

Twin and family studies have revealed that genetic factors account for a substantial percentage of variance in antisocial and criminal behaviors (Plomin, 1990; Rowe & Farrington, 1997). For instance, Grove and colleague's (1990) analysis of 32 sets of monozygotic (MZ) twins who were reared apart found that genetic factors accounted for 45% of the variance in drug use, 41% of variance in childhood antisocial behavior, and 28% of the variance in adulthood antisocial behavior. Meta-analyses of twin and adoption studies have also shown that the heritability of antisocial and criminal behaviors range from approximately .20 to .60 (Walters, 1992). Mason and Frick's (1994) meta-analysis of 21 heritability estimates from 12 twin studies revealed that 48% of variance in antisocial behavior is attributed to genetic effects. These studies converge to show that genetic factors are important to the development of antisocial and criminal behavior.

While studies from psychiatry and behavioral genetics show that genetic factors are relevant to the study of crime, few criminologists are familiar with the process of genetic expression, as well as the concepts and terminology from molecular genetics. In light of this unfamiliarity, the current chapter will provide a brief overview of molecular genetics in four sections. First, this chapter will describe the basic characteristics of genes, such as how genetic information is acquired and where this information is housed in the body. Second, this chapter will describe how genetic factors influence behavior via the production of different proteins during the processes of transcription and translation. Third, this chapter will discuss the different ways in which genes may be related to criminal behaviors. The different types of genetic expression include a one gene one disorder relationship (OGOD), pleiotropy, polygeny, epistatis, a gene-environment interaction, and a gene-environment correlation (Beaver, 2008b). Fourth, this chapter will describe the functions of five candidate genetic polymorphisms, and it will review the evidence linking these five genetic variants to criminal behavior. The five genetic polymorphisms that will be reviewed include polymorphisms in a dopamine transporter gene (DAT1), two dopamine receptor genes (DRD2 and DRD4), a serotonin transporter gene (5HTTLPR), and a monoamine oxidase gene (MAOA). Finally, this chapter will review evidence that shows that gender may condition the effects of the five candidate genes on antisocial behaviors. This chapter will also discuss the potential reasons why genetic polymorphisms may have differential effects on males and females antisocial behavior.

Basic Characteristics of Genes
Acquiring chromosomes and genes.

Genes are located on chromosomes. Humans have a total of 46 chromosomes or 23 pairs of chromosomes in the nucleus of each somatic cell. The 46 chromosomes are acquired from parents; the mother provides 23 chromosomes and the father provides the complementary 23 chromosomes. Unlike somatic cells (i.e., non-sex cells), the mother's and the father's mature sex cell contains only 23 chromosomes (22 autosomes or chromosomes that are similar across gender and 1 sex chromosome), instead of 46 chromosomes each. The mother and the father's sex cells reduce the number of chromosomes from 46 to 23 through a process called meiosis. Meiosis is a cell division process in which genetic information is exchanged and recombined within a parent's cell, and then the cell divides to produce sex cells with only 23 chromosomes. Meiosis is important for two interrelated reasons: (1) meiosis produces unique genetic combinations that give rise to variation in individual characteristics, and (2) abnormalities during meiosis can produce genetic mutations, which may lead to physical deformities or mental deficits.

During the meiosis process, two chromosomes within a nucleus align next to each other. Each chromosome contains genes that correspond to genes located on the other chromosome; thus, each chromosome contains the same gene in the same location. While each chromosome contains the same gene, the genes do not always share the same sets of genetic information. That is, a gene from one chromosome may contain genetic instructions for brown hair, while the gene from the other chromosome may contain instructions for blond hair. After the chromosomes align to each other, there is a break in an arm of the chromosome (i.e., chromosome 1) and the corresponding arm in the adjacent chromosome 'crosses over' to join chromosome 1. This crossing over process results in the recombination of DNA on the chromosomes, which may produce variation in individual characteristics (Lewis, 2001; Walsh, 1995). It is estimated that DNA from the 23 chromosomes can recombine in 8,388,608 ways (2^{23}), producing a wide range of variation in individual traits. Thus, offspring will not be a perfect admixture or blend of their parents DNA because both parents' cells begin recombining and altering DNA sequences before fertilization.

Once the sperm fertilizes the egg, the father's 23 chromosomes align with the corresponding 23 maternal chromosomes and combine to form a zygote. A zygote then undergoes a rapid sequence of cell division that eventually creates an embryo and then a fetus. Each cell within the fetus contains two copies of the genome, or 23 pairs of chromosomes (Lewis, 2001). The genome provides genetic instructions that directly aid in a person's physiological and neurological development.

Structure of chromosomes, genes, and DNA.

Before discussing how genes influence behavior, it is important to review how chromosomes, genes, and DNA are related to one another. As previously discussed, chromosomes are located within the nucleus of a cell, and genes are located on the chromosomes. Genes are units that provide instructions for the production of specific proteins. The Human Genome Project estimates that there are between 20,000 and 25,000 genes within the human body. Genes provide instructions for the production of proteins through DNA sequences. Each gene contains deoxyribonucleic acid or DNA. Thus, chromosomes are the larger structure that contains genes, and genes are comprised of DNA (Figure 3.1).

In order for thousands of genes to be compacted into a chromosome (and then placing one copy of each chromosome into a cell's nucleus), DNA strands wind themselves around structures called histones. A histone is a positively charged protein that regulates the expression of DNA sequences.

Figure 3.1 Illustration of chromosome, gene, and DNA

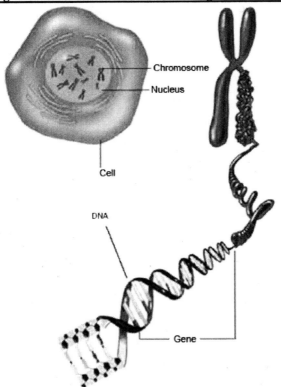

http://publications.nigms.nih.gov/thenewgenetics/images/ch1_dnagenes .jpg

Figure 3.2 Illustration of the pairing of sugar, phosphate, and nitrogen base

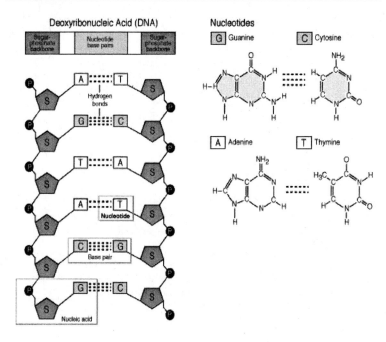

http://www.tutorvista.com/biology/nucleotide-bases-in-dna

Since DNA is negatively charged, the positive charge of the histone pulls the DNA very close to the histone and prevents transcriptional factors from accessing the initiation sites of genes. As previously discussed, attaching an acetyl group to a histone loosens the DNA from the histone by making the histone more negatively charged, and this process allows genetic expression. Removal of an acetyl group causes the DNA to pull very tightly around the histone and this process prevents genetic expression. Thus, modification of a histone can affect genetic expression (i.e., whether a gene is 'turned on' or 'turned off').

DNA or deoxyribonucleic acid is a nucleotide or a chemical building block that contains a sugar, a phosphate, and a nitrogen base (A, C, T, G). The sugar and phosphate join together to form a long chain, with the nitrogen base protruding from the sugar-phosphate backbone (Figure 3.2). It is useful to think of the chain as one side of a zipper. A zipper has metal teeth or hooks (i.e., nitrogen bases) that are attached to a seamless cloth strip (i.e., sugar-phosphate backbone). Similar to a zipper, the nitrogen bases (or metal teeth) can only be paired with complementary nitrogen bases. That is, adenine (A) can only be paired with thymine (T), and cytosine (C) can only be paired with guanine (G). The complementary nitrogen base pairs are chemically attracted to one another, and they are held together by hydrogen bonds. This repeated pairing of complementary nitrogen bases produces the double helix (Lewis, 2001).

Nitrogen bases can be arranged in a sequence, which will give genetic instructions for a particular function. For instance, a DNA sequence of GCC will correspond to a complementary sequence of CGG, which will code for the amino acid glycine. The sequence of GCC and the complementary sequence of CGG is referred to as a nitrogen base pair. It is estimated that there are 3 billion base pair sequences within the human genome, and that approximately 1 to 10 percent of those base pairs vary between individuals (Wright, Tibbetts, & Daigle, 2008). The differences in base pairs may produce variation in individuals' cognitive skills and behaviors.

Genetic variation.

As previously discussed, each sex cell contains only 23 chromosomes (instead of 46 chromosomes), and each chromosome contains only one DNA sequence for a particular gene. That is, each sex cell contains only half of the genetic information that is necessary to have a complete single gene. Each DNA sequence or variant is referred to as an allele. When gametes combine, their offspring have two chromosomes or two DNA sequences for a particular gene. Thus, each gene has two alleles, one allele that is maternally inherited and one allele that is paternally inherited. The two alleles represent a person's genotype.

Figure 3.3 Punnett squares

Panel A.

	B	B
B	BB	BB
b	Bb	Bb

Panel B.

	B	b
B	BB	Bb
b	Bb	bb

For the majority of genes, there is only one allele or genetic sequence available in the population. This means that offspring will inherit the same allele from each of their parents. There are other genes, however, that have more than one allele available in the population. Genes that have more than one variant or allele available in the population are referred to as polymorphic. More specifically, "a variant in sequence that is present in at least 1 percent of a population is called a polymorphism" (Lewis, 2001: p. 6). When a gene is polymorphic, the probability that offspring will have the same alleles is less than 100 percent. For instance, offspring who have one parent with black hair (BB) and one parent with brown hair (Bb) has a 50 percent chance of having brown hair (Bb), and a 50 percent chance of having black hair (BB) (Figure 3.3 panel A). Individuals who have two copies of the same allele are referred to as homozygous, while individuals with two different alleles are referred to as heterozygous. In the current example, offspring who have black hair would be homozygous for the B allele (BB genotype), while offspring with brown hair would be referred to as heterozygous (Bb). A second example will show that offspring can have a heterozygous genotype for hair color, or they may be homozygous for the B allele (BB genotype) or homozygous for the b allele (bb genotype). Offspring who have two parents with brown hair (Bb) have a 50 percent chance of having brown hair (Bb), a 25 percent chance of having black hair (BB), and a 25 percent chance of having blond hair (bb) (Figure 3.3 panel B). This example shows that multiple allelic combinations are possible when a gene is polymorphic.

Different alleles or genetic polymorphisms are the result of differences in DNA sequences. These differences can be either differences in the content of the DNA sequence (i.e., nucleotide differences) or differences in the length of the DNA sequence. There are three types of genetic polymorphisms: single nucleotide polymorphisms (SNPs), microsatellites, and minisatellites or variable number of tandem repeat (VNTR) polymorphisms (Beaver, 2008b). SNPs are polymorphisms that arise due to a difference in the content of the DNA sequence. More specifically, "a SNP is a site on the DNA which a single base-pair varies from person to person" (Kwok & Gu, 1998). This means that SNPs can occur when a single nucleotide is absent from a sequence (i.e., deletions), when an extra single nucleotide is present in a sequence (i.e., insertions), or when one nucleotide is substituted for another nucleotide. SNPs are the most frequently occurring polymorphism. It is estimated that a SNP occurs every 1000 base pairs (Haddley, Vasiliou, Ali, Paredes, Bubb, & Quinn, 2008; Landegren, Nilsson, & Kwok, 1998). An example of a SNP is the TaqIA polymorphism on the DRD2 gene. The dopamine receptor gene (DRD2) has a SNP located downstream of the 3' untranslated region. This polymorphism has a C to T (TCG to TTG) substitution in a nonfunctional or noncoding region of the gene. The TTG codon corresponds to the A1 allele, and the TCG codon corresponds to the A2 allele (Haberstick & Smolen, 2004).

The second type of polymorphism is a microsatellite. Microsatellites are polymorphisms that arise due to differences in the length of a DNA sequence. More specifically, microsatellites occur when a short nucleotide sequence (less than four nucleotides) is repeated a variable number of times. For instance, a CAG microsatellite is located on an androgen receptor gene. This short nucleotide sequence can be repeated up to 29 times. Studies have shown that men who have less than 22 repeats of the CAG sequence have a higher risk of prostate cancer than males who have 22 or more repeats of the sequence (Irvine, Yu, Ross, & Coetzee, 1995). Finally, the last type of polymorphism is a minisatellite. Minisatellites are also polymorphisms that occur when nucleotide sequences differ in length. However, unlike microsatellites, minisatellites can have nucleotide sequences that differ in 10 or more nucleotides (Haddley et al., 2008). Minisatellites are also referred to as variable number tandem repeat (VNTR) polymorphisms. For instance, a dopamine transporter gene (DAT1) has a 40 base pair VNTR polymorphism:

AGGAGCGTGTCCTATCCCCGGACGCATGCAGGGCCCCCAC

(Mill et al., 2005b). This 40 base pair sequence can be repeated three to eleven times. In sum, polymorphisms may arise due to either content or length differences in DNA sequences.

Function of DNA.

DNA influences physiological and neurological functioning via the production of proteins. That is, DNA sequences (i..e, nucleotide sequences) provide genetic instructions for the production of amino acids. The processes by which DNA influences protein production are referred to as transcription and translation. During transcription, the genetic instructions found in the DNA sequence are replicated, and then these instructions can be read or translated by a ribosome during the transcription process. The first step of transcription begins with an enzyme (i.e., RNA polymerase) unzipping the DNA strand, leaving one side of the DNA strand exposed (Figure 3.5). Free floating DNA nucleotides are then attracted to the exposed strand of DNA, and the complementary bases begin to pair up with the exposed nitrogen bases. Similar to the original strand of DNA, cytosine is paired with guanine (G), and thymine (T) is paired with adenine (A), but now adenine (A) is paired with uracil (U) (Box 3.1). These complementary nucleotides form a new strand or sequence that is referred to as pre-messenger ribonucleic acid (pre-mRNA).

Box 3.1: Why is uracil used in RNA and thymine is used in DNA?

The simpliest answer to this question is that thymine is less susceptible to mutation than uracil. Since DNA is somewhat rigid and less adaptive than RNA, thymine is used in place of uracil to protect the integrity of the DNA strand.

Uracil is actually a precursor to thymine. Uracil is converted into thymine by a process called methylation. Methylation protects thymine from enzymes that may degrade or break down DNA and RNA molecules. Furthermore, methylation forces thymine to only pair with adenine rather than any other base. Thymine's precursor, uracil, can pair with any base including itself. This is incredibly beneficial when the body must adapt to new bacteria or chemical challenges via RNA. However, using uracil in DNA (rather than thymine) would decrease the efficiency and accuracy of the DNA replication process. Thus, thymine is used in DNA due to its stability and lack of vulnerability, while uracil is used in RNA due to its flexibility.

Before the genetic instructions in the pre-mRNA can be executed, the pre-mRNA strand undergoes a process called splicing, where non-coding regions of mRNA (referred to as introns) are removed from the instruction sequence. Genes consist of coding regions—referred to as exons—and they also consist of introns, which are sections of a DNA sequence that do not directly influence protein synthesis. Introns are removed from the pre-mRNA prior to the mRNA entering the cytoplasm for translation. More specifically, a spliceosome attaches to the pre-mRNA, where it will begin to remove the introns and bind the remaining exons together to form mRNA. Once the introns are removed, the mRNA ventures out into the cytoplasm, where the sequence will be used in the translation process.

Once in the cytoplasm, the mRNA attaches to a ribosomal subunit where the sequence is decoded or read. This is the first step in the translation process (Figure 3.6). Next, the ribosome begins to read the mRNA, three characters or bases at a time. Three continuous bases on an mRNA strand are referred to as a codon. Each codon corresponds to a particular amino acid, and amino acids are located on transfer RNA (tRNA) molecules. As each codon is read, tRNA brings the codon's complementary amino acid to the ribosome and releases the amino acid to the ribosome. This first amino acid is the beginning of the protein chain that will be built in the ribosome. As the ribosome reads off each codon, a new amino acid is added to the growing polypeptide or protein chain until the ribosome reaches a stop codon (UGA, UAG, or UAA). These codons do not have a complementary amino acid, and this causes the ribosome to stop production of the protein. At this point, the ribosome and tRNA will separate, and the polypeptide or protein strand is released into the cytoplasm. This polypeptide chain then attaches to other protein chains to form tissues, enzymes, hormones, and neurotransmitters (Plomin, 1990).

Figure 3.4. Illustration of transcription

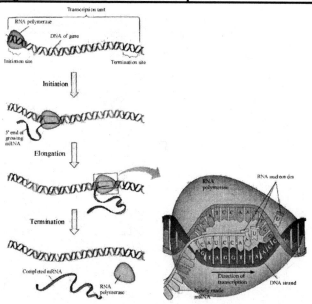

http://www.dadamo.com/wiki/wiki.pl/RNA_(ribonucleic_acid)/Glycoli pids/Transcription_(DNA_transcription)

Figure 3.5. Illustration of translation

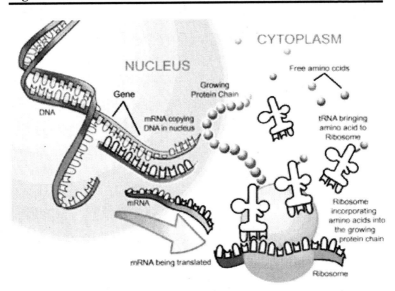

http://www.scq.ubc.ca/wp-content/translation1.gif

Genetic associations.

There are a number of ways in which genes may be related to variation in cognitive or behavioral functioning. This section will review six ways in which genes can be directly and indirectly related to different observable traits, or phenotypes. First, a single gene may increase one's risk of developing one specific type of disorder or trait. This type of relationship is often referred to as a one gene, one disorder (OGOD) association (Beaver, 2008b). Fragile X syndrome is an example of an OGOD. Fragile X syndrome occurs when a DNA sequence of CGG is excessively repeated in the FRM1 gene. Individuals without fragile X syndrome usually have 6 to 50 repeats of the CGG sequence in the FRM1 gene, while those with the syndrome have 200 to 2,000 repeats (Lewis, 2001).

Second, a single phenotype may be a function of multiple genes or polymorphisms. This type of genetic association is referred to as polygeny. For instance, Comings and colleagues (2000b) found that twelve genes were significantly related to attention deficit disorder diagnoses. This does not suggest that all twelve genes must be present for symptoms of ADHD to surface. Instead, this finding indicates that different alleles (i.e., risk alleles) of all twelve genes increase the likelihood that one will exhibit ADHD symptoms. That is, some individuals with ADHD may carry only three risk alleles, while another individual with ADHD may carry seven risk alleles. Each additional risk allele increases the probability that an individual will exhibit a certain phenotype.

Third, a single gene may increase one's risk of developing multiple types of behaviors or observable traits. This type of genetic expression is referred to as pleiotropy. For instance, a polymorphism in the dopamine receptor gene (DRD2) has been linked to substance abuse, obesity, depression, migraine headaches, posttraumatic stress syndrome, and schizophrenia (Noble, 2003). Pleiotropy can occur for a variety of reasons including: (a) when a polymorphism influences a protein that is involved in multiple biochemical processes; (b) one section of a gene overlaps with another gene, resulting in only half of the protein being synthesized; and/or (c) alternative splicing patterns in which an intron may be left in mRNA or an exon is erroneously removed from the pre-mRNA (Pyeritz, 1989). These processes cause the gene to have effects on multiple types of observable traits. In statistical terms, pleiotropy refers to the additive effects of genes on a phenotype.

Fourth, unlike pleiotropy, different genes may interact with one another to increase the likelihood of a certain phenotype. More specifically, one gene may either enhance or mask the expression of another gene. This type of genetic expression is referred to as epistasis. Beaver and colleagues (2007a) recently reported that dopamine receptor gene (DRD2) interacted with dopamine receptor gene (DRD4) to increase the likelihood of antisocial behavior during adolescence and adulthood. Additional studies have also reported epistatis between genes that are involved in the same chemical processes, such as an interaction between serotonin transporter gene (5HTTLR) and a monoamine oxidase A affecting serotonergic functioning (Murphy et al., 2003; Passamonti et al., 2008).

Fifth, genes may interact with environmental factors to increase the likelihood of a particular behavior or observable trait. This is referred to as gene-environment interaction. This suggests that a genetic polymorphism will only lead to a particular outcome when it is paired with a certain environment. When the genetic polymorphism is not paired with a certain environment, it will not significantly influence a phenotype. The most well-known example of a gene-environment interaction comes from Caspi et al.'s (2002) analysis of youths from the Dunedin Multidisciplinary Health and Development Study. Their analyses revealed that a monoamine oxidase A polymorphism (MAOA) did not have a significant direct effect on antisocial behavior. However, MAOA did lead to higher levels of antisocial and violent behavior when carriers of the polymorphism had experienced childhood maltreatment. Thus, the genetic polymorphism only exerted an effect on maladaptive behavior when it was paired with a high-risk environment. Numerous other studies have reported similar findings (Eley et al., 2004; Haberstick et al., 2005; Tuvblad, Grann, & Lichtenstein, 2006; Widom & Brzustowicz, 2006).

Finally, genetic factors may indirectly influence criminal behavior via exposure to certain environments. That is, a person's genotype may increase the likelihood that he or she will be exposed to a criminogenic environment, which in turn will increase the probability of offending. This type of genetic expression is referred to as a gene-environment correlation. Gene-environment correlations recognize that individuals' exposure to environments is not random, and that individuals may play a role in shaping the types of environments they are exposed to. For instance, people who are hostile and confrontational may be more likely to find themselves in aggressive, physically violent situations than people who are less confrontational. This may be because hostile individuals evoke negative, aggressive reactions from others, or it may be that hostile individuals seek out situations that lend themselves to violence (i.e., drug dealing).

There are three types of gene-environment correlations: active, evocative, and passive. Active gene-environment correlations occur when individuals select themselves into environments that are most compatible with their genetic predispositions or tendencies. People are more likely to select themselves into environments that "allow, encourage, and reward their genetically based traits" (Wright et al., 2008: 178). For instance, individuals are more likely to choose romantic partners who have similar qualities, rather than choosing a partner who has completely different qualities. Indeed, Caspi and Herbener (1990) found that women were more likely to marry men that were similar to them in terms of personality, and these women were significantly more likely to be satisfied in their marriages. Also, partners who married individuals with a similar personality reported they were more likely to display consistency in their own personality across middle adulthood. Thus, individuals are more likely to select themselves into relationships and environments that compliment their genetic tendencies, and this selection increases the likelihood that their genetic predispositions will be expressed.

Evocative gene-environment correlations occur when individuals' elicit certain responses from their environment based on their genetically influenced traits. For instance, parenting theories such as Patterson's (1982) coercion theory acknowledge that children who have a difficult temperament are more likely to elicit erratic and negative reactions from their parents than more mild tempered children. A recent study by Beaver and Wright (2007) confirmed that children have a strong effect on parents' rearing practices. In their analysis of data from the Cambridge Study, they found that children's antisocial behavior at wave 2 influenced parents' socialization at wave 2, but parents' socialization did not influence children's antisocial behavior. Other studies have also noted that people with behavioral problems are more likely to be rejected by their peers and teachers (Hokanson & Butler, 1992; Joiner & Metalsky, 1995; Schaeffer, Petras, Ialongo, Poduska, & Kellam, 2003).

Passive gene-environment correlations occur when individuals' inherit a certain behavioral style from their parents, and they are also exposed to family environments that foster expression of that specific genetic tendency. That is, parents' may provide offspring with genes that increase the likelihood of antisocial behavior, and an environment that provides optimal expression of those genes. For instance, youths may inherit an inclination towards deviant or antisocial behavior from their antisocial parents. In turn, antisocial parents may be more likely to reinforce their child's misbehavior by using coercive, inconsistent, and harsh punishments (Patterson, 1982; Unnever, Cullen, & Agnew, 2007). The passive gene-environment correlation reflects the fact that parents' genotypes help create the family environment, and parents also pass these genotypes on to their children.

Neurotransmission or Synaptic Communication

Genetic polymorphisms may regulate various cell structures and chemicals in the body. The genetic polymorphisms that are the focus of this study are those polymorphisms that are related to neurotransmission. Neurotransmission is the chemical and electrical processes that facilitate communication between neurons or nerve cells within the central nervous system. Neurons consist of four general structures: cell body, nucleus, dendrites, and axons (Figure 3.7). The cell body or soma provides the general structure of the neuron and it houses the cell's nucleus. Remember that DNA is stored in the nucleus of a cell, and therefore protein synthesis occurs within the soma. The dendrites are short branches or 'communication wires' that receive information from other neurons. Once this information is received, it is processed by the nucleus and then sent down to the axon. The axon then sends the message across a gap (i.e., synapse) to the dendrite of an adjacent neuron. Thus, chemical and electrical messages are received by dendrites, processed by the nucleus, sent down to the axon, and then transmitted across a synaptic gap where it is received by an adjacent neuron.

This basic process is how neurotransmitters are processed throughout the brain. Neurotransmitters are "biological chemicals that carry the impulse from one neuron to another" (Wright et al., 2008; pg. 127). Neurotransmitters are stored at the end of an axon, and they are released when the electrical impulse from the cell body reaches a certain threshold. Once released, neurotransmitters cross over the synaptic cleft or gap to reach the adjacent neuron. The adjacent dendrite has specialized receptors that 'capture' the neurotransmitters. It is important to note that most receptors are specialized, and only correspond to particular types of neurotransmitters. Therefore, there are dopamine receptors, serotonin receptors, norepinephrine receptors, and so forth. Once the adjacent dendrite receives the chemical message, the ion channels on the dendrite open up and the message is reprocessed and retransmitted to the post synaptic neuron (Brown, 1976) (Figure 3.8).

Neurotransmitters may linger in the synaptic cleft after the message has been transmitted to the adjacent neuron. These neurotransmitters must be removed from the synaptic cleft, in order to ensure that future messages can be clearly transmitted without interference or noise. There are two ways that neurotransmitters can be removed from the synaptic cleft: (1) reuptake, or (2) degradation. During the reuptake process, transporters 'capture' the neurotransmitters and return them to the presynaptic neuron for later neurotransmission. The second way that neurotransmitters can be removed is through degradation. After a message is sent to the adjacent neuron, enzymes can be released from the axon of the presynaptic neuron. Enzymes degrade or break down neurontransmitters into inactive chemical compounds. Reuptake and degradation processes are important because they help maintain an optimal level of neurotransmitters within the brain. If the brain has too few transporters and degradation enzymes, neurotransmitters will build up in the synaptic cleft and interfere with the transmission of chemical messages. On the other hand, too many transporters or enzymes cause a deficiency in certain neurotransmitters, which results in the under-transmission of messages. Thus, an appropriate level of transporters and degradation enzymes are necessary for optimal neurotransmission.

Dopamine, Serotonin, and Monoamine Oxidase Genes
Dopamine.

Dopamine is an excitatory neurotransmitter that is manufactured in the hypothalamus, substantia nigra, and the ventral tegmental area. An appropriate level of dopamine is needed in order to ensure optimal cognitive performance. Small to moderate increases dopamine are associated with increases in cognitive activity and the ability to stay focused on a task. However, significantly higher levels of dopamine lead to aggression and hypersensitivity to external stimuli, while significant reductions in dopamine are linked to depression and the inability to concentrate. Thus, the effects of dopamine are curvilinear in that significantly high and low levels are associated with maladaptive behaviors, while a moderate level is linked to optimal cognitive functioning.

Figure 3.6. Illustration of a neuron

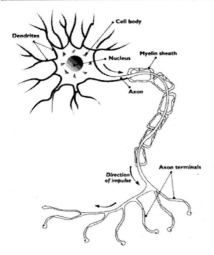

http://teens.drugabuse.gov/mom/tg_nerves.asp

Figure 3.7. Illustration of neurotransmission

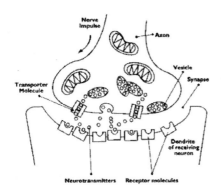

http://teens.drugabuse.gov/mom/tg_nerves.asp

Dopamine has been linked to criminal behavior and substance use due to its role in the body's reward/pleasure system. When people engage in pleasurable or relaxing activities, a large dose of dopamine is released in the brain (especially subsections of the limbic system such as the nucleus accumbens), and they experience a "high" or euphoric feeling (Blum, Cull, Braverman, & Comings, 1996; Reif & Lesch, 2003). This pleasurable sensation motivates people to repeat such activities in order to get that "high" feeling again. Thus, dopamine is at the heart of reinforcement or reward seeking behaviors.

Researchers have hypothesized that some individuals may suffer from a condition referred to as reward deficiency syndrome (Blum et al., 1996). Reward deficiency syndrome occurs when individuals require a significantly higher level of stimulation to achieve the same level of satisfaction or pleasure that others would experience at a lower level of stimulation. It is expected that individuals with reward deficiency syndrome may engage in behaviors that stimulate the dopaminergic system (i.e., sexual behaviors, over-eating, substance use) more so than individuals who do not experience reward deficiency syndrome. That is, individuals with reward deficiency syndrome may have lower levels of dopaminergic neurotransmission, and they may compensate for this deficiency by engaging in addictive and compulsive behaviors.

It is hypothesized that individuals with reward deficiency syndrome will be more likely to engage in addictive and compulsive behaviors, than risky behaviors in general. This is because addictive and compulsive behaviors may correspond to dysfunctions within the limbic system, while general risky behaviors may correspond to deficits in the prefrontal cortex. The limbic system is responsible for the expression of emotions, while the prefrontal cortex is responsible for executive functions, such as decision-making, regulation of emotions, and concentration. Thus, behaviors that are more emotionally satisfying may be linked to the limbic system more so than behaviors that are impulsive or risky. This does not suggest that there is no overlap between these types of behaviors, because many antisocial behaviors have an emotional and an impulsive component. However, some behaviors (i.e., substance use, aggression, gambling) may be more emotional than others (i.e., selling drugs, burglary, writing a bad check). There are various lines of evidence that support the link between dopamine and aggressive and criminal behavior (Fishbein, 1990). For instance, pharmacological studies have revealed that the prevalence and incidence of aggressive behavior decreased when dopamine antagonists (i.e., reduces dopamine activity), such as haloperidol, were administered to aggressive subjects (de Almeida, Ferrari, Parmigiani, & Miczek, 2005). Masi's (2004) literature review found that administration of haloperidol corresponded to decreases in hyperactivity, negativism, and angry affect among autistic children and adolescents. Results from animal models have also reported similar findings (Sweidan, Edinger, & Siegel, 1991). Sweidan et al. (1991) found that administration of dopamine agonists increased aggressive behavior among cats (i.e., hissing, striking), while administration of the dopamine antagonists haloperidol and sulpiride reduced aggressive behaviors. These findings suggest that pharmacological remedies can be used to decrease dopamine activity in the brain, and subsequently decrease the likelihood of aggressive and criminal behavior.

Animal studies have also found that higher dopamine levels are associated with aggressive behavior (Louilot, Le Moal, & Simon, 1986). A series of novel studies examined dopamine turnover levels in mice immediately before, during, and after an aggressive confrontation. Ferrari and colleagues (2003) exposed mice to confrontational and aggressive situations for ten days at a regularly scheduled time. The authors measured dopamine activity in the nucleus accumbens and prefrontal cortex immediately before, during, and after the confrontational situations. They found that dopamine levels increased 60 to 70 percent in the prefrontal cortex before regularly scheduled confrontations, while serotonin levels decreased by 30 percent before the confrontation. Dopamine activity levels also increased in the nucleus accumbens during and after a scheduled encounter. Other studies have also reported that dopamine activity increases in the nucleus accumbens after a confrontation (Haney, Noda, Kream, & Miczek, 1990; van Erp & Miczek, 2000). These studies suggest that dopamine may be important for preparing one for an aggressive attack (by energizing them), as well as by rewarding them when they successfully attack another subject.

Researchers have also used other indicators of dopamine activity to examine the link between dopamine and antisocial behavior. For instance, studies have investigated the relationship between antisocial behavior and a dopamine by-product, homovanillic acid (HVA) (Virkkunen, Goldman, Nielsen, & Linnoila, 1989). Enzymes, such as monoamine oxidase and catechol-O-methyltransferase, break down dopamine neurotransmitters and help convert dopamine into the metabolite HVA. Since HVA is a derivative of dopamine, it is frequently used as a proxy for dopamine activity. Studies have revealed that HVA levels are negatively associated with antisocial behaviors (Linnoila, Virkkunen, Scheinin, Nuutila, Rimon, & Goodwin, 1983; van Goozen, Matthys, Cohen-Kettenis, Westenberg, & van Engeland, 1999). For instance, Gabel and colleague's (1993) analysis of 22 boys in a residential treatment center reported that youths with conduct disorders had significantly lower levels of HVA than non-conduct disordered youths. The authors hypothesized that lower levels of HVA may reflect a dopamine deficiency, which may lead to poor concentration and poor motor skills. Poor concentration may then increase the probability that youths will display antisocial behavior.

In sum, studies have revealed that dopamine activity levels are associated with criminal and antisocial behaviors. However, it is important to note that the different lines of evidence do not agree on the direction of this relationship. Pharmacological and animal studies have reported a positive relationship between dopamine levels and aggression, while other studies have reported a negative relationship between dopamine metabolites and antisocial behavior. These findings show that the relationship between dopamine and antisocial behavior is complex, and often curvilinear.

In light of the evidence between dopamine and antisocial behavior, molecular genetics have begun to investigate whether polymorphisms in dopamine genes are related to criminal and violent behaviors. Research has focused primarily on three polymorphisms in the dopaminergic genes: a dopamine transporter polymorphism (DAT1) and two dopamine receptor gene polymorphisms (DRD2 and DRD4) (Guo, Roettger, & Shih, 2007a). The next sections will describe the functioning of each polymorphism and how it affects dopaminergic activity. In addition, it will review the research that examines the effects of each polymorphism on antisocial and criminal behavior.

Dopamine transporter polymorphism (DAT1).

Dopamine transporters are responsible for removing dopamine neurotransmitters from the synaptic cleft, and returning them to the presynaptic neuron during reuptake (Giros & Caron, 1993). Too many dopamine transporters may result in a dopamine deficiency, which places one at risk for a host of maladaptive outcomes such as depression and an inability to concentrate (Kapur & Mann, 1992). On the other hand, too few dopamine transporters may result in an excess of dopamine within the synaptic cleft. The build-up of dopamine within the synaptic cleft may correspond to higher levels of dopamine activity and neurotransmission, which has been linked to hypersensitivity to stimuli and criminal behavior. However, as will be discussed in other sections, there is evidence that the body may try to offset the negative effects of too few transporters by decreasing the activity of receptors on post-synaptic neurons (David et al., 2005). More specifically, animal studies have shown that postsynaptic dopamine receptors become down-regulated or desensitized when dopamine transporters fail to remove an appropriate amount of dopamine from the synaptic cleft (Giros, Jaber, Jones, Wightman, & Caron, 1996). Thus, too few dopamine transporters, in general, may correspond to higher levels of dopamine activity and a higher probability of criminal behavior, but this may not always be the case.

The availability of dopamine transporter protein is regulated by the dopamine transporter gene (DAT1). The DAT1 gene is located on the short arm of chromosome 5, and it includes numerous VNTR or minisatellite polymorphisms (Haddley et al., 2008). One VNTR polymorphism that has received attention within the literature is the 3'UTR VNTR polymorphism. The DAT1 gene has a 40 base pair VNTR polymorphism that can be repeated 3 to 11 times. The 9 repeat (9R) and 10 repeat (10R) alleles are the most frequently occurring alleles for multiple populations (Kang, Palmatier, & Kidd, 1999). The 40bp VNTR is located on the 3' untranslated region of the gene. This is important because polymorphisms in the untranslated or non-coding regions of a gene have not been shown to influence protein structure. Yet, polymorphisms in the 3' untranslated region can affect other aspects of protein production, such as efficiency of transcription or efficiency of translation (Conne, Stutz, & Vassalli, 2000). This means that the polymorphism may not influence the content of the protein (or products of the transcription and translation process), but it may influence the amount of the DA transporter protein.

Indeed, studies have revealed that the 3' UTR polymorphism in DAT1 influences the efficiency of transcription. For instance, Brookes and colleague's (2007) analysis of post-mortem tissue revealed that the 10R allele was associated with higher levels of DAT1 transcription in the midbrain. A study revealed that the 10R allele corresponded to higher levels of DAT1 mRNA in the cerebellum and temporal lobe (Mill, Asherson, Browes, D'Souza, & Craig, 2002). Other studies have found that the 3' UTR influences the amount of messenger RNA available for translation (Haddley et al., 2008). In light of the evidence that the 3' UTR influences the amount of mRNA, it is not surprising that the polymorphism also influences the amount of DAT1 protein. Heinz et al.'s (2000) analysis of 14 abstinent alcoholics and 11 age-matched controls revealed that individuals who carried two copies of the 10R (10/10 genotype) had approximately 22 percent more DAT1 protein available than those who carried only one copy of the 10R (9/10 genotype). Other studies have also found that the 10R allele is associated with higher levels of DAT1 protein (Cheon, Ryu, Kim, & Cho, 2005; Fuke, Suo, Takahashi, Koike, Sasagawa, & Ishiura, 2001; VanNess, Owens, & Kilts, 2005), yet there are some studies who have not found an association between the 3' UTR polymorphism and dopamine transporter protein (Martinez et al., 2001; Mill et al., 2005b). Overall, the evidence suggests that the 10R allele of the 3' UTR DAT1 polymorphism is associated with a higher number of dopamine transporters than those who do not carry a copy of the 10R. Conversely, the 9R allele corresponds to fewer dopamine transporters, which may lead to an excess of dopamine in the synaptic cleft.

In sum, a dopamine transporter is responsible for returning any excess dopamine to the presynaptic neuron after neurotransmission is complete. The 3' UTR polymorphism of the dopamine transporter gene (DAT1) codes for the production of dopamine transporters that are used to remove any excess dopamine during reuptake. The most common variants of the 3' UTR DAT1 polymorphism is the 9-repeat allele and the 10-repeat allele. Studies suggest that the 10-repeat allele corresponds to more dopamine transporters within the brain, which would hypothetically lead to lower levels of dopamine activity (i.e., more removal of dopamine from synaptic cleft, less dopamine available to adjacent neurons). Lower levels of dopamine have been linked to higher levels of depression, inattention, and poor motor skills. On the other hand, the 9 repeat allele corresponds to fewer dopamine transporters, which suggests that more dopamine would be available for neurotransmission; thus, one may have higher levels of dopamine activity. High levels of dopamine activity have been linked to higher levels of impulsivity, novelty seeking, and hypersensitivity to neutral or negative stimuli (Dagher & Robbins, 2009).

Studies have found that the 3' UTR DAT1 polymorphism is associated with a host of maladaptive outcomes, such as mood disorders, conduct disorder, and criminal behavior. While research has found that the 3' UTR DAT1 polymorphism is related to mood disorders, the evidence is mixed and inconsistent. For instance, Rowe et al. (1998) found that children who carried one or more copies of the 10R allele displayed more mood disorders than those who did not carry the 10R allele. A recent meta-analysis also reported that 3' UTR VNTR polymorphism was associated with a higher risk of depressive disorders, but the authors found that the 9R allele heightened the risk of depression (Lopez et al., 2007). Other studies, however, have not found a relationship between the 3' UTR VNTR polymorphism and internalizing disorders (Frisch et al., 1999; Manki et al., 1996).

The DAT1 VNTR polymorphism has also been linked to higher levels of attention deficit hyperactivity disorder (ADHD) and conduct disorder (CD) (Gill, Daly, Heron, Hawi, & Fitzgerald, 1997). A study of 336 unrelated Caucasians revealed that the 10R allele was associated with ADHD and CD, but the 10R was not associated with oppositional defiant disorder (Comings et al., 2000a, 2000b). Barr et al.'s (2001) transmission disequilibrium analysis of 102 nuclear families revealed that the 10R allele was related to ADHD. A retrospective study found that mothers with the 10/10 genotype reported significantly higher levels of inattention problems than mothers with the 9/10 or 9/9 genotypes (Rowe, Stever, Chase, Sherman, Abramowitz, & Waldman, 2001). Finally, Mill et al.'s (2005a) analysis of male DZ twin pairs revealed that the 10R was associated with higher levels of ADHD. While a substantial number of studies have reported that the 10R is associated with externalizing behaviors, other studies have reported that it is the 9R allele that heightens the risk of externalizing behavior (Young et al., 2002). Still, other analyses have failed to find any relationship between the VNTR 3' UTR polymorphism and ADHD or CD (Bakker et al., 2005; Holmes et al., 2000).

Research has shown that the 3' UTR VNTR DAT1 polymorphism is associated with higher levels of alcohol problems (Samochowiec et al., 2006), especially severe alcohol problems. Sander et al.'s (1997) analysis of 293 alcoholics and 93 healthy controls found that the frequency of the 9R allele was significantly higher among alcoholics with delirium and withdrawal seizures compared to non-alcoholic controls. A study of 48 alcohol dependent individuals revealed that withdrawal symptoms were significantly higher among alcoholics with the 9R allele compared to those without the 9R allele (Schmidt, Harms, Kuhn, Rommelspacher, & Sander, 1998). An analysis of 120 French alcohol dependent patients revealed that patients who carried the 9R allele reported significantly more delirium tremors and withdrawal seizures than those who did not carry the 9R allele (Gorwood, Limosin, Batel, Hamon, Ades, & Boni, 2003). Hopfer et al.'s (2005) analysis of data from the Add Health genetic sample showed that the 10R allele was associated with higher levels of alcohol consumption. Other studies, however, have not found a relationship between DAT1 and alcohol use (Bau et al., 2001; Franke et al., 1999; Heinz et al., 2000; Parsian & Zhang, 1997; Samochowiec et al., 2008).

In light of the evidence linking the 3' UTR VNTR DAT1 polymorphism to antisocial behaviors such as ADHD and substance use, researchers have begun to explore whether this polymorphism influences other types of antisocial behaviors, such as violent and criminal behavior (Chen et al., 2005). Similar to previous studies, the VNTR polymorphism is linked to violent and criminal behaviors, but the studies do not agree on which allele confer an increased risk of antisocial behavior. Gerra et al. (2005) found that irritability and aggressive behavior was higher among individuals with the 9/9 genotype compared to the 9/10 and 10/10 genotypes. In addition, the authors found that the frequency of the 9R allele was significantly higher among violent offenders than nonoffenders. Guo et al.'s (2007a) analysis of the Add Health genetic sample revealed that subjects with the 10/10 and 9/10 genotypes had trajectories of serious delinquency that were almost two times higher than subjects with the 9/9 genotype. Finally, Chen et al. (2007) compared the DAT1 genotype frequencies of 30 super normal controls to the genotypes from 11 adolescents who were diagnosed with impulsive-aggressive behavior or pathological aggression. They found that all 11 (100 percent) diagnosed subjects carried the 10R allele, whereas only 38 percent of the controls carried one or more copies of the 10R allele.

Dopamine (D2) Receptor Polymorphism (DRD2).

Dopamine receptors are located on postsynaptic neurons and they are responsible for capturing or receiving dopamine neurotransmitters from presynaptic neurons. When dopamine receptors are dense, dopamine neurotransmitters can be easily captured and the 'message' is adequately received. However, when dopamine receptors are sparse, few dopamine neurotransmitter molecules are received by the postsynaptic neuron and dopaminergic neurotransmission is limited. To compensate for the sparse dopamine receptors, the body begins overproducing dopamine neurotransmitters in an effort to flood the synapse, and increase the odds that the receptors will receive a dopamine molecule (Laakso et al., 2005). Thus, the body attempts to offset the negative effects of sparse dopamine receptors in an effort to maintain equilibrium.

The availability of dopamine receptors is regulated by dopamine receptor genes. Unlike the gene regulating the dopamine transporter protein, there are numerous dopamine receptor genes that influence the availability of dopamine receptors. One dopamine receptor gene that has received attention within the literature is the DRD2 gene. The DRD2 gene is located on chromosome 11. It contains numerous polymorphisms in the noncoding region of the gene, including a restriction fragment length polymorphism (RLFP) located 2500bp downstream from the gene's coding region. This polymorphism is labeled as TaqIA RLFP, and it contains a C to T substitution (TCGA to

TTGA) that removes the TaqI site (Haberstick & Smolen, 2004). This mutation produces two alleles: the A1 allele and the A2 allele.

The TaqIA polymorphism has been shown to influence the density of D2 receptors within the striatum and nucleus accumbens (Noble, Gottschalk, Fallon, Ritchie, & Wu, 1997; Thompson et al., 1997). An analysis of alcoholic and nonalcoholic subjects revealed that the number of D2 receptors in the caudate nucleus was approximately 30 percent lower in subjects who carried one or more copies of the A1 allele (Noble, Blu, Ritchie, Montgomery, & Sheridan, 1991). The authors also found, however, that the binding of dopamine neurotransmitters to receptors did not differ between alleles. This suggests that the TaqIA polymorphism influences the number of dopamine receptors, but does not influence whether the receptors 'capture' the neurotransmitter. Other studies have reported similar results (Jönsson et al., 1999; Pohjalainen et al., 1998; Ritchie & Noble, 2003), however studies have also failed to find that the TaqIA polymorphism influences the number of dopamine receptors (Laruelle, Gelernter, & Innis, 1998).

One interpretation of these findings is that the A1 allele corresponds to fewer dopamine receptors, which subsequently may lead to lower levels of dopaminergic neurotransmission. As previously discussed, lower levels of dopaminergic neurotransmission are associated with higher levels of depression, trouble concentrating, poor motor skills, and reward deficiency syndrome. Reward deficiency syndrome may increase the likelihood that individuals will engage in addictive or compulsive behaviors, in order to increase dopaminergic neurotransmission (Blum et al., 1996). An alternative interpretation of these findings is that the A1 allele corresponds to fewer dopamine receptors, but that carriers of the A1 allele have higher levels of dopamine activity because they have higher levels of dopamine synthesis (Laakso et al., 2005). The increased amounts of dopamine may then be processed by either D2 receptors or by other dopamine receptors, such as D1 receptors (Klein, Neumann, Reuter, Hennig, vonCramon, & Ullsperger, 2007). As a result, carriers of the A1 allele will have higher levels of dopamine activity—which may lead to impulsivity and aggression—and they may be more sensitive to surges of dopamine that may come from using alcohol or drugs (Dagher & Robbins, 2009).

In sum, a dopamine receptor is responsible for 'capturing' a dopamine molecule from a presynaptic neuron, so that it may 'pass along' the dopaminergic message. The TaqIA DRD2 polymorphism codes for the production of a dopamine D2 receptor. This polymorphism has two variants: the A2 allele and the A1 allele. The A1 allele is associated with fewer dopamine receptors within the striatum; thus, there will be fewer receptors to 'capture' the dopamine molecules and overall dopamine activity will be reduced. As will be discussed below, the A1 allele has been linked to higher levels of substance abuse, impulsivity, and aggression. There are two hypotheses about how the A1 allele increases individuals' risk of substance abuse and impulsivity. The first hypothesis, the reward deficiency perspective, argues that individuals with the A1 allele will require higher levels of stimulation to receive the same pleasure (i.e., dopamine activity) that individuals with the A2 allele because carriers of the A1 allele suffer from hypodopaminergic functioning (Blum et al., 2000). Thus, individuals who carry the A1 allele will be more likely to engage in addictive, compulsive, and risky behaviors because these are some of the most pleasurable and exciting behaviors that will provide the largest doses of dopamine (Blum et al., 1996). The second hypothesis states that A1 carriers may have an over-active dopaminergic system because the A1 allele is associated with increased dopamine synthesis. As a result, the higher levels of dopamine are processed by dopamine receptors (either D2 or other versions of dopamine receptors), and individuals will engage in behaviors that are characteristic of high dopamine activity, such as impulsivity, novelty seeking, and addictive behaviors (Dagher & Robbins, 2009).

In light of the evidence linking the TaqIA polymorphism to dopaminergic functioning, researchers have begun investigating whether the TaqIA polymorphism is related with behaviors that stimulate the dopaminergic system. Numerous studies have examined whether the A1 allele increases individuals' susceptibility to alcoholism and substance use (Cook & Gurling, 1994; Noble et al., 1991; Noble, 1991). For instance, Blum et al. (1991) found that the frequency of the A1 allele was significantly higher among alcoholics, especially chronic alcoholics, compared to healthy controls. Other case control studies have also revealed that the frequency of the A1 allele is significantly higher among alcoholics than healthy controls (Amadéo et al., 1993; Arinami et al., 1993; Berggren et al., 2006; Ishiguro et al., 1998; Kono et al., 1997; Lawford et al., 1997). In addition to the positive results from case control studies, meta-analyses have found that the A1 allele is associated with a heightened risk of alcoholism (Noble, 1993, 1998; Pato, Macciardi, Pato, Verga, & Kennedy, 1993). A recent meta-analysis of 44 studies that included a total of 9,382 subjects revealed that individuals who carry one or more copies of the A1 allele (A1/A1 and A2/A1 genotype) were almost one-and-a-half times more likely to be dependent upon alcohol than those who do not carry the A1 allele (A2/A2 genotype) (Smith, Watson, Gates, Ball, & Foxcroft, 2008). Studies have also shown that the A1 allele is more strongly linked to severe alcohol problems, rather than to less severe problems (Connor, Young, Lawford, Ritchie, & Noble, 2002; Noble, 1998; Ponce et al., 2003).

Despite the numerous studies that support the association between the A1 allele and alcohol use or alcoholism, other studies have reported either no association (Amadéo et al., 2000; Konishi, Calvillo, Leng, Lin, & Wan, 2004; Lu et al., 1996; Suarez, Parsian, Hampe, Todd, Reich, & Cloninger, 1994; Shaikh et al., 2001; Turner et al., 1992) or a negative relationship (Hallikainen et al., 2003; Munafò, Johnstone, Welsh, & Walton, 2005). The two studies that reported a negative relationship focused on alcohol consumption as the outcome variable rather than a diagnosis of alcohol dependence; thus, the negative effects may be due to differences in the outcome variable.

The A1 allele has also been associated with other maladaptive behaviors, such as psychological distress, gambling, and aggression (Chen et al., 2005; Noble, 2003). Comings et al.'s (2001) analysis of data on 31 different genes from 139 pathological gamblers and 139 matched controls revealed that the A1 allele was more prevalent among pathological gamblers than controls. A study of Caucasian adolescent subjects found that subjects who were diagnosed with impulsive-aggressive behavioral problems were more likely to carry the A1 allele than healthy and super normal controls (Chen et al., 2007). Finally, Guo, Roettger, and Shih's (2007) analysis of data from the Add Health sample revealed that individuals with the A1/A2 genotype had trajectories of serious delinquency that were approximately 20 percent higher than individuals with the A2/A2 genotype. In sum, the A1 allele has been linked to a host of maladaptive traits, including substance abuse, aggression, depression, and gambling.

It is important to note that this polymorphism is located in the noncoding region of the gene. This means that the TaqIA polymorphism will not directly influence protein structure, but it may affect other processes such as transcription and translation. Many scholars have hypothesized that the TaqIA polymorphism is in linkage with a functional polymorphism that is located on the DRD2 gene (Gelernter, Kranzler, Cubells, Ichinose, & Nagatsu, 1998; Hitzemann, 1998; Ritchie & Noble, 2003). 'In linkage' refers to a situation where polymorphisms are non-randomly inherited together; thus, if you inherit one gene, you are more likely to inherit another gene. This suggests that any association between the TaqIA DRD2 polymorphism and an observable trait may be confounded by an additional polymorphism.

Dopamine (D4) receptor gene (DRD4).

Similar to dopamine D2 receptors, dopamine D4 receptors are also responsible for capturing dopamine neurotransmitters that are released from presynaptic neurons. However, unlike D2 receptors that are densely located in the striatum, D4 receptors are found largely in the prefrontal cortex, hippocampus, hypothalamus, and dorsal medial thalamus (Primus et al., 1997). This suggests that D4 receptors may be important for the filtering, integration, and storage of information, while the D2 receptors may play a larger role in reward and learning processes (Klein et al., 2007).

The density and functioning of the D4 receptors may be contingent upon proteins that are regulated by the D4 receptor gene (DRD4). DRD4 is located on chromosome 11p15.5 and it contains various functional polymorphisms. One polymorphism that has received a significant attention is a 48 base pair polymorphism that is located in the third exon. The 48 bp polymorphism can be repeated 2 to 11 times (Van Tol et al., 1992). The most prevalent allele is the 4 repeat allele, followed by the 7 repeat, and then the 2 repeat allele (Chang, Kidd,

Livak, Pakstis, & Kidd, 1996). Unlike other polymorphisms that are discussed in this study, the 48 bp polymorphism in DRD4 varies in both the number of repeats and the order in which the repeats appear (Lichter, Barr, Kennedy, VanTol, Kidd, & Livak, 1993). The functional consequences of the 48 bp polymorphism are less well understood than those of other polymorphisms. Scholars have hypothesized that the 48 bp polymorphism may influence the availability and the functioning of D4 receptors. Schoots and Van Tol (2003) found that the 7R allele is associated with less transcriptional efficiency and lower RNA stability. The polymorphism may also influence the availability of D4 receptors via the efficiency and effectiveness of protein folding. After a protein chain is created during the translation process, the protein rapidly folds over and over again until it makes the corresponding chemical molecule. Proteins that are not rapidly folded are degraded by enzymes. Van Craenenbroeck and colleagues' (2005) analyses suggested that the shorter variants of the 48 bp polymorphism (i.e., the 2R) are folded more efficiently and effectively than longer alleles. Thus, proteins from the 7R and higher repeat alleles may be degraded and result in a fewer number of D4 receptors that are available in the brain. Scholars have also hypothesized that the number of alleles may correspond to differences in binding affinity (Asghari et al., 1994) and intracellular responses or sensitivity to dopamine (i.e., signaling efficiency) (Asghari, Sanyal, Buchwaldt, Paterson, Jovanovic, & Van Tol, 1995), with the 7R inhibiting intracellular responses more so than the 2R or 4R. These results suggest that the 48 bp polymorphism may also regulate the functioning and/or signaling efficiency of the D4 receptors. It is important to note, however, that the evidence pointing to functional differences between genotypes is sparse, and it is unclear: (a) if there truly are functional differences between the alleles/repeats, and (b) how large these differences are across genotypes.

In sum, similar to the D2 receptors, the D4 receptors are responsible for receiving dopaminergic 'messages' from adjacent neurons. However, unlike the D2 receptors, the D4 receptors are distributed in areas outside of the striatum, such as the hippocampus, hypothalamus, prefrontal cortex, amygdala, and dorsal medial thalamus (Primus et al., 1997). Therefore, it is expected that the D4 receptors are important for working memory, attentional processes, motor skills, stress reactivity, and regulation of emotions (Falzone, Gelman, Young, Grandy, Low, & Rubinstein, 2002; Kreek, Nielsen, Butelman, & LaForge, 2005; Zhang et al., 2004a), more so than reward and motivational processes. The density of the D4 receptors is a function of the DRD4 gene. The DRD4 gene has a 48 bp polymorphism that can be repeated 2 to 11 times, with the most prevalent repeats being the 2-repeat, the 4-repeat, and the 7-repeat. The 7-repeat allele has been shown to correspond to fewer D4 receptors, which would suggest that dopamine activity would be lower among carriers of the 7R allele. However, as discussed below, studies have shown that the 7R allele is associated with behaviors characteristic of high dopamine activity levels, such as novelty seeking, ADHD, schizophrenia, and hypersensitivity to external stimuli. A theory linking the 7R allele to hyperactive dopaminergic functioning has not yet been proposed in the literature; thus, future research will need to explore the functional significance of the 48 bp polymorphism.

While research is still exploring the functional significance of the 48 bp polymorphism in DRD4, molecular genetic studies have revealed that this polymorphism is related to a variety of maladaptive traits (Comings et al., 2001). For instance, studies have reported that the 48 bp polymorphism is associated with an increased risk of mood disorders (Aguirre, Apiquián, Fresán, & Cruz-Fuentes, 2007; Garriock et al., 2006; Zalsman et al., 2004). Lopez-Leon and colleagues' (2005) meta-analysis of twelve studies revealed that the frequency of the 7R was significantly higher among those diagnosed with unipolar disorders, and the 2R allele was more prevalent among individuals with comorbid unipolar and bipolar disorders. Other studies have found that DRD4 is related to personality traits such as harm avoidance (Hill, Zezza, Wipprecht, Locke, & Neiswanger, 1999) and novelty seeking (Lee et al., 2003). Becker and colleague's (2005) analysis of 303 at-risk high school students found that males who carried one or more copies of the 7R allele scored significantly higher on indices of novelty seeking and harm avoidance. DRD4, however, was not significantly related to novelty seeking and harm avoidance for females. A meta-analysis of 48 studies also reported that DRD4 was not related to approach related traits, such as novelty seeking, extraversion, and impulsivity (Munafò, Yalcin, Willis-Owen, & Flint, 2008).

A large body of research has also reported that the 48 bp DRD4 polymorphism confers an increased risk of attention deficit hyperactivity disorder. A meta-analysis of 36 case control and family based association studies revealed that the 5R and 7R were associated a higher prevalence of ADHD, while shorter alleles (4R) decreased the likelihood of ADHD (Li, Sham, Owen, & He, 2006). Faraone and colleagues' (2001) meta-analysis of case control and family based association studies also found that the odds of being diagnosed with ADHD were significantly higher among those who carried one or more copies of the 7R. Additional case control studies support the hypothesis that the 7R increases the risk of ADHD compared to the shorter variants of the 48 bp polymorphism (4R and less) (El-Faddagh, Laucht, Maras, Vöhringer, & Schmidt, 2004; Holmes et al., 2000; Rowe et al., 2001; Swanson et al., 1998; Todd et al., 2005). Family based association studies have also reported that the 7R allele is associated with ADHD (Barr et al., 2000; Swanson et al., 1998). The significant effect of DRD4 on ADHD has been reported in studies that vary in age group and ethnicity (Arcos-Burgos et al., 2004; Kirley et al., 2004). Other studies, however, have not found a significant relationship between DRD4 and ADHD (Bakker et al., 2005; Castellanos et al., 1998; Comings et al., 2000; Eisenberg et al., 2000).

Finally, studies have revealed that the prevalence and frequency of alcohol and drug misuse is significantly higher among individuals who carry one or more copies of the 7R allele (Hill et al., 1999; McGeary, Esposito-Smythers, Spirito, & Monti, 2007). For instance, Franke et al.'s (2000) analysis of 218 alcoholics and 197 ethnically matched controls found that the frequency of the 7R was significantly higher among alcoholics than healthy controls. Vandenbergh et al. (2000) also found that the quantity and frequency of drug use was significantly higher among individuals who carried one or more copies of the long alleles (6R and greater) compared to short alleles (2R to 5R alleles). A study of university students found that individuals who carried the 7R allele reported higher levels of alcohol craving after alcohol consumption than students who did not carry the 7R (Hopfer et al., 2005; Hutchinson, McGeary, Smolen, Bryan, & Swift, 2002). Other studies, however, have not found an association between the 48 bp polymorphism and substance use (Parsian, Chakraverty, Fisher, & Cloninger, 1997; Sander et al., 1997).

Serotonin.

Serotonin is an inhibitory neurotransmitter synthesized in various regions of the brain and inside the intestinal tract. Serotonergic neurons are densely located in the hindbrain (i.e., raphe nucleus) and various sections of the midbrain such as the caudate, pineal gland, and hypothalamus (Jacobs & Azmitia, 1992; Lucki, 1998; Nishizawa et al., 1997). These neurons are responsible for synthesizing serotonin and serotonergic neurotransmission within the central nervous system. Serotonin that is synthesized in the central nervous system may influence cognitive processes, and ultimately affect human behavior. On the other hand, it remains open to empirical investigation whether serotonin that is synthesized within the intestine (and housed within blood platelets) affects serotonergic neurotransmission. This is because intestinally synthesized serotonin cannot cross over the blood-brain barrier. It may be that intestinally synthesized serotonin influences the chemical precursors to serotonin, such as L-tryptophan, which can cross the blood brain barrier.

Given that serotonin is considered an inhibitory neurotransmitter, it is not surprising that serotonin has been implicated in the inhibition or control of behavior (Reif & Lesch, 2003). It is believed that lower levels of serotonin activity correspond to higher levels of substance use, impulsivity, aggression, depression, and an increased sensitivity to stress (Lucki, 1998). On the other hand, serotonin levels that are too high may lead to over-controlled behaviors such as obsessive compulsive disorder and anorexia nervosa (Jarry & Vaccarino, 1996; Oades, Oades, Röpcke, & Eggers, 1994). Thus, similar to dopamine, serotonin levels must be within the moderate range in order to ensure optimal functioning.

Studies have used three different indicators of serotonergic functioning to examine the relationship between serotonin and human behavior. These three indicators include serotonin metabolite (5HIAA), serotonin agonists (i.e., fenfluramine), and whole blood or blood platelet samples. Similar to dopamine, serotonin neurotransmitters are metabolized by monoamine oxidase enzymes (MAOA and MAOB). These enzymes break down serotonin molecules into inactive compounds that are referred to as metabolites. The metabolite for serotonin is 5HIAA.

Numerous studies have shown that 5HIAA concentrations are typically lower among violent, substance using, depressed, and/or impulsive individuals (Asberg, Thoren, Traskman, Bertilsson, & Ringerger, 1976; Asberg, 1997; Linnoila et al., 1983; Virkkunen, Goldman, Nielsen, & Linnoila, 1995). For instance, an analysis of 26 military men found a moderate, yet significant, negative correlation between 5HIAA and aggression ($r = -.078$) (Brown, Goodwin, Ballenger, Goyer, & Major, 1979). Clarke, Murphy, and Constantino's (1999) analysis of infants revealed that infants who had low 5HIAA levels exhibited significantly more externalizing behaviors at 30 months of age than those infants who did not have low levels of 5HIAA.

Other studies have also reported a negative relationship between 5HIAA and misconduct in childhood and adolescence. Van Goozen and colleagues (1999) found that 5HIAA levels were significantly lower among youths who were diagnosed with oppositional defiant disorder compared to healthy controls. Also, 5HIAA was negatively correlated with aggression and delinquency. Finally, Moore, Scarpa, and Raine's (2002) meta-analysis of 20 studies found a moderate negative association between 5HIAA and antisocial behavior (effect size = $-.45$). While numerous studies have reported a negative correlation between 5HIAA and maladaptive behaviors, other studies have reported either no association (Coccaro, Kavoussi, Trestman, Gabriel, Cooper, & Siever, 1997) or a positive correlation (Castellanos et al., 1994).

Another method for assessing serotonergic functioning is to administer a serotonin agonist and then measure hormonal responses to the drug. It is known that stimulation of the serotonergic system causes the body to release large doses of hormones. Researchers can stimulate the serotonergic system through an agonist, and then use hormone levels as an indicator of serotonergic functioning. For instance, researchers assess serotonin activity by giving subjects fenfluramine (i.e., a serotonin agonist) and then measuring changes in subjects'

cortisol and prolactin levels. It is expected that lower levels of prolactin
or cortisol correspond to higher levels of aggression, impulsivity, or
depression.

Indeed, studies have revealed that prolactin and cortisol levels are
negatively correlated with measures of aggression and impulsivity
(Coccaro et al., 1997; Moss, Yao, & Panzak, 1990). Coccaro and
colleague's (1996) analysis of 14 males with personality disorders
revealed negative relationships between prolactin responses to
fenfluramine and three different measures of aggression. The three
measures of aggression included two self-reported inventories and one
behavioral measure that was observed in a laboratory setting. Other
case control studies have also reported a significant relationship
between prolactin responses and aggression, impulsivity, and substance
abuse (Dolan, Anderson, & Deakin, 2001). However, some studies
have found no relationship between hormone levels (i.e., prolactin and
cortisol) and aggression (Stoff, Pasatiempo, Yeung, Cooper, Bridger, &
Rabinovich, 1992), or they have reported a positive relationship
(Fishbein, Lozovsky, & Jaffee, 1989; Halperin et al., 1994).

Finally, researchers may assess serotonergic functioning by
measuring serotonin levels within blood platelets or whole blood
samples. As previously discussed, blood serotonin is synthesized
within the gastrointestinal tract, while CNS serotonin is synthesized in
the hindbrain. In light of the differences in origin between these two
measures of serotonin, it is possible that the functions of blood
serotonin differ from those of CNS serotonin. Despite the potential
differences in origin and function, blood serotonin and CNS serotonin
can provide researchers with the same basic type of information. That
is, researchers can collect information on serotonin uptake, receptors,
and metabolism from both serotonin neurons and blood samples
(Hrdina, 1994). This suggests that blood samples may be used as a
proxy for CNS serotonergic functioning, yet there is still reason to
believe the functional processes of these elements may be different.

The research linking blood and platelet serotonin levels to
antisocial behavior is mixed. Several studies have shown a negative
relationship between antisocial behavior and platelet 5HT uptake
(Patkar, Gottheil, Berrettini, Hill, Thornton, & Weinstein, 2003) or
whole blood 5HT levels (Hanna, Yuwiler, & Coates, 1995). For

instance, Stoff and colleagues (1987) reported that decreases in 5HT uptake sites on blood platelets corresponded to higher levels of conduct disorder, aggression, and externalizing behavior among children. Other studies, however, have reported positive relationships between whole blood 5HT levels and antisocial behaviors (Hughes, Petty, Sheikha, & Kramer, 1996; Unis et al., 1997). An analysis of 43 male juvenile offenders found that 5HT whole blood concentrations were significantly higher in adolescents who were diagnosed with conduct disorder (Unis et al., 1997). Moffitt et al.'s (1998) analysis of 781 young adult men and women found that increases in whole blood 5HT levels corresponded to significantly higher levels of violent offending for males, but not for females. Thus, the evidence linking 5HT concentrations in whole blood samples and blood platelets to antisocial behavior is mixed and inconclusive.

Serotonin transporter polymorphism (5HTTLPR).

Serotonin transporters are responsible for capturing serotonin neurotransmitters that are lingering in the synaptic cleft, and returning these neurotransmitters to the presynaptic neuron. If there too few serotonin transporters, serotonin neurotransmitters may begin building up in the synaptic cleft, which may interfere with future neurotransmission. On the other hand, if there are too many serotonin transporters, there may not be enough serotonin neurotransmitters to effectively transmit the chemical message. It is important to remember that neurotransmitter transporters are only one part of a larger system. Therefore, even though transporters may not be functioning properly, the body will attempt to compensate for this dysfunction by adjusting another element of the larger system (i.e., receptors).

The protein that creates serotonin transporters is regulated by the serotonin transporter gene (5HTT). The 5HTT is located on chromosome 17q11.2. One polymorphism that has received a substantial amount of attention in the literature is the 44 base pair insertion/deletion polymorphism. The 44bp polymorphism is located upstream from the transcription initiation site, and consists of a short allele (deletion) and a long allele (insertion).

The 44bp polymorphism has been implicated in the transcriptional efficiency of the promoter region of the 5HTT gene (Canli & Lesch,

2007; Heils et al., 1996). Lesch et al. (1996) found that human cells that included one or more copies of the short allele had lower concentrations of 5HTT mRNA, and subsequently reduced transcriptional efficiency. Their analyses also revealed that 5HT reuptake was 1.9 to 2.2 times lower in cells that carried the short allele. These results suggest that the short allele corresponds to lower levels of serotonin transporters, which (hypothetically) would lead to higher levels of serotonin in the synaptic cleft and higher levels of serotonin neurotransmission. However, this is not the case. Research has found that 5HT (presynaptic and postsynaptic) receptors become downregulated, as a way to offset the effects of the short allele. Therefore, even though individuals with the short allele have higher levels of serotonin within the synaptic cleft, post-synaptic receptors become desensitized and downregulated in order to slow down serotonergic neurotransmission (David et al., 2005). This may produce lower levels of overall serotonin activity. Williams et al.'s (2001) analysis of 54 adults supports this hypothesis. Their analyses found that individuals who were homozygous for the short allele had cerebral spinal fluid (CSF) levels of the serotonin metabolite (5HIAA) that were 50% lower than those of persons who carried one or more copies of the long allele. Thus, individuals with the short allele are expected to have lower levels of serotonin neurotransmission.

Results from mice knockout models confirm those from analyses of human cells. Bengel et al. (1998) found that -/- mice (short/short genotype) had fewer serotonin transporters and lower levels of 5HT concentrations in various brain regions, including the frontal cortex, hippocampus, striatum, and brain stem. However, the efficiency of reuptake did not significantly vary by genotype. In line with the hypothesis that the short allele is related to downregulation of 5HT receptors, Fabre et al.'s (2000) analyses revealed that -/- mice had lower levels of 5HT1A and 5HT1B receptor protein and mRNA levels in various brain regions. Furthermore, studies have shown that the body may attempt to compensate for lower levels of serotonergic neurotransmission by over-producing serotonin neurotransmitters. Kim et al. (2005) found that -/- mice had 5HT synthesis rates that were 30 to 60 percent higher than synthesis rates of +/+ mice (long/long genotype). They also found that, despite the over-production of 5HT neurotransmitters, -/- mice had 5HT concentrations that were 55 to 70 percent lower than +/+ mice. The evidence from human and animal models converge to show that the short allele is associated with lower levels of serotongeric neurotransmission, perhaps because post-synaptic receptors downregulate themselves to deal with the large increases in serotonin.

In sum, serotonin transporters are responsible for returning any excess serotonin back to the presynaptic neuron after neurotransmission is complete. A 44 bp insertion/deletion polymorphism in the 5HTT gene has been shown to regulate the number of serotonin transporters. The deletion variant or short allele has been linked to fewer serotonin transporters, less reuptake, decreased expression of serotonin receptors, and lower concentrations of serotonin. As stated above, lower levels of serotonin have been linked to higher levels of aggressive, impulsive, and criminal behavior.

In light of evidence showing that the short allele corresponds to lower levels of serotonin activity, researchers have begun to examine whether the short allele is linked to a variety of maladaptive outcomes. Studies have shown that the 5HTTLPR polymorphism is associated with depression, neuroticism, harm avoidance, and anxiety (Baca-Garcia, Vaquero, Diaz-Sastre, Saiz-Ruiz, Fernandez-Piqueras, & de Leon, 2002; Brummett, Siegler, McQuoid, Svenson, Marchuk, & Steffens, 2003; Lesch et al., 1996; López-León et al., 2007; Wilhelm et al., 2007). Gelernter and colleagues' (1998) analysis of 322 subjects found that males who carried one or more copies of the short allele had higher levels of harm avoidance than males with the L/L genotype. Interestingly, their analyses also showed that females who were homozygous for the long allele (L/L genotype) had higher harm avoidance scores than females who carried one or more copies of the short allele. Other studies have also reported gender specific effects of 5HTTLPR on depression, anxiety, and neuroticism (Brummett et al., 2003; Flory, Manuck, Ferrell, Dent, Peters, & Muldoon, 1999). For instance, Du, Bakish, and Hrdina's (2000) analyzed data from 186 normal subjects found that the short allele was significantly associated with neuroticism scores for males, but it was not associated with neuroticism scores for females. Gonda and colleagues' (2005) analysis of 128 healthy females, however, revealed that females with the short allele reported significantly higher levels of depression than females who were homozygous for the long allele. Thus, the evidence on the association between 5HTTLPR and measures of psychological distress is mixed, and the relationships often vary by gender. Research has also shown that the 5HTTLPR polymorphism is significantly related to attention deficit hyperactivity disorder, oppositional defiant disorder, aggression, and violence (Comings et al., 2000; Haberstick, Smolen, & Hewitt, 2006; Liao, Hong, Shih, & Tsai, 2004; Manor et al., 2001). A case control study of extremely aggressive children and healthy controls revealed that the short allele was more prevalent among aggressive children (Beitchman et al., 2003). An analysis of incarcerated Caucasian males revealed that the short allele was more prevalent among inmates who frequently engaged in physically violent behavior (Retz, Retz-Junginger, Supprian, Thorne, & Rösler, 2004). The authors also found that the short allele was more prevalent among violent offenders who had a history of attention deficit hyperactivity disorder than non-violent offenders with a history of ADHD. Other studies have found that the long allele is associated with higher levels of ADHD (Kent et al., 2002). Beitchman et al. (2003) found that aggressive children with ADHD were more likely to carry one or more copies of the long allele than those without ADHD. Cadoret et al. (2003) found that females with the long allele were more likely to show signs of conduct disorder, ADHD, and aggression than females without the long allele. For males, however, the short allele increased the likelihood of conduct disorder, ADHD, and aggression. Thus, the evidence on externalizing types of behaviors is mixed, and the effect of 5HTTLPR on externalizing behavior often varies by gender.

Research has shown that the short allele of 5HTTLPR is associated with higher levels of alcohol consumption, alcohol problems, and ethanol tolerance (Matsushita, Yoshino, Murayama, Kimura, Muramatsu, & Higuchi, 2001; Türker et al., 1998). Herman and colleagues' (2003) analysis of 204 Caucasian subjects found that individuals who were homozygous for the short allele consumed more alcohol per occasion, engaged in binge drinking more frequently, and reported getting intoxicated more frequently than subjects who were not homozygous for the short allele. Other studies, however, have found no association between 5HTTLPR and alcohol use (Hopfer et al., 2005), or they have found that the relationship varies by gender. Munafò et al. (2005) found that males who were homozygous and heterozygous for the short allele consumed higher levels of alcohol than males who were homozygous for the long allele. For females, however, only females who were heterozygous for the short allele reported significantly higher levels of alcohol consumption.

Monoamine Oxidase A.

Monoamine oxidase A (MAOA) is a mitochondrial enzyme that is responsible for degrading neurotransmitters that linger in the synaptic cleft after a chemical message has been transmitted to a post-synaptic neuron (Roth, Breakefield, & Castiglione, 1976). MAOA neurons are heavily located in regions responsible for the synthesis and processing of catecholamines such as nucleus locus coeruleus, substantia nigra, and periventricular region of the hypothalamus (Shih, Chen, & Ridd, 1999; Westlund, Denney, Kochersperger, Rose, & Abell, 1985). The enzyme MAOA primarily degrades serotonin and norepinephrine, but it can also degrade dopamine neurotransmitters (Ellis, 1991). Since MAOA is responsible for clearing out the synaptic cleft after neurotransmission, it has been hypothesized that lower levels of MAOA activity may result in an excess of neurotransmitters within the synaptic cleft. The excess number of neurotransmitters may then interfere with the transmission of chemical messages. On the other hand, too many MAOA molecules may result in neurotransmitter deficiencies, which may also lead to aberrant behavior.

Studies have shown that low MAOA activity is significantly related to under-controlled behaviors, such as sensation seeking, substance use, impulsivity, aggression, and criminal behavior (Ellis, 1991; Shih et al., 1999; Shih & Thompson, 1999). Brunner and colleagues' (1993) analysis of youths from a Dutch kindred revealed that males were mentally disabled and they engaged in a variety of antisocial behavior, such as exhibition, impulsive aggression, and attempted rape. The authors analyzed the MAOA metabolite levels from the males over a twenty-four hour period and found that the antisocial males suffered from an MAOA deficiency. Additional analyses revealed that these MAOA deficient males suffered from a C to T point mutation in the eighth exon of the MAOA gene. The authors concluded that the MAOA polymorphism resulted in MAOA deficiency, which subsequently explained why the males exhibited behavioral problems.

Results from knockout mice studies have also shown that MAOA deficiency is linked to maladaptive behaviors (Shih et al., 1999). Cases et al.'s (1995) found that MAOA deficient mice were more sensitive to the effects of stimuli than mice who were not MAOA deficient. MAOA deficient mice would tremble, become fearful, and attempt to bury themselves under woodchips to escape stimuli. In addition, the authors found that MAOA deficient mice had concentrations of serotonin that were nine times higher than serotonin levels in non-MAOA deficient mice. Finally, the results showed that MAOA deficiency caused architectural changes in the mice pup's brains. The brains of MAOA deficient mice showed significantly higher levels of 5HT sites in the locus coeruleus and nigral complex, regions that are rich with catecholaminergic neurons. These regions did not show higher levels of tryptophan hydroxylase, an enzyme that is necessary for the synthesis of serotonin. The authors concluded that the increased number of 5HT sites in the locus coeruleus and nigral complex may reflect higher levels of 5HT uptake rather than an increased synthesis of 5HT.

Human studies have also shown that MAOA deficiency may lead to structural and functional changes in the brain. Meyer-Lindenberg et al.'s (2006) analysis of healthy volunteers revealed that the volume of limbic structures was significantly reduced among individuals who carried one or more copies of the low activity allele of the MAOA gene. In addition, individuals who carried one or more copies of the low activity allele showed greater amygdale responses and lower prefrontal cortex responses when presented with emotional stimuli. This suggests that individuals who carry the low activity allele may emotionally react to a situation without fully assessing and processing the stimuli; thus, they are likely to react emotionally, rather than rationally.

Monoamine oxidase A polymorphism.

The MAOA gene is located on the X-chromosome at position Xp11.3-11.4. It contains several polymorphisms, but the literature has begun to focus on a 30bp VNTR polymorphism in the promoter region of the gene. The 30bp VNTR consists of five repetitions of the six nucleotide sequence: ACC(A/G/C)G(C/T) (Sabol, Hu, & Hamer, 1998). The 30bp sequence can be repeated 2, 3, 3.5, 4 or 5 times. The 2 and 3 repeat alleles are referred to as low activity alleles, and these are believed to confer an increased risk for antisocial behavior (Caspi et al., 2002). Studies have shown that the 3.5 and 4 repeat alleles are transcribed more efficiently than the 3 and 5 repeat alleles (Deckert, 1999). More specifically, Sabol et al. (1998) found that the transcriptional efficiency of the 3.5 and 4 repeat alleles was two to ten times that of the 3 and 5 repeat alleles.

The low activity alleles (2 and 3 repeat) may correspond to lower levels of MAOA, which may lead to less degradation of neurotransmitters (i.e., lower metabolite levels) and greater concentrations of neurotransmitters within the brain. This hypothesis can be deduced from studies on humans and mice knockouts. Zalsman and colleagues (2005) found that the low activity allele was related to lower levels of dopamine metabolites (HVA) in males; thus, lower levels of MAOA corresponded to less degradation of dopamine neurotransmitters. This may suggest that the low activity allele is related to greater concentrations of serotonin, dopamine, and norepinephrine in the brain. Indeed, mice knockout studies have revealed that mice lacking the MAOA gene (i.e., a proxy for the low activity allele) have higher levels of serotonin, dopamine, and norepinephrine, while wild type mice (i.e., a distant proxy for the high activity allele) have lower levels of such neurotransmitters (Shih, 2004). Thus, it may be hypothesized that the low activity allele reduces degradation of neurotransmitters and creates chemical imbalances that increase the likelihood of antisocial behaviors.

Studies have shown that the 3 repeat allele or low activity allele is related to various antisocial behaviors (Lawson et al., 2003; Samochowiec et al., 1999). Contini and colleague's (2006) analysis of 125 Brazilian alcoholics and 235 healthy controls revealed that the 3 repeat or low activity allele was significantly associated with an earlier onset of alcoholism, alcohol dependence, polydrug use among alcoholics, and a higher number of antisocial behaviors. Guo, Wilhelmsen, and Hamilton (2007b) found that MAOA was related to adult alcohol use, but not adolescent alcohol use. Other studies have also found that the 3 repeat allele is significantly associated with alcoholism (Parsian, Cloninger, Sinha, & Zhang, 2003), especially alcoholics who also meet the criteria for antisocial personality disorder (Samochowiec et al., 1999; Schmidt et al., 2000). Other studies, however, have failed to replicate these results (Koller, Bondy, Preuss, Bottlender, & Soyka, 2003; Lu, Lee, Ko, Lin, Chen, & Shih, 2002; Lu, Lee, Ko, Lin, Chen, & Shih, 2003). There has been some research on the association between the 30bp VNTR and aggression. However, unlike previous studies which implicated the 3 repeat allele as the risk allele, these studies have shown that the high activity alleles (3.5 and 4 repeat) confer an increased risk of aggression. Manuck and colleagues (2000) analyzed data from 110 men from the community and found that the 3.5 repeat and 4 repeat alleles were associated with higher scores on inventories of aggression and impulsivity. Beitchman and colleagues (2004) examined the relationship between MAOA and aggression using data from 50 psychiatrically referred male children and ethnically matched adult males. Their analyses revealed that persistently aggressive children were more likely to carry the 4 repeat allele (or high activity allele) than the healthy controls. The results from these studies suggest that the high activity allele may confer an increased risk of aggression and impulsivity.

Summary of the Dopaminergic, Serotonergic, and Monoamine Oxidase A Polymorphisms.

The dopaminergic, serotonergic, and monoamine oxidase polymorphisms described above regulate specific aspects of the neurotransmission process. The dopamine transporter polymorphism codes for the transporters that are responsible for clearing dopamine from the synaptic cleft and returning it to the presynaptic neuron. The dopamine receptor polymorphisms, on the other hand, code for proteins that create dopamine receptors on postsynaptic neurons. The serotonin transporter polymorphism codes for proteins that make up the serotonin transporters. Similar to dopamine transporters, serotonin transporters capture serotonin molecules from the synaptic cleft and return them to the presynaptic neuron. Finally, the monoamine oxidase A polymorphism codes for the monoamine oxidase A enzyme, which is responsible for degrading excess neurotransmitters after transmission. While these polymorphisms code for specific elements, it would be erroneous to create hypotheses based on a single element without reference to the other elements of the system, as well as the body's need to maintain equilibrium. For instance, the 9 repeat allele of the DAT1 polymorphism has been linked to lower levels of dopamine transporter protein (Fuke et al., 2001; VanNess et al., 2005), which would suggest that more dopamine would accumulate within the synaptic cleft and overall dopamine activity levels would be higher. However, this is not the case due to the body's need to maintain equilibrium. When too much dopamine accumulates in the synaptic cleft, the dopamine receptors on the post-synaptic neuron may downregulate themselves in an effort to slow down dopamine neurotransmission. Thus, while researchers using secondary data sources with genetic markers can make general assumptions about the functioning of a polymorphism, it is impossible to understand the full functioning of those polymorphisms without more sophisticated methods.

Sex Differences in the Effects of Dopaminergic, Serotonergic, and Monoamine Oxidase A Polymorphisms on Antisocial Behaviors
While males and females have similar genomes, the ways in which these genes express themselves and influence behavior differs. That is, males and females share many of the same genes, yet there are substantial differences in the activity of these genes (i.e., the efficiency in producing a protein). For instance, studies of mice have shown that there are sex differences in the expression of genes that code for proteins used in the liver (Clodfelter, Holloway, Hodor, Park, Ray, & Waxman, 2006; Delongchamp, Velasco, Dial, & Harris, 2005), skeletal muscle (Welle, Tawil, & Thornton, 2008), and fat tissues (Rodríguez, Ribot, Rodríguez, & Palou, 2004). Research has also shown that sex conditions the expression of genes within the brain (Ilia, Sugiyama, & Price, 2003; Rinn & Snyder, 2005; Treister, Richards, Lombardi, Rowley, Jensen, & Sullivan, 2005). Yang et al.'s (2006) analysis of 334 mice found that 355 genes are expressed more highly in male's brains and 257 genes were expressed more highly in female's brain.

Dewing, Shi, Horvath, and Vilain (2003) analyzed mice embryos and found that 36 genes were expressed at a higher rate in the female brain, while 18 genes were expressed at a higher rate in the male brain. Vawter et al. (2004) analyzed 20 post mortem brains and found that the XIST gene was expressed at a higher rate in the anterior cingulate and cerebellum of females, while five genes were expressed at a higher rate in male's anterior cingulate, cerebellum, and dorsal lateral prefrontal cortex. Finally, Weickert et al. (2009) examined 55,000 transcripts of genes that are expressed in the prefrontal cortex and found a significant gender difference in 130 of the transcripts. The study also revealed a significant gender difference in 25 genes located on sex chromosomes and 58 autosomal genes.

The literature on sex differences in general gene expression would suggest that the dopaminergic, serotonergic, and monoamine oxidase A genes may have different effects on antisocial behavior for males and females. Indeed, studies have revealed that sex conditions the effects DAT1, DRD2, DRD4, 5HTTLPR, and MAOA polymorphisms on antisocial behavior. It is important to note, however, that these findings are limited and often contradictory. Thus, there is a need for replication in the future.

The effects of the dopaminergic polymorphisms on antisocial behavior have been shown to vary by sex. For instance, Rowe and colleagues (2001) found that females who were homozygous for the 10R allele reported higher levels of inattention and conduct disorder than females who were not homozygous for the 10R allele. However, the DAT1 polymorphism was not related to fathers' retrospective reports of conduct disorder. Andersen and Teicher (2000) found that males had a greater increase in DRD2 receptors during prepubertal development than females, and this may explain the higher prevalence of ADHD among adolescent boys relative to adolescent girls.

Other researchers have reported that the 48 bp DRD4 polymorphism has different effects on males and females antisocial behavior. Results from a high risk community sample of youths found that males who carried the 7R allele reported higher levels of novelty seeking and harm avoidance than males who did not carry the 7R, but DRD4 was not related to measures of temperament for females (Becker et al., 2005). Ham et al. (2006) analyzed data from Korean medical students and found that DRD4 was related to GPA and reward dependence for males, but not females. A study of Caucasian substance abusers found that male substance users were more likely to carry one or more copies of the long DRD4 alleles (7R and greater) than female substance users (Vandenbergh et al., 2000). A recent study of 263 Russian adolescents revealed that males with the 7R reported higher levels of delinquency, higher levels of thrill seeking, and being more prone to a short temper, than females carrying the 7R (Dmitrieva, Chen, Greenberger, Ogunseitan, & Ding, 2010). Thus, it appears that the DRD4 polymorphism may have a stronger effect on males' antisocial behavior than females' antisocial behavior.

A substantial number of studies have investigated whether the effects of 5HTTLPR on antisocial behavior are invariant by gender (Munafò et al., 2005). Two studies have found that the short allele confers an increased risk of externalizing behaviors for males, but it is the long allele that increases the risk of externalizing behaviors for females. Gelernter et al. (1998) found that the short allele was associated with higher scores on a harm avoidance inventory for males, while the long allele was associated with harm avoidance for females. Cadoret et al. (2003) also found that the short allele was associated with higher levels of conduct disorder, aggression, and ADHD for males, while the long allele increased females' risk of engaging in conduct disorder, aggression, and ADHD.

Studies of internalizing symptoms have reported mixed results. Research has found that males who carried the short allele were less likely to report symptoms of anxiety than males who did not carry the short allele (Flory et al., 1999; Brummett, Siegler, McQuoid, Svenson, Marchuk, & Steffens, 2003). The 5HTTLPR polymorphism, however, was not associated with anxiety for females in either of the two studies. Du et al.'s (2000) analysis of healthy subjects found that neuroticism scores were significantly higher among males who carried the short allele, but 5HTTLPR was not associated with females' neuroticism scores.

Finally, there is some evidence to suggest that the MAOA polymorphism should have a stronger effect on males' behavior than females' behavior. Brunner et al.'s (1993) analysis of the Dutch kindred found that low MAOA activity was associated with mental disability, impulsivity, and aggression for males, but not females. One reason why variants in MAOA may have a stronger effect on males is that the MAOA gene is located on the X chromosome. Genetic polymorphisms on the X chromosome may have a stronger effect on males than females because genetic abnormalities on the X chromosome may be inactivated or offset for females, but not for males. As discussed in the following sections, X linked polymorphisms such as MAOA may have a more profound effect for males than females due to biological processes, such as X-inactivation, lack of a homolog, and genomic imprinting (Bainbridge, 2003).

Sex-Based Differences in Gene Expression—a focus on the X chromosome

Scholars have noted that genes located on the X chromosomes may have a stronger effect on the behavioral and physiological functioning of males than females. There are at least two reasons why the transmission of genes on the X chromosome differentially affect males compared to females (Vaske, Wright, Boisvert, & Beaver, 2010). First, X-linked alleles may have gender specific effects on behavior because of sex differences in chromosomes (Nguyen & Disteche, 2006). Males acquire an X chromosome from their mother and a Y chromosome from their father. Females, on the other hand, acquire an X chromosome from their mother and an X chromosome from their father. Each cell within the female body, however, (theoretically) contains only one fully active X chromosome rather than two. This reduction from two X chromosomes to only one fully active X chromosome is referred to as X-inactivation or X-silencing (Lyon, 1961). In order to prevent genetic 'overload', an X-linked gene called the *XIST* gene randomly switches on in either the paternal or maternal X chromosome during embryonic development, and it silences or inactivates the "chosen" chromosome. If an X-linked trait is dominant (i.e., color blindness, hemophilia)—meaning that only one allele is necessary for the genotype to be expressed as a phenotype—then it is expected that males will be more affected by the gene than females because there is not a chance that the harmful genetic X-linked trait will be silenced. That is, there is a chance that a harmful genetic mutation will be silenced in females, but there is no such alternative for males. Thus, males will show signs of an X-linked dominant disorder, while females may or may not show signs of the disorder depending upon the results of X-inactivation.

Second, approximately 10 to 15 percent of X chromosomes may escape inactivation (Carrel & Willard, 2005), and there is a possibility that active X chromosomes will contain an "advantageous" allele that will offset the effects of an active "disadvantageous" allele. For instance, if a female has two active X chromosomes and one chromosome contains a "disadvantageous" allele, there is a possibility that she may have an "advantageous" allele on the other X chromosome, and this will mask or moderate the negative consequences of the "disadvantageous" allele. Another scenario could be that both X chromosomes with "disadvantageous" alleles would be active, and this could cause serious harm to the female. Despite the latter scenario, males may have a lower probability of having a "backup" allele to offset any negative effects. The possibility of a "backup" allele for X linked polymorphisms is lower among males because they may not have a complementary allele on the X or Y chromosome. If a gene is X linked and males only receive one X chromosome, they have a zero probability of having an "advantageous" allele on a second X chromosome to offset negative effects. Similarly, many X linked genes do not have complementary alleles on the Y chromosome; thus, there is not a chance that an "advantageous" allele lies on the Y chromosome to offset the negative effects of a "disadvantageous" X linked allele. In sum, it is believed that "disadvantageous" X linked alleles may have a stronger effect on males than females because the probability of having a "backup" allele on the X or Y chromosome is lower for males than females.

Genetic markers may also have different effects for males and females because of differences in gene expression. Gene expression may differ due to the origin of the chromosome (i.e., paternal or maternal) and differences in sex hormones (Ostrer, 2001). First, sex specific effects of genes may arise due to genomic imprinting (Iwasa & Pomiankowski, 2001; Skuse, 2006). Genomic imprinting occurs when a gene is either "silenced" or "switched on" due to whether the gene was inherited from the mother or from the father. Skuse et al. (1997) analyzed data from 80 females who had Turner's syndrome. Turner's syndrome is a chromosomal condition where either all or a significant proportion of an X chromosome is missing; thus X-inactivation cannot occur and the likelihood of expressing the one X chromosome is close to 100 percent (depending upon the extent of missing information on the second X chromosome). Skuse et al.'s (1997) analysis revealed that females who inherited the paternal X chromosome had higher verbal IQ's, were better socially adjusted, and scored higher on behavioral inhibition tasks than females who inherited the maternal X chromosome. The authors hypothesized that an "advantageous" allele may be located on the paternal X chromosome, and the locus of that "advantageous" allele is methylated or silenced on the maternal X chromosome. Similarly, maternally inherited X-chromosomes may carry "disadvantageous" alleles that place females and males at risk for a host of behavioral problems (Ostrer, 2001; Lynn & Davies, 2007). Since males inherit the X-chromosome from their mothers (without the likelihood of X-inactivation and a low probability of having a "backup" allele), it is expected that maladaptive X-linked imprinted genes will have a stronger effect on males' behavior than females' behavior due to genomic imprinting (combined with a lack of inactivation and a low probability of having a "backup" allele) (Skuse, 2006; Xu & Disteche, 2006).

Second, sex hormones may influence the transcription of genes. A substantial body of literature has shown that estrogens and androgens significantly influence functioning of the serotonergic, dopaminergic, and monoamine oxidase systems (Amin, Canli, & Epperson, 2005; Cahill, 2006; McEwen, 1999; Warren, Tedford, & Flynn, 1979). For instance, research findings suggest that estrogen influences the synthesis, transport, and degradation of serotonin (Joffe & Cohen, 1998; Rubinow, Schmidt, & Roca, 1998). More specifically, studies have shown that females typically have lower levels of 5HT synthesis, greater turnover of serotonin (5HIAA), and fewer serotonin receptors within the brain than males (Fischette, Biegon, & McEwen, 1983; Rubinow et al., 1998). Studies of ovarectomized monkeys found that the administration of estrogen decreased serotonin transporter mRNA (Bethea, Mirkes, Su, & Michelson, 2002; Pecins-Thompson, Brown, & Bethea, 1998). Biver et al.'s (1996) analysis of twenty-two healthy males and females revealed that the binding potential (i.e., affinity) of serotonin receptors ($5HT_{2r}$) was significantly higher among males than females. Additional analyses have also shown that male sex hormones, androgens, may have a positive effect on the density of serotonin receptors (Fink, Sumner, Rosie, Wilson, & McQueen, 1999; Fischette et al., 1983).

Studies have found that sex hormones may significantly influence the functioning of dopamine and monoamine oxidase systems. LeSaux and Paolo (2006) found that removing the ovaries of rats lead to a significant increase in the binding of dopamine transporters in the striatum. This suggests that the transportation of dopamine back to the presynaptic neuron will increase as estrogen (receptor) levels decrease. Other studies have found that increases in estrogen levels are related to higher levels of dopamine synthesis and dopamine activity (Beyer, Pilgrim, & Reisert, 1991; Ma et al., 1993; Becker, 1999). These studies generally show that dopaminergic functioning is significantly influenced by estrogen, but not androgens. However, estrogens *and* androgens may influence the functioning of enzymes such as monoamine oxidase A (Buckholtz & Meyer-Lindenberg, 2008; Ellis, 1991; Warren et al., 1979). Studies have shown that the administration of estrogen and progesterone to ovarectomized monkeys significantly decreases MAOA mRNA, but generally have little effect on MAOB (Gundlah, Lu, & Bethea, 2002; Smith, Henderson, Abell, & Bethea, 2004). Researchers have hypothesized that increases in testosterone may decrease monoamine oxidase levels (Sjöberg et al., 2008).

The mechanism underlying the relationship between sex hormones and neurotransmitter activity may be genetically mediated. It is believed that estrogen may influence the transcription and translation of proteins that are necessary for the synthesis of neurotransmitters and enzymes (i.e., MAOA). More specifically, estrogen receptor molecules are transcription factors that can bind to the promoter region on a DNA strand via mRNA (Katzenelienbogen, O'Malley, & Katzenelienbogen, 1996; Lasiuk & Hegadoren, 2007). Once the estrogen molecule binds to the promoter region, it can then affect the transcription and translation of DNA sequences that are used to create proteins. These proteins can be used to synthesize neurotransmitters, enzymes, transporters, receptors, growth factors, and neuropeptides (Rubinow et al., 1998). Similarly, androgen and estrogen molecules may bind to the promoter region of the MAOA gene and decrease the transcriptional efficiency of the MAOA gene (Gundlah et al., 2002). This may lead to lower levels of the MAOA enzyme within the brain, and subsequently influence behavior (Ou, Chen, & Shih, 2006). The above discussion suggests that genetic expression may differ for males and females due to genomic imprinting (especially on X chromosomes) and gender differences in sex hormones. It would be erroneous to think, however, that these processes occur in a vacuum. That is, that these processes are separate and do not interact. This is not how the human body functions, it is a large process that is interdependent upon various subprocesses. The next section will discuss two examples of how the X linked genes and sex hormones may come together to influence behavior.

When gene transmission collides with gender and gene expression.

There is some research that shows that sex hormones may moderate the effects of X linked polymorphisms on antisocial behavior. For instance, Sjöberg et al. (2008) found that MAOA interacted with testosterone to influence antisocial behavior and aggression among males. Males who carried a low activity allele and who had higher levels of testosterone reported higher levels of aggression and were more likely to be diagnosed with antisocial personality disorder than males with the high activity allele and high testosterone. Sjöberg and colleagues also found that males with the low activity allele and high testosterone levels had lower MAOA metabolites than low activity allele/low testosterone males, suggesting that high levels of testosterone may further suppress transcription of the low activity MAOA allele. From this study, it may be suggested that males with the low activity allele will have lower levels of MAOA activity (and perhaps less degradation of neurotransmitters) than females with the low activity allele because of males' higher levels of testosterone. Further, as discussed above, males may be even more at-risk for neuropsychological problems from X linked polymorphisms (such as MAOA) due to the inability to inactivate "disadvantageous" alleles such as the low activity allele; thus, males' higher level of testosterone may further exacerbate their level of risk associated with X linked "disadvantageous" alleles.

Studies have also suggested that testosterone may interact with another X linked gene—the androgen receptor gene—to influence antisocial behavior. Androgen receptors are densely populated in the amygdala, and these receptors are responsible for processing androgens, such as testosterone. The androgen receptor CAG polymorphism has a short allele which is associated with hyperactive androgen receptor activity (i.e., greater processing of androgens), and a long allele which is associated with lower androgen receptor activity. Vermeersch and colleagues (2010) found that nonaggressive risk-taking, dominance, and aggressive risk-taking were higher among high testosterone males who carried the short allele, relative to high testosterone males with the long allele and low testosterone males with the short allele. It is not known whether the interaction has a stronger neurobiological effect for males than females. It may be hypothesized, however, that the interaction will have a stronger effect on males because of the theoretical reasons (i.e., no inactivation of X linked gene) and the stronger effect observed with MAOA.

Take home messages:

- DNA contains nitrogen bases (A, C, G, T), and variations in these nitrogen bases give rise to differences in physiology and neuropsychology, which may lead to differences in cognition and behavior.

- Genetic variations or polymorphisms in genes related to dopamine, serotonin, and monoamine oxidase systems may correspond to variations in internalizing behaviors, aggression, antisocial behavior, and substance use. More specifically, these variations include polymorphisms in the DAT1, DRD2, DRD4, 5HTTLPR, and MAOA genes. Research suggests that maladaptive behaviors are associated with the 9R or 10R alleles of DAT1, A1 allele of DRD2, 7 or more repeat allele of DRD4, short allele of 5HTTLPR, and low activity allele of MAOA.

- Gender differences in genetic transmission or genetic expression may occur due to genes located on sex chromosomes, genomic imprinting (and parent of origin effects), and sex hormones. For instance, "disadvantageous" alleles on the X chromosome may have a stronger effect on males than females because males do not have the opportunity for X inactivation, males have a lower probability of a "backup" allele on the X or Y chromosome, and the genomic imprinting of an "advantageous" locus on the maternal X chromosome.

CHAPTER FOUR
The Integration of Behavioral Genetics and Criminological Hypotheses of Victimization & Criminal Behavior

Criminologists have been reluctant to incorporate biology and genetics into their theories of offending. This is understandable given scholars past inclinations to attribute offending to biological inferiorities (Lombroso & Ferrera, 2004). However, recent findings from the field of behavioral genetics may help researchers address some unanswered questions from criminologists' empirical work. For instance, criminologists have noted that although victimization increases the risk of offending for females, a substantial percentage of victimized females do not go on to commit crime (Widom, 1989a). This suggests that some additional factor(s) are needed to explain why some victimized women engage in crime while others do not. Perhaps women who have a genetic propensity towards antisocial behavior are more likely to respond to victimization with crime, whereas other women respond in alternative ways (i.e., depression, seeking counseling).

A large body of research has explored whether genetic polymorphisms explain why some individuals respond to stressful life events, such as victimization, with depression while others do not (Caspi et al., 2003; Cervillia et al., 2007; Cicchetti et al., 2007; Eley et al., 2004; Elovainio et al., 2007; Kaufman et al., 2004; Kendler, Kuhn, Vittum, Prescott, & Riley, 2005; Lenze et al., 2005; Mandelli, Serretti, Marino, Pirovano, Calati, & Colombo, 2007; Scheid et al., 2007;

97

Sjöberg et al., 2006; Taylor, Way, Welch, Hilmert, Lehman, & Eisenberger, 2006; Vaske, Makarios, Boisvert, Beaver, & Wright, 2008; Wilhelm et al., 2006; Zalsman et al., 2006). For instance, Kim-Cohen et al. (2006) found that boys who carried the low activity allele of the MAOA gene were more likely to respond to physical abuse with depression than males who carried the high activity allele. Other studies have shown that genetic polymorphisms in the serotonin and MAOA genes condition the effects of victimization on criminal behavior (Haberstick et al., 2005). These studies converge to show that genetic polymorphisms may explain why individuals respond differently to similar types of stimuli (i.e., victimization).

The current chapter will review findings from the behavioral genetics field, and it will integrate these findings into the current feminist hypotheses that link victimization to criminal behavior. As previously stated, it appears as if a substantial percentage of youths are resilient to the criminogenic effects of victimization. Genetics may partially explain why some youths are more sensitive to the effects of victimization, while other youths are relatively immune or resilient to such stimuli. This chapter will also review evidence on gene-environment correlations related to victimization and childhood abuse. There is some evidence that youths who have a genetic propensity towards antisocial behavior are more likely to evoke harsh or physically abusive responses from their environment (Beaver & Wright, 2007; Patterson, 1982). In addition, youths who are genetically inclined towards antisocial behavior may actively seek out high risk environments that subsequently increase their likelihood of victimization. The integration of gene-environment correlations into the feminist literature may help explain why some individuals are more likely to be recipients of violence, while others are not.

Resilience to Victimization
Studies have shown that victimization generally increase the risk of offending for males and females. However, a substantial percentage of abused youths do not engage in criminal behavior (Cicchetti et al., 1993; Kurtz et al., 1991; Seccombe, 2002). For instance, Widom (1989a, 1989b) compared the arrest rates of 667 abused children to those from 667 non-abused children matched on gender, age, race, and

socioeconomic status. She found that abused children were more likely to be arrested during adolescence and adulthood than non-abused children. Her analyses also revealed, however, that 26 percent of abused children were arrested as a juvenile, 29 percent were arrested during adulthood, and 11 percent were ever arrested for a violent crime. This shows that a substantial percentage of abused youths (around 70 percent) were not arrested during adolescence or adulthood, especially for violent crimes.

McGloin and Widom (2001) extended Widom's (1989) analyses to examine whether abused children (n= 667) exhibited resilience in other domains. They found that, of the abused youths, approximately 19 percent were successfully employed in adulthood, 74 percent had never been homeless, 48 percent had graduated from high school, and 48 percent did not show signs of a psychiatric disorder. In addition, approximately 38 percent of abused youths did not abuse substances, 43 percent were not arrested in adulthood, and 67 percent did not engage in violence. The prevalence of substance abuse was comparable across abused and non-abused children. Finally, their results revealed that abused females were more successful across a range of prosocial outcomes than abused males; thus, females exhibited more resilience to abuse and neglect than males. This is similar to findings from Werner and Smith (1989).

Studies have also shown that males demonstrate resilience to the effects of childhood abuse and maltreatment. Stouthamer-Loeber and colleagues (2001) examined whether childhood maltreatment predicted boys' progression into the authority conflict, overt, and covert behavior pathways. Their analyses revealed that abused males were more likely to engage in behaviors in the authority conflict and overt pathways. However, they found that approximately 50 percent of abused males did not advance to the highest steps of the overt pathway. This suggests that childhood maltreatment may increase the risk for less serious forms of behavior, but it may not increase males' risk of engaging in more serious criminal behaviors.

In light of the studies showing that a substantial percentage of youths are resilient to stressful circumstances, research has begun to explore whether genetic factors may explain variation in individuals' responses to victimization. The diathesis stress hypothesis argues that individuals with certain genetic backgrounds are more sensitive to the effects of stressful events and circumstances than individuals with a different genetic background (Hammen, Ellicott, Gitlin, & Jamison, 1989; Monroe & Simons, 1991). Research has provided some support for diathesis stress hypothesis (Caspi et al., 2003; Elovanio et al., 2007; Vaske et al., 2008). For instance, Grabe et al.'s (2005) analysis of 1,005 adults found that females who carried one or more copies of the 5HTTLPR short allele were more sensitive to the depressogenic effects of unemployment than females who did not carry the short allele. Unemployment and the 5HTTLPR genotype did not have direct effects on depression among females. This suggests that unemployment may increase females' risk of depression only when it is paired with the 5HTTLPR (s/l or s/s) genotype.

Before moving into the discussion of the moderating effects of genetic factors, it is important to note that individuals' resiliency to victimization may be a function of various factors, including sociological, psychological, and biological factors. For instance, previous research has noted that social support from parents and social institutions (i.e., criminal justice and social service agencies) may moderate the effects of victimization on criminal behavior (Aceves & Cookston, 2007). Further, females who have high levels of self-esteem may be more resilient to the effects of victimization than females with low levels of self-esteem (Carlson, McNutt, Choi, & Rose, 2002). Thus, individuals' response to victimization may depend upon sociological and psychological factors. While these moderating effects are not disputable, it can also be argued that criminological research has failed to examine which biological factors condition the effects of victimization on offending. It is the goal of this study to explore whether genetic polymorphisms related to neurotransmission moderate the influence of victimization on antisocial behaviors.

Neurobiological Mechanisms Underlying Gene X Victimization Interactions

Before discussing the empirical research on gene X victimization interactio, it is important to understand why one would theoretically expect the genetic polymorphisms to moderate the effects of victimization on criminal behavior. It is expected that the candidate genes in the current analyses may exacerbate the negative neurobiological effects of victimization that were discussed in Chapter 2. As noted in Chapter 2, research suggests that individuals who experience childhood abuse or victimization during adolescence are more likely to engage in antisocial behaviors because they have too much arousal and too few inhibitory mechanisms. More specifically, abused and victimized individuals may have a hyperactive hypothalamic-pituitary-adrenal (HPA) and higher levels of dopamine activity, coupled with low levels of serotonin and deficits in the hippocampus and prefrontal cortex. If individuals carry genetic polymorphisms that are associated with greater HPA axis activity, higher levels of dopamine, lower serotonin levels, or structural brain deficits, then victimization experiences may exacerbate these initial propensities and exponentially increase their risk of antisocial behavior.

In light of the evidence showing that maltreatment has a negative effect on the dopaminergic and serotonergic systems, it may be hypothesized that genetic polymorphisms related to the dopaminergic and serotonergic systems may exacerbate the negative effects of maltreatment. For instance, it may be expected that victimized individuals who carry the A1 allele of DRD2 will have higher rates of offending and substance use because both victimization and the A1 allele may be linked to higher levels of dopamine activity (Dagher & Robbins, 2009; Laasko et al., 2005). It could be that the simultaneous presence of the A1 allele and victimization leads to unusually high levels of dopamine activity in the striatum, which subsequently increases the likelihood of impulsivity, hyperactive behaviors (i.e., ADHD), substance use, and aggressive behaviors. Similarly, it may be expected that 5HTTLPR may exacerbate the effects of abuse and victimization on antisocial behavior because both factors may lead to lower levels of serotonin activity in the hippocampus, striatum, and frontal cortex (Bengel et al., 1998; Ichise et al., 2006).

It may also be hypothesized that the MAOA polymorphism may contribute to the over-arousal of victimized individuals. Unlike previous polymorphisms, however, the mechanisms underlying this effect may be less well understood. For instance, previous studies have shown that the low activity allele corresponds to greater amygdala responses and lower prefrontal cortex responses to negative stimuli; thus, suggesting that individuals with the low activity allele are more sensitive to the effects of negative stimuli (Meyer-Lindenberg et al.,

2006). However, studies have also show that the high activity allele is
linked to higher levels of aggression and impulsivity (Manuck et al.,
2000). These conflicting results may reflect the fact MAOA is
responsible for degrading both inhibitory (i.e., serotonin) and excitatory
(i.e., norepinephrine) neurotransmitters. Therefore, neglected
individuals who carry the low activity allele may be more likely to
engage in antisocial behavior because they have high levels of
norepinephrine (i.e., excitatory neurotransmitters). On the other hand,
victimized individuals who carry the high activity allele may be more
likely to engage in antisocial behaviors because they have low
concentrations of serotonin.

**Empirical Research on Gene X Victimization Interactions on
Antisocial Behavior**
An emerging line of research has begun to explore whether genetic
polymorphisms moderate the effects of victimization on antisocial
behaviors. To my knowledge, there are currently eleven studies that
have examined the interaction between genetic factors and
victimization/abuse on criminal behavior. The first study to examine
the interaction between a genetic polymorphism and victimization on
criminal behavior was conducted by Caspi et al. (2002). Caspi et al.
(2002) analyzed data from male subjects in the Dunedin
Multidisciplinary Health and Development study to examine whether
the MAOA polymorphism moderated the effects of childhood
maltreatment on adolescent conduct disorder, convictions for violent
crimes during adulthood, adulthood antisocial personality disorder, and
self-reported disposition towards violence. The Dunedin study is a
prospective birth cohort study that followed youths from age 3 till age
26. Childhood maltreatment was assessed by combining responses
from interviewer observations at age 3, parent reports at ages 7 and 9,
and retrospective reports from subjects at age 26. The items in the
childhood maltreatment scale assessed mother's rough handling of the
child, physical punishment, neglect (i.e., "unkempt appearance of
child"), and sexual abuse. Their results found that MAOA was not
significantly related to any of the four antisocial behavior outcomes,
while maltreatment had a significant direct effect on all four outcomes.
However, logistic and ordinary least square regression results revealed

that MAOA interacted with maltreatment to predict all four outcomes. More specifically, males who carried the low activity allele of the MAOA gene were more likely to respond to maltreatment with higher levels of adolescent conduct disorder, violent crime convictions, antisocial personality disorder, and disposition towards violence.

Foley et al. (2004) examined whether a polymorphism in the MAOA gene moderated the effects of childhood adversity on adolescent conduct disorder. Their sample consisted of 514 Caucasian male twins age 8 to 17 from the Virginia Twin Study for Adolescent Behavioral Development study. Childhood adversity was a composite scale of three subscales: parent reported parental neglect, child reported exposure to interparental violence, and child reported inconsistent parental discipline. Similar to Caspi et al. (2002), logistic regression results revealed that the main effect of MAOA on conduct disorder was non-significant, while the main effect of childhood adversity was significant. In addition, Foley et al. (2004) found that greater childhood adversity lead to higher levels of conduct disorder among males who carried the low activity allele, but not among males who carried the high activity allele.

Haberstick et al. (2005) used data from 774 Caucasian males from the National Longitudinal Study of Adolescent Health to examine whether a polymorphism in the MAOA gene moderated the effects of childhood maltreatment and adolescent victimization on adolescent conduct problems and adulthood convictions. Childhood maltreatment was a retrospective measure that assessed whether subjects had been neglected or abused before entry into sixth grade. Regression results revealed that MAOA did not have a significant effect on self-reported conduct problems or adulthood convictions, and childhood maltreatment did not significantly influence adulthood convictions. In addition, MAOA did not interact with childhood maltreatment to predict adolescent conduct problems or adulthood convictions.

Jaffee et al. (2005) analyzed data from 1,116 twin pairs from the Environmental Risk Longitudinal Twin Study (E-Risk Study) to examine whether genetic factors moderated the effects of physical maltreatment on conduct problems. The E-Risk study is a study of high-risk same sex twins that were interviewed between the ages of 5 to 7. Childhood maltreatment was assessed by asking two probe questions and then following up with additional questions. The two probe questions were: "When (subject) was a toddler, do you remember a time when s/he was disciplined severely enough that s/he may have been hurt?" and "Did you worry that you or someone else (such as a babysitter, a relative or a neighbor) may have harmed or hurt (name) during those years?" Genetic risk was determined by combining information regarding zygosity and whether the subject was diagnosed with conduct disorder. More specifically, subjects were considered to have the highest genetic risk if they were part of a MZ twin pair and their co-twin was diagnosed with conduct disorder (genetic risk score = 3). Subjects were considered high-medium risk if they were part of a DZ twin pair and their co-twin was diagnosed with conduct disorder (genetic risk score = 2). Subjects were considered medium risk if they were part of a DZ twin pair and their co-twin was not diagnosed with conduct disorder (genetic risk score = 1). Finally, subjects were considered low risk if they were part of an MZ twin pair and their co-twin was not diagnosed with conduct disorder (genetic risk score = 0). This measure of genetic risk is based on two assumptions: (1) conduct disorder is a partially heritable trait, and (2) MZ twins share 100 percent of their DNA. Therefore, genetic risk will be considered highest if a twin is part of a MZ pair and the co-twin is diagnosed with conduct disorder. Ordinary least squares regression revealed that genetic risk and physical maltreatment had significant independent effects on levels of conduct problems. In addition, genetic risk moderated the effects of physical maltreatment on conduct problems. Their analyses revealed that the probability of being diagnosed with conduct disorder was highest among subjects who had been physically maltreated and who had the highest genetic risk. The probability of conduct disorder incrementally decreased as the authors moved from highest genetic risk to lowest genetic risk. Results revealed that the gene X environment interaction was invariant by gender.

Huizinga et al. (2006) analyzed data from 277 Caucasian males age 11 to 15 from the National Youth Survey Family Study (NYSFS) to examine whether a polymorphism in the MAOA gene conditioned the effects of maltreatment and adolescent violent victimization on a variety of adolescent and adulthood antisocial outcomes. The NYSFS is a prospective, on-going study that began collecting data on youths age 11-15 in 1976. Data for Huizinga et al.'s analysis came from adults who were age 37 to age 41 in 2002. The measure of childhood maltreatment included one question that was asked to subjects between ages 11 and 17: "Have you been beaten up by your mother, stepmother, father, or stepfather" within the past year? Adolescent violent victimization included items that asked whether the subject had been the victim of a serious assault, robbery, or sexual assault between ages 11 and 17. The variable was dichotomized so that a score of 0 corresponded to the bottom 75 percent of the distribution for violent victimization, and a score of 1 reflected the top 25 percent. Huizinga et al. (2006) included six measures of antisocial outcomes: adolescent conduct disorder, arrest for a violent offense as an adult, disposition towards violence as an adult, antisocial personality disorder symptoms during adulthood, a composite problem behavior index, and life course problem behavior measure. Logistic and ordinary least squares regression results revealed that MAOA did not have a direct significant effect on any of the six outcomes. Maltreatment had a direct effect on adolescent conduct disorder, violent arrest, antisocial personality disorder, composite problem behavior index, and life course problem behavior. The interaction between maltreatment and MAOA did not significantly predict any of the six outcomes.

Kaufman et al.'s (2007) analyzed data from 76 maltreated children and 51 matched controls to examine whether 5HTTLPR moderated the effects of childhood maltreatment on alcohol abuse. Maltreated children were identified through social service referrals to foster care. The results revealed that maltreated youths with the S/L genotype were more likely to have an early onset for alcohol use than maltreated youths with the L/L genotype.

Young et al. (2006) examined whether the 30bp polymorphism in the MAOA gene moderated the effects of childhood neglect, verbal/psychological abuse, physical abuse, and sexual abuse on adolescent conduct problems. To investigate this hypothesis, the authors used data from 247 male adolescents who were entering a residential treatment program based on referrals for persistent conduct problems or substance use. The four categories of childhood maltreatment were assessed through the Colorado Adolescent Rearing Inventory interview. Ordinary least squares regression results revealed that childhood maltreatment had a significant positive effect on adolescent conduct problems, but the direct effect of MAOA was not significant. In addition, none of the interactions between MAOA and the four maltreatment domains were significant.

Widom and Brzustowicz (2006) examined whether the 30bp polymorphism in the MAOA conditioned the effects of abuse/neglect on juvenile and lifetime antisocial behavior. The authors used data from a prospective cohort of abused youths and a matched control sample that was followed from 1986 to 2004. Unlike previous studies, the authors used an officially reported measure of abuse rather than a self-report, parent report, or interviewer observations. Cases were included in the abused group if: (1) there was a judgment in juvenile or adult criminal courts for charges of physical abuse, sexual abuse, or neglect between the years of 1967 and 1971, and (2) the youth had to be 11 years old or less at the time of incident. Members of the control group were matched to those in the abuse group based on gender, age, race, and socioeconomic status. Regression analyses revealed that MAOA did not have a significant direct effect on juvenile or lifetime antisocial behavior, but abuse was a significant predictor of both juvenile and lifetime antisocial behavior scores. However, MAOA interacted with abuse to predict higher levels of juvenile and lifetime antisocial behavior. More specifically, abused subjects who carried the low activity allele of MAOA had higher levels of juvenile and lifetime antisocial behavior than subjects who carried the high activity allele. The significant interaction between MAOA and abuse/neglect was found for Caucasians, but not non-whites (African Americans, Hispanics, American Indians, Pacific Islanders, and others). Further, the same pattern of results were found for Caucasian males and females.

Beaver (2008a) analyzed data from the National Longitudinal Study of Adolescent Health to examine whether dopaminergic polymorphisms moderated the effects of childhood sexual abuse on adolescent violent delinquency for males and females. Childhood sexual abuse was retrospectively assessed with one question that asked whether their parents or any other adult had ever touched them sexually or forced them to have sexual relations prior to entering the sixth grade. Genetic risk was assessed by combining scores from the DAT1, DRD2, and DRD4 polymorphisms. Negative binomial results revealed that genetic risk moderated the effects of childhood sexual abuse on violent delinquency for males, but not females. For females, neither the main effects nor interactive effects of genetic risk and childhood sexual abuse had a significant effect on violent delinquency.

Brendgen and colleagues (2008) analyzed data from 506 six year old twins that were part of a longitudinal, prospective birth cohort study of twins born in the Montreal area between November 1995 and July 1998. The authors examined whether genetic factors moderated the effects of peer victimization on aggressive behavior among males and females. Peer victimization was assessed through peer nominated reports of whether the subject "gets hit or pushed by other kids" and whether the subject "gets called names by other kids." The authors also assessed aggressive behavior through peer nominated reports and teacher reports. Genetic risk was determined by the same method used by Jaffee et al. (2005), except youths were considered aggressive if they scored in the top 25th percentile of the aggression measure. Results from their multi-level model revealed that genetic risk and peer victimization had significant direct effects on aggressive behavior for males and females. The authors also found that genetic risk interacted with peer victimization to predict aggressive behavior for females only. Specifically, peer victimization had the strongest effect on aggressive behavior for girls when genetic risk was at its highest level. The effects of peer victimization on aggressive behavior decreased as one moved from the highest genetic risk level to the lowest level of genetic risk.

Finally, Ducci et al. (2008) examined whether the polymorphisms in the MAOA and MAOB genes conditioned the effects of childhood sexual abuse on alcoholism and alcoholism with antisocial personality disorder diagnosis. To investigate this hypothesis, the authors analyzed data from 291 women from a Southwest American Indian tribe. Women were considered sexually abused if they answered yes to the following question: "Were you ever sexually abused or molested as a child before the age of 16?" Results revealed that women who evidenced signs of alcoholism with antisocial personality disorder were more likely to carry the low activity allele than women who did not show signs of alcoholism. In addition, the authors found that sexually abused females who were homozygous for the low activity exhibited more signs of alcoholism with antisocial personality disorder than sexually abused females who were homozygous for the high activity allele. The 30bp polymorphism did not significantly predict higher levels of alcoholism or co-morbid alcoholism for females who were not sexually abused. Ducci et al. (2007) also found that MAOA interacted with childhood sexual abuse to predict higher levels of antisocial personality disorder. In sum, the results from gene X victimization studies reveal that genetic factors moderate the effects of victimization on antisocial and criminal behavior. A significant interaction between genetic polymorphisms and victimization were found in eight out of the eleven studies. This suggests that genetic polymorphisms may help explain why some victimized individuals engage in criminal behavior, while others do not. Despite the consistency in interaction effects across studies, there are at least three limitations to the current literature. First, the studies primarily focus on one genetic polymorphism— MAOA. This is surprising in light of the evidence that other polymorphisms, such as the 5HTTLPR and DRD2 polymorphisms, moderate the effects of stressful life events on disorders, such as depression and violent delinquency (Caspi et al., 2003; Cicchetti et al., 2007; Beaver, 2008a; Vaske et al., 2008). Given that victimization is considered a stressful life event, it is important to examine whether additional polymorphisms interact with victimization to influence antisocial and criminal behaviors.

Second, five of the eleven studies only include one gender (either males or females) in their analyses. Studies that do include both genders in their analyses show that either the interaction is significant for both genders (Jaffee et al., 2005; Widom & Brzustowicz, 2006), or the interaction is only significant for one gender (either males or females) (Beaver, 2008a; Brendgen et al., 2008). Thus, the evidence is mixed whether gene X victimization interactions are consistent across genders. The mixed results may partially be due to differences in which genetic polymorphism is examined (i.e., MAOA vs. dopaminergic polymorphisms), as well as which form of victimization is included in the analyses. This leads to the third limitation of the current literature.

Finally, all eleven studies only include one type of victimization (i.e., childhood maltreatment, peer victimization) within their analyses, and none of the studies examine whether genetic polymorphisms moderate the effects of intimate partner violence on antisocial behavior. Thus, there has not been a systematic evaluation of how genetic polymorphisms may interact with various forms of victimization to influence criminal behavior. Further, many of the gene X victimization studies only examine a composite measure of childhood maltreatment, instead of separating out neglect, physical abuse, and sexual abuse. Studies from the feminist criminological literature have shown that neglect has a stronger effect on delinquent and criminal behavior than physical and sexual abuse (Kingree, Phan, & Thompson, 2003; Widom & Ames, 1994). Thus, true gene X victimization relationships may be masked when researchers use aggregated measures of childhood maltreatment.

Gene-Environment Correlations (rGE) Related to Victimization
Scholars have noted that individuals are not randomly exposed to certain environments (Farrell & Pease, 1993). That is, individuals' behaviors and lifestyles may influence the likelihood that they will be exposed to certain environments (Hindelang, Gottfredson, & Garofalo, 1978). For instance, studies have shown that individuals who spend more time outside of the home, either working or seeking out entertainment, are more likely to be violently victimized than individuals who spend less time outside of the home (Miethe, Stafford, & Long, 1987). This suggests that individuals' behavioral and lifestyle choices may increase their risk of victimization.

In addition to the lifestyle theory of victimization, researchers have argued that certain personality traits or behaviors may increase one's risk of victimization (Schreck, Wright, & Miller, 2002). More specifically, it is expected that individuals who are low in self-control and who are prone to aggression may be more likely to evoke negative responses from their environments (Schreck, 1999; Wolfgang, 1957). For instance, people who are distrustful of their environment and who believe that others are generally out to 'get them' will respond to a minor social violation (i.e., cutting them off in traffic, stepping on their shoes) with a much greater intensity than individuals who do not perceive the world as distrustful. Individuals may also increase their risk of victimization by selecting themselves into a high-risk environment. Studies have repeatedly shown that individuals who frequent bars at-night are more likely to be victimized than individuals who do not frequent bars (Miethe et al., 1987). Incidentally, individuals who frequent bars may score lower on inventories of self-control and behavioral inhibition than individuals who do not frequent bars. Thus, individuals with low self-control may be more likely to place themselves into risky situations (i.e., bars) that increase their chance of victimization (Schreck, 1999).

Because many antisocial personality traits are genetically influenced (Plomin, 1990; Rutter, 2006; Walsh, 1995), it is expected that genetic factors may explain some of the variation in the prevalence and frequency of victimization. Indeed, twin studies have revealed that genetic factors explain a substantial percentage of variation in stressful life events and circumstances (Jockin, McGue, & Lykken, 1996; Kendler, Kessler, & Neale, 1993; McGue & Lykken, 1992; McGuffin, Katz, & Bebbington, 1988; Thapar & McGuffin, 1996; Wang, Trivedi, Treiber, & Snieder, 2005). Wierzbicki (1989) found that genetic factors explained approximately 30 to 40 percent of the variation in the prevalence and frequency of unpleasant life experiences. Plomin and colleague's (1990) analysis of twins from the Swedish Adoption Twin Study of Aging found that genetic factors explain 43 percent of the variation in controllable events, such as divorce, deterioration of marriage, paying a fine for minor law violation, and deterioration of financial status. An analysis of 222 monozygotic twin pairs and 184 dizygotic twin pairs found that the heritability coefficient for assaultive trauma (i.e., being robbed, being beat up, or sexually assaulted) was .20 (Stein, Jang, Taylor, Vernon, & Livesley, 2002). Finally, Hines and Saudino's (2004) analysis of monozygotic and dizygotic twin pairs revealed that approximately 25 percent of the variation in psychological intimate partner violence was a function of genetic factors. Other studies have also reported that genetic factors explain approximately 20 to 30 percent of the variation in exposure to stressful and violent events (Jaffee et al., 2005; Kendler, 2001). This suggests that individuals' exposure to certain environments vary as a function of their genotype (rGE).

While evidence from twin studies shows that genetic factors may explain variation in stressful life events (such as victimization), research that has examined the effects of specific genetic polymorphisms on victimization is mixed. Studies have found that the 5HTTLPR is not significantly related to exposure to stressful life events (Caspi et al., 2003; Kendler et al., 2005) or childhood adversity

(Surtees et al., 2006). Research has also revealed that the 30 bp VNTR in the MAOA gene was not related to childhood adversity (Foley et al., 2004), childhood physical abuse and maltreatment (Cicchetti et al., 2007; Kim-Cohen et al., 2006), and adolescent victimization (Haberstick et al., 2005). Recent studies, however, have revealed that dopaminergic polymorphisms are related to levels of violent victimization. Beaver and colleague's (2007) analysis of the Add Health data revealed that the TaqIA polymorphism in DRD2 significantly increased the likelihood of violent victimization among youths who had a low number of delinquent peers. Vaske, Wright, and Beaver (2008) found that the DRD2 polymorphism distinguished between Caucasian male offenders who have been violently victimized and Caucasian male offenders who have not been violently victimized. However, Vaske et al.'s (2008) analysis revealed that the DRD2 TaqIA polymorphism did not significantly predict higher levels of violent victimization or witnessed violence for Caucasian females, African American females, or African American males. Thus, evidence on gene-environment correlations from molecular genetic studies is mixed and the effects may vary by gender-race subgroups.

In sum, results from twin studies revealed that genetic factors explain a substantial amount of variation in life events, such as victimization. However, the results from molecular genetic studies have provided limited support for the hypothesis that genetic factors are linked to victimization. There is a reason for the incongruence between twin study findings and molecular genetics study findings of gene-environment correlations. Biometric analyses from twin studies are capturing, hypothetically, the additive and dominant effects of various genetic (potential) effects on victimization. On the other hand, molecular genetic studies frequently examine the additive effect of one genetic polymorphism on victimization. It is likely that numerous genetic polymorphisms are working in tandem, either through polygenic or epistatic processes, to influence the likelihood of victimization.

Integration of Behavioral Genetics Findings with Gender-Specific Hypotheses of Victimization
Integrating behavioral genetics into gender specific hypotheses of victimization on crime may explain resiliency *within* genders (gene X

environment interaction). That is, genetic information may explain why some victimized females engage in criminal behavior, while other victimized females do not. Genetic factors may explain individual differences in resiliency if victimized females (or males) that have one genotype are less likely to engage in crime than victimized females (or males) that have a different genotype.

Behavioral genetics may also help researchers explain variation or individual differences in resiliency *between* genders (sex X gene X environment interaction). A gene X environment interaction suggests that people with *different genotypes* may respond differently to the same environmental factors. A sex X gene X environment interaction suggests that males and females with the *same genotype* may respond differently to the same social stimuli. For instance, scholars have noted that at-risk males seem to be more sensitive to the criminogenic effects of negative environmental factors (i.e., broken home) than at-risk females (Cowie, Cowie, & Slater, 1968; Werner & Smith, 1989). Recent research has provided some support for this hypothesis. Beaver's (2008a) recent analyses of the Add Health data revealed that males and females with the same level of genetic risk may respond differently to childhood sexual abuse. His analyses showed that sexually abused males who have higher levels of genetic risk (related to the dopaminergic system) are more likely to engage in violent crime than sexually abused males who have lower levels of genetic risk (Beaver, 2008a). In addition, sexually abused females who have higher levels of genetic risk are not more likely to engage in violent crime. Beaver's (2008a) findings suggest that sexually abused males who have dysfunctions in the dopaminergic system may be more likely to engage in violent behavior than sexually abused females who have dysfunctions in the dopaminergic system (as proxied by dopaminergic polymorphisms).

If sex or gender explains why individuals with the same genotype respond differently to the same stimuli, the next question to ask is *why* does sex or gender explain this difference. There are at least two potential reasons for a sex X gene X environment interaction. First, males and females may have the same biological or genetic risk factor, but these factors may operate differently between the genders. For instance, research has noted that there are gender differences in gene expression within the human brain (Rinn & Snyder, 2005; Vawter et al., 2004). There is some evidence that suggests that the DRD2 gene may be differentially expressed in the brains of males and females (Andersen, Rutstein, Benzo, Hostetter, & Teicher, 1997; Andersen, Thompson, Krenzel, & Teicher, 2002), and that this difference may increase females' sensitivity to the effects of victimization. Andersen and Teicher (2000) found that the density of D2 receptors increased approximately 150 percent at the onset of puberty for males, but D2 receptors only increased 30 percent for females. This finding suggests that the DRD2 gene may be expressed at a lower rate in adolescent females compared to males. If adolescent females generally have fewer D2 receptors, relative to males, it may be expected that victimized females who carry the A1 allele would display more behaviors associated with low dopamine activity (i.e., trouble concentrating, depression) than victimized males who carry the A1 allele. This is expected because both victimization and DRD2 A1 allele may correspond to a lower density of D2 receptors in the brain and lower levels of dopamine activity (Champagne & Curley, 2008; Petronis et al., 2003), which subsequently can lead to higher levels of depression and greater involvement in addictive or compulsive behaviors (Blum et al., 1996). Thus, lower levels of dopamine activity may be a function of the A1 allele of DRD2, victimization status, and being female; all three factors contribute to lower density of D2 receptors and lower levels of dopamine activity.

The second reason why sex or gender may condition gene X environment interactions is that one gender may have protective factors that offset the gene X environment effects (while the other gender does not have the same level of protective factors). That is, sex or gender may act as a proxy for some unmeasured protective factors. The protective factors may either be biological, psychological, or sociological in nature. For instance, recent research has shown that females have a larger orbitofrontal cortex (i.e., area related to identifying and regulating emotions) relative to the amygdala (i.e., seat of negative emotion) than males (Gur, Gunning-Dixon, Bilker, & Gur, 2002). This finding suggests that females may be less likely to engage in aggressive behavior due to their capability to better regulate their negative emotions, compared to males. Applying this finding to the current discussion, genetically at-risk females who are victimized may not act on their anger or frustration due their increased capacity to regulate such emotions. On the other hand, genetically at-risk males who are victimized, on average, may act on their negative emotions due to their genetic vulnerability to antisocial behavior and their decreased capacity to regulate such emotions. These hypotheses do not suggest that females always have a larger orbitofrontal cortex (OFC) than males, but that the volume of the OFC is typically larger than males' OFC. Thus, some males may have a larger OFC, and this may act as a protective factor for those males.

At-risk females may also be less likely to respond to victimization with violent or externalizing behavior, compared to at-risk males, because females generally have higher hypothalamic-pituitary-adrenal (HPA) axis activity (Young, Korszun, Figueiredo, Banks-Solomon, & Herman, 2007). Higher levels of HPA axis activity have been linked to greater anxiety and shyness, while lower levels of HPA axis activity are correlated with higher levels of impulsivity and inattention (Hong, Shin, Lee, Oh, & Noh, 2003). Many researchers have argued that a hyperactive HPA axis may be advantageous in many ways (Zhang, Parent, Weaver, & Meaney, 2004b). For instance, a hyperactive HPA axis may lead to avoidance behaviors, so that individuals with an overactive HPA axis may avoid high risk situations that facilitate criminal behavior (Meaney, 2001). Since victimization and abuse also increase HPA axis activity (Champagne & Curley, 2008), it may be expected that victimized females may be less likely to engage in externalizing behaviors than victimized males due to their higher baseline level of HPA axis activity. While a hyperactive HPA axis is advantageous in some ways, it can also be disadvantageous. That is, females may be less likely to engage in externalizing behaviors, especially as a response to victimization, but females may be more likely to display symptoms of anxiety and use illicit substances to reduce their levels of anxiety.

Research Questions
Genetic factors may influence the likelihood of criminal behavior via higher levels of victimization (rGE). Twin studies have shown that genetic factors account for a substantial proportion of variation in the prevalence and frequency of life events, such as victimization.

However, evidence of gene-victimization correlations in molecular genetics studies has been mixed. The current study extends upon previous research by examining whether the dopaminergic, serotonergic, and monoamine oxidase A polymorphisms explain variation in victimization, as well as whether the average level of victimization is a function of the polymorphisms.

Research question one: **Are dopaminergic, serotonergic, and monoamine oxidase A polymorphisms related to youths' levels of childhood neglect, childhood physical abuse, adolescent violent victimization and adolescent intimate partner violence (gene-environment correlations)?**

Research question two: **Do the gene-environment correlations vary by gender?**

It is also likely that genetic factors may help explain the variation in individuals' responses to victimization (Haberstick et al., 2005). Recent research has revealed that dopaminergic, serotonergic, and monoamine oxidase A genetic polymorphisms moderate the effects of neglect, maltreatment, physical abuse, sexual abuse, and violent victimization on antisocial behaviors. However, studies typically examine whether genetic factors condition one form of abuse (i.e., sexual abuse) without consideration of other forms of victimization (i.e., adolescent violent victimization). Therefore, the current study extends upon previous research by investigating whether polymorphisms in the dopaminergic, serotonergic, and monoamine oxidase A genes condition the effects of various forms of victimization.

Research question three: **Do dopaminergic, serotonergic, and monoamine oxidase A polymorphisms moderate the effects childhood neglect, childhood sexual abuse, childhood physical abuse, adolescent violent victimization, and adolescent intimate partner violence on a wide range of antisocial behaviors?**

Previous studies generally have not investigated whether the gene X environment interactions are invariant by gender (Foley et al., 2004; Haberstick et al., 2005; Huizinga et al., 2006). In light of the evidence showing gender differences in genetic expression and responses to stressful life circumstances (Kendler, Thornton, & Prescott, 2001; Silberg et al., 1999), the current study explores whether the moderating effects of genetic factors are invariant across gender.

Research question four: **Do the moderating effects of dopaminergic, serotonergic, and monoamine oxidase A polymorphisms vary by gender?**

CHAPTER FIVE
Methods

Data for the current project come from the National Longitudinal Study of Adolescent Health (Add Health) dataset. This dataset includes a rich array of genetic and environmental variables that are not commonly found in other general population studies. In addition, this longitudinal study tracks respondents' from adolescence into adulthood. This feature allows researchers to explore transitions into adulthood and investigate potential causal processes over time. Due to these considerations, the Add Health dataset is used to examine the interplay between genes and environment in the etiology of offending.

The National Longitudinal Study of Adolescent Health
The National Longitudinal Study of Adolescent Health (Add Health) is a prospective, nationally representative study of youths in grades seven through twelve. The Add Health includes three waves of data. The first wave of data included information from an in-school survey and in-home interview that were administered between 1994 and 1995. Youths were approximately 11 to 19 years old during wave I data collection. The second wave of questionnaires was administered between 1995 and 1996, when youths were between the ages of 12 and 20. Finally, the third wave of data included in-home interview data that were collected between August 2001 and April 2002, when respondents were between the ages of 18 and 26. The Add Health researchers administered questionnaires to school administrators, youths, and parents during the study. This was done in order to gather information on the multiple contexts that surrounded the youth as he or she entered into adulthood. Before describing these questionnaires, it is important

discuss the research and sampling design employed by Add Health researchers.

Research and Sampling Design

The Add Health study employed multistage stratified sampling techniques to obtain a final sample of 132 schools (80 high schools, 52 middle and junior high schools). The initial sampling frame consisted of 26,666 high schools that were listed in the Quality Education Data, Inc. (QED) database. To qualify as a high school, the school was defined as either a private or public school that enrolled at least thirty students and included an eleventh grade (Tourangeau & Shin, 1999). These high schools were then stratified into clusters based on the following factors: enrollment size (125 or fewer, 126 to 350, 351 to 775, 776 or more students), school type (public, parochial, private), geographic region (Northeast, Midwest, South, West), level of urbanicity (urban, suburban, rural), and percent white (0, 1 to 66, 67 to 93, and 94 to 100) (Tourangeau & Shin, 1999). Using these clusters, Add Health researchers systematically selected 80 high schools with the probability of selection being proportional to enrollment size. Of the 80 high schools selected for the final sample, 52 schools agreed to participate in the study; 28 schools refused to cooperate. These 28 high schools were replaced by a high school that was similar to the refusal school in terms of school size, school type, urbanicity, percent white, grade span, percent black, geographic region, and census division (Tourangeau & Shin, 1999). If the replacement school refused to cooperate, the Add Health researchers selected another replacement school that was similar to the original refusal school on the eight dimensions. This process was completed until researchers had a final sample of 80 high schools.

High school administrators were asked to provide the name(s) of middle and junior high schools that contributed at least five students to incoming freshman classes at the selected high school. These contributing middle and junior high schools included "feeder" schools. A single feeder school was selected for each high school included in the sample. A total of 56 feeder schools were selected, with their probability of selection being proportional to the percentage of incoming high school students that came from that feeder school

(Chantala, 2006). For instance, if 35 percent of all incoming high school students came from Feeder school A, then Feeder school A's probability of selection in the final sample was .35. Of the 56 selected feeder schools, 52 feeder schools agreed to participate in the study. Thus, the final sample included 132 schools (80 high schools, 52 middle and junior high schools).

Selection Biases in Sampling of Schools.

There are three selection biases in Add Health's sampling of middle and high schools. First, some schools were originally sampled from the sampling frame (QED database), but then it was discovered that these schools did not meet sampling criteria. For instance, some high schools did not have an 11th grade. The ineligible schools were eliminated from the sample and a replacement school with similar characteristics was selected into the sample. Second, a feeder school was only selected into the sample if the high school to which they sent their graduates was selected into the sample; thus, the feeder school's probability of selection was conditional upon the high school's selection into the sample. Finally, four feeder schools refused to cooperate in the study, and these schools were not replaced. Due to these considerations, sampling weights must be used when analyzing the Add Health data for descriptive purposes. It is noted that sampling weights should not be used when estimating coefficients in multivariate models.

Three Waves of Data.

Wave I In-School Survey.

Students enrolled in the 132 sampled schools were invited to complete the wave I in-school survey. Add Health researchers administered the in-school surveys to students in grades seven through twelve between September 1994 and April 1995. The self-report surveys were administered to students who obtained parental consent during a selected class period that was 45 to 60 minutes in length. Students who were absent on the day of survey administration were not eligible for the study. A total of 90,118 students completed the in-school survey (Chantala & Tabor, 1999). The survey questions tapped into youths' individual demographics, family characteristics, friendship networks, involvement in extracurricular activities, problems at school, substance use, health and emotional problems, and physical activity.

Selection Biases in Wave I In-School Samples.
There are four selection biases associated with the wave I in-school survey. First, four schools refused to allow students to complete in-school surveys. These schools, however, did allow students to be sampled from the school rosters, so that the students were eligible for the in-home interviews. Second, the identifying information from some in-school surveys was deleted. Due to this limitation, it is impossible link the student questionnaire data with the aggregate school-level data from these schools. Third, the sampling frame contained inaccurate data for some sampled schools. For instance, QED noted that students were in the 12th grade for one school, yet the students were actually still in middle school. This influenced the probability of selection, so that it varied across gender-grade combinations. Finally, youths who were not enrolled in school (i.e., drop outs, home schooled) were not eligible for the sample.

Wave I In-Home Interview.

A subsample of students enrolled at the 80 high school and 52 middle schools were selected to participate in the wave I in-home interview process. In order to be eligible for selection into the subsample, students had to be listed on the school roster for the 1994-1995 academic year. Add Health researchers then stratified the school roster by gender and grade level, and selected a total of 27,559 students (Tourangeau & Shin, 1999). A total of 20,745 youths completed the in-home interview between April 1995 and December 1995 (Chantala & Tabor, 1999). Questions included in this interview inquired about subject's health and emotional problems, school activities and performance, family structure, relationships, substance use, delinquent activities, and aspirations and expectations.

The final wave I in-home sample consisted of a number of subsamples. The following subsamples were included in the wave I in-home interview process: a core sample, a physically disabled subsample, a saturation or school network subsample, ethnic subsamples (Chinese, Cuban, Puerto Rican, and educated African Americans), and a sibling subsample. The core sample consisted of 12,105 respondents who were listed on the school rosters. Subjects for the core sample were selected randomly from school rosters that were stratified on gender and grade level. The core sample is intended to be a nationally representative sample of youths in grades seven through twelve between 1994 and 1995.

In addition to the core sample, researchers oversampled 589 students who reported that they had a physical disability during the in-school survey. This sample was dropped in subsequent waves, however, because in-home interviewers discovered that many of these students did not have a physical disability. A saturation or school network subsample was also included in the wave I data. This subsample consisted of all youths who attended two large schools and fourteen schools with less than 300 enrolled students. This subsample allowed researchers to collect data on social friendship networks within the schools. Finally, specific ethnic groups were oversampled to be included in the wave I in-home interview process. These ethnic groups included: 334 Chinese youths, 450 Cuban youths, 437 Puerto Rican youths, and 1,038 African American youths who had a parent with a college degree.

During wave I, Add Health researchers also oversampled siblings to be included in a genetic supplemental sample. Siblings were identified during wave 1 in-school surveys and in-home interviews. In these questionnaires, respondents were asked whether any other household members were enrolled in grades 7 thru 12. For each identified sibling, the respondent reported the sibling's sex and whether the sibling had the same biological mother and biological father as the respondent. Identified siblings and original respondents were then added to the genetic supplemental sample. The final genetic subsample included 2,658 twins, 208 non-twin siblings of twins, 1,611 full siblings, 1,177 half siblings, and 491 non-related siblings. Non-related siblings were youths who lived in the same household as the respondent, but he or she did not have the same biological mother and biological father as the respondent. This included step-siblings, adopted children, and foster children (Harris, Florey, Tabor, Bearman, Jones, & Urdy, 2003; Tourangeau & Shin, 1999). Youths who were selected into the genetic supplemental sample participated in the in-home interviews for waves I thru III.

In-home interviews were conducted in the youth's home and typically lasted between one to two hours. Questionnaires were administered through Computer Assisted Personal Interview (CAPI) and Audio Computer Assisted Self-Interview (ACASI) methods. With CAPI methods, interviewers read aloud the survey questions and manually entered in the subject's response on a secure laptop. The CAPI method was used to collect data about topics that were less sensitive in nature. Other topics, such as criminal activity, were more sensitive in nature and required researchers to choose an alternative method of data collection. Respondents answered these questions through the ACASI method. The ACASI method allows respondents to listen to pre-recorded questions on earphones, and then key in their response on the computer. This method was chosen because studies have shown that the ACASI reduces social desirability bias when gathering information on particularly sensitive topics, such as information on sexual behaviors and criminal behavior (Couper, Singer, & Tourangeau, 2003; Ghanem, Hutton, Zenilman, Zimba, & Erbelding, 2005).

The wave I in-home interviews also included a parent questionnaire. One parent (typically the mother) completed a 40 minute paper-and-pencil survey that contained questions regarding their employment, financial situation, involvement in activities, neighborhood conditions, health, marriage, substance abuse, parent-child relationship, and information about the child. A total of 17,700 parents completed the parent questionnaire between April 1995 and December 1995.

Selection Biases in Wave I In-Home Samples.

In addition to the selection biases that 'carry over' from the in-school survey, there are five selection biases associated with the in-home samples (core and/or supplemental subsamples). First, thirteen schools did not submit their school rosters and complete their in-school surveys by the original deadline date. Cases from these thirteen schools were not eligible for selection into the core sample. Second, the probability of selection into the core sample varied by school size. In larger schools, students were randomly selected into the core sample. In smaller schools, however, all students were selected to participate in the core sample if two-third or more would have been randomly selected for the core. Third, students who did not complete an in-school survey were not eligible for the core sample and supplemental subsamples. Fourth, youths who were not enrolled in middle or high school (i.e., drop outs, home schooled) were not eligible for the in-home samples.

The last selection bias is associated only with the sibling subsample. The final selection bias is that selection into the sibling subsample varied by type of sibling. All adoptee, twin, and brother-sister full sibling pairs were automatically selected into the sibling subsample, but half sibling pairs (n= 597 pairs) were randomly selected from all half-siblings identified in the in-school survey (n= 2,443 pairs). Also, brother-brother and sister-sister full sibling pairs were selected into the sibling subsample through convenience sampling. It was originally assumed that the in-school surveys would yield at least 250 brother-brother and 250 sister-sister sibling pairs. These sibling pairs were underrepresented in the sibling subsample. Due to this issue, Add Health researchers purposefully sampled these sibling pairs from other samples (core, PAIRS, non-genetic subsamples, or wave I in-school sample).

Wave II In-Home Interview.

All youths who took part in the wave I in-home interview and/or who were selected into the genetic supplemental sample were invited to participate in wave II in-home interviews. There were, however, two groups of individuals who were excluded from the wave II in-home interview process: (a) youths who were in the 12th grade during wave I and who were not included in the genetic supplemental sample, and (b) physically disabled youths who were oversampled during wave I. A total of 14,738 youths (71 percent) from the original sample completed wave II in-home interviews (Chantala & Tabor, 1999; Tourangeau & Shin, 1999). Wave II in-home interviews were administered between April through August 1996. Similar to wave I in-home interviews, the wave II in-home questionnaires were administered through CAPI and ACASI methods. Questions included in the wave II in-home questionnaire covered topics such as subject's health and emotional problems, nutrition, family dynamics, relationships, intimate partner violence, and risky behaviors.

Selection Biases in Wave II In-Home Samples

There are three selection biases associated with the wave II in-home samples. First, as previously noted, all subjects who were in 12th grade during wave I were not interviewed during wave II, except those subjects who were part of the sibling subsample. Second, twins and siblings who were not included in wave I but who were in grades 7 through 12 in wave II were included in the sibling subsample. This difference in sample composition may affect results when comparing outcomes across waves. Finally, approximately 29 percent of the wave I respondents did not participate in wave II in-home interviews, either due to previously discussed selection processes (i.e., wave I 12th graders) or attrition (Chantala & Tabor, 1999). Again, this may influence results when comparing findings across waves.

Wave III In-Home Interview.

All youths who completed the wave I in-home interviews were invited to participate in the wave III in-home interview process, with the exception of respondents who were located outside the country. Respondents who were residing in correctional facilities were eligible for the study, and Add Health researchers made a special effort to locate and interview these respondents. Only 29 subjects (.001 percent) were interviewed in prison, but it was noted that 103 individuals could not be interviewed because they were incarcerated (Chantala, Kalsbeek, & Andraca, 2004). A total of 15,170 (73 percent) wave I respondents were retained at wave III. During wave III, Add Health researchers also collected data from respondents' romantic partners. Approximately 50 percent of respondents were asked whether they were married, cohabiting, or dating someone from the opposite sex. A total of 1,507 partners participated in the wave III in-home interview process.

Wave III in-home interviews were conducted in the respondent's home and typically lasted on average 134 minutes. Similar to the previous waves, respondents answered series of questions using CAPI and ACASI methods. Unlike the previous waves though, the content of the questions was altered to reflect respondents' transition from adolescence to adulthood. That is, the social contexts (i.e., spouse, employment) that influence respondents' behavior as an adult may differ from those contexts that influenced behavior during adolescence (i.e., peer relationships). To account for these changes in life circumstances, the wave III in-home questionnaire included questions regarding marriage and cohabitation, employment, education, criminal behavior, and health and emotional problems. The interview also includes items pertaining to childhood maltreatment and ADHD.

Wave III DNA Sample.

Respondents who reported that they had a full sibling or twin in wave I were eligible to participate in the DNA subsample. That is, full siblings and twins who were part of the genetic supplemental sample in wave I were asked to participate in the wave III DNA sample. A total of 3,787 respondents were asked to submit a saliva sample for genetic analysis, and 2,574 respondents submitted a saliva sample. Before submitting a saliva sample, respondents were required to sign informed consent forms. Subjects were also not provided any additional compensation for participating in the DNA sample. University of Colorado researchers targeted six polymorphisms for genetic analysis: a dopamine transporter gene (DAT1), two dopamine receptor genes (DRD2 and DRD4), a serotonin transporter gene (5-HTT), cytochrome P450, and monoamine oxidase A (MAOA).

Selection Biases in Wave III In-Home Samples.

In addition to the selection biases of samples in previous waves, the main limitation in the wave III samples is attrition. Chantala and colleagues (2004) note that 783 wave I cases were deemed ineligible for wave III in-home surveys, and 4,792 were eligible but not interviewed. Subjects were deemed ineligible in wave III because they were not part of the probability sample, they were not part of the genetic subsample, or they were deceased. Subjects who were eligible but not interviewed did not participate in the study because subject could not be located (n= 2,330) or was unavailable (n= 748), there was a language barrier (n= 9), subject was incarcerated (n= 103) or institutionalized (n= 3), subject was in the military (n= 187), subject was out of the country (n =202), subject was physically or mentally incapable (n= 41) or the subject was unwilling to participate (n =1,160). Descriptive statistics from Add Health researchers shows that response rates were not significantly lower in the genetic subsample than in the probability core sample.

DNA Collection, Extraction, and Genotyping Procedures
DNA collection procedures.

Add Health researchers used a combination of cytology brush and mouthwash methods to collect DNA samples from respondents. The DNA samples from each method were initially collected and prepared separately, but then later combined for genetic analysis. The cytology brush method required respondents to rub a cytology brush on the inner cheek and gums for 20 seconds. Once this was completed, the tip of the cytology brush was placed into a 2 ml screw tap tube that contained 200 µl of lysis buffer (1 percent isopropyl alcohol [v/v] in 50 mM Tris-HCl, 1 mM EDTA and 1 percent sodium dodecyl sulfate, pH 8.0). The mouthwash method required respondents to rinse 10 ml of 4 percent sucrose for 30 seconds, and then dispense the liquid into a 50 ml conical test tube. The tube was sealed with parafilm and labeled as "wash 1." Respondents were then instructed to repeat the process with another 10 ml of 4 percent sucrose. This second mouthwash sample was labeled as "wash 2." The cytology brush and mouthwash tubes were then packaged in ice to maintain a temperature of 4°C until it was received at Dr. David Rowe's laboratory at the University of Arizona (Add Health Biomarker Team, no date).

DNA extraction procedures.

DNA was extracted from buccal cells in the laboratory of Dr. David Rowe at the University of Arizona. On the first day of DNA extraction, 1 ml of lysis buffer (6 M guanidine-HCl, 100 mM Tris-HCl and 10 mM EDTA, pH 7.5) and 25 µl of proteinase K (10mg/ml) were added to the tubes containing the cytology brushes. The lysis buffer and proteinase K allow DNA to be isolated from the cell by breaking down the cell membrane. These tubes were then placed in a rotating incubator and stored overnight at 55°C. In addition to preparing the cytology brush specimens, the research assistants also began preparing the mouthwash samples for genetic analyses. The mouthwash samples ("wash 1" and "wash 2") were combined and centrifuged at 1,800 revolutions per minute for 10 minutes. This separated buccal cells from the liquid. Once this was complete, the supernatant fluid was removed and a pellet of buccal cells remained at the bottom of the 50 ml conical test tube. In order to resuspend the pellet, 1 ml of lysis buffer was added to the pellet. The pellet was then transferred to a new 2 ml tube, and 25 μl of proteinase K (10mg/ml) was added to the new tube. These tubes were incubated overnight at 55°C (Add Health Biomarker Team, no date).

On the second day, cytology brushes were removed from their 2 ml tubes. 200 μl of binding matrix (10 mM sodium acetate and .1g/ml diatomaceous earth [Sigma] in lysis buffer) was added to the cytology brush tubes and to the combined wash tube. The tubes were placed in a rotating incubator for 15 minutes at room temperature, and then centrifuged for 2 minutes at maximum speed. The supernatant was discarded and 1 ml of wash buffer (50 percent ethanol [v/v] in 400 mM sodium chloride, 20 mM Tris-HCl and 2 mM EDTA, pH 7.5) was added to each pellet of buccal cells (i.e., one pellet from the brush sample and one pellet from the combined mouthwash sample). The tubes were placed in a rotating incubator for 15 minutes at room temperature, and then centrifuged for 2 minutes at maximum speed. The supernatant was removed and the pellets were vacuum dried overnight (Add Health Biomarker Team, no date).

Finally, on the third day, 200 μl of elution buffer (10 mM Tris-HCl, .1 mM EDTA, pH 8.8) was added to each dried pellet. The tubes were placed in a rotating incubator for 30 minutes at 55°C, and then centrifuged for 2 minutes at maximum speed. The supernatant fluid containing the DNA from each subject's cytology brush tube and wash tube were combined into a .5 ml tube. An average of 58 ± 1 μg of DNA was extracted for each subject. The .5 ml tubes were then packaged to maintain a temperature of 4°C and sent to the Institute for Behavioral Genetics at the University of Colorado.

Genotyping.

Researchers at the Institute for Behavioral Genetics used polymerase chain reaction (PCR) methods to genotype the DAT1, DRD2, DRD4, 5HTT, and MAOA genes. PCR is a procedure that is used to replicate a strand of DNA. This method allows researchers to create billions and billions of duplicates of a single DNA strand. This is advantageous because a greater number of DNA copies increases the reliability of deciphering a genetic sequence. The PCR technique works similarly to how living organisms naturally replicate their DNA. Due to the similarities between the two processes, the next section will discuss how living organisms naturally replicate their DNA, followed by a discussion of the PCR technique.

The DNA replication process can be described in a series of four steps. First, an enzyme, helicase, attaches to a section of DNA referred to as the initiation site. As it attaches to the initiation site, it begins to unwind the DNA helix and separates the two DNA strands from each other. Second, the enzyme RNA primase synthesizes an RNA primer to initiate the replication process. A primer is a sequence of RNA nucleotides that complement the first sequence of DNA bases on each 'unzipped' strand of DNA. This complementary sequence of nucleotides binds to the 'unzipped' strand of DNA and initiates the duplication process. Third, once the beginning of the sequence is "primed" or initiated, DNA polymerase moves along the 'unzipped' strand of DNA. As DNA polymerase moves along the original strand of DNA, it binds DNA nucleotides (A, C, T, or G) that complement the bases on the exposed or 'unzipped' strand of DNA. Finally, the enzyme ligase seals together the original and replicated strand.

Similar to DNA replication that occurs naturally in organisms, the PCR technique duplicates DNA fragments through a process of separating DNA strands, priming, and synthesizing nucleotide sequences with polymerase (Figure 5.1). The components required for the PCR process include: the DNA region that is to be replicated, a large supply of free floating DNA bases (A, C, T, and G), a primer sequence, and Taq1 polymerase. These components are placed into a test tube that holds .2 to .5 ml. Once the test tube is prepared for analysis, the PCR process is executed in three steps. The first step, referred to as denaturation, involves heating the test tube to 90°C-96°C in order to separate the two DNA strands from each other. After the DNA strands are separated, the primers can be activated to initiate the replication process. To activate the primers, the test tube is cooled down to 55°C. This step, referred to as annealing, allows the primers to bind to the targeted DNA regions and the primers begin attaching complementary nucleotides to the original strand of DNA. Finally, the last step of the PCR process is the extension or elongation step. This step entails heating the test tube to 75°C, so that the Taq1 polymerase can continue the replication process by binding complementary nucleotides to the 'unzipped' strand of DNA. The Taq1 polymerase continues to attach complementary nucleotides until it reaches the end of the targeted sequence of DNA. At this point, the first cycle of the PCR process is complete and there will be two copies of targeted DNA. This PCR process is repeated for numerous cycles until there are billions of copies of the targeted DNA region.

Once the targeted DNA region is replicated for each subject, these regions must be inspected for differences in allele length. That is, the targeted DNA region may be longer for some subjects (in allele length) compared to other subjects' DNA region, and this difference may translate into behavioral and cognitive differences later in analysis. Before analyzing the relationship between differences in allele length and cognition or behavior, it is necessary to measure the variation in allele length. Electrophoresis is a technique used to examine differences in the length of DNA strands. In electrophoresis, samples of the PCR products are placed in a block of agarose gel or polyacrylamide gel. Next, the gel block is placed inside of an electrophoresis box where an electrical charge is added to two opposite sides of the box; a negative charge is placed on the end containing the DNA samples and a positive charge is placed on the opposite end. Since DNA molecules are negatively charged, the DNA strands will be repelled from the negatively charged end of the electrophoresis box and they will move towards the positively charged side. The DNA strands will naturally sort themselves according to length because shorter strands will move more quickly through the gel than the longer strands. Finally, the gel block is removed from the electrophoresis box, a stain (typically ethidium bromide) is added to the gel, and the gel block placed on an ultraviolet light. This allows the researcher to visually inspect for differences in allele length of genetic markers, such as the DAT1, DRD2, DRD4, 5HTTLPR, and MAOA markers.

Figure 5.1. Illustration of polymerase chain reaction method

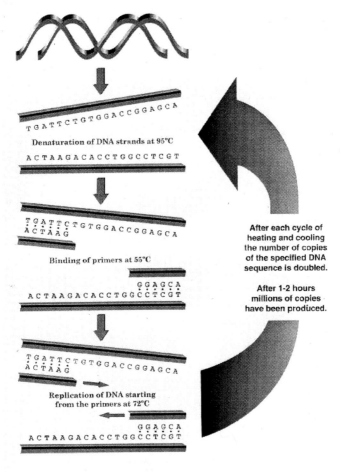

http://fungus.org.uk/cv/dna1cv.htm

Dopamine Transporter Polymorphism (DAT1).

The DAT1 gene (locus symbol: SLC6A3) maps to chromosome 5p15.3. The location of a gene (i.e., 5p15.3) is written as (chromosome #) (p arm or q arm) (position on chromosome). As shown in figure 5.2, a chromosome has a short arm that is referred to as the 'p arm', and it has a long arm that is referred to as the 'q arm'. The 'p' or 'q' listed after the chromosome number tells the reader if the gene is on the short or the long arm of the chromosome. The remaining number tells the reader exactly where on the 'p' or 'q' arm the gene lies. The ideogram (Figure 5.3) shows that the DAT1 gene is located on the short arm of chromosome 5, in the first light band (near position 5p15.32). The light bands of chromosomes (referred to as euchromatin) contain more protein encoding genes, while the dark bands (referred to as heterochromatin) are important for maintaining the chromosome's structure.

Genes contain DNA sequences (i.e., sequences of base pairs—A, C, T, G) that can be repeated and vary in length. DAT1 contains a 40 base pair variable number of tandem repeat (VNTR) polymorphism in the 3' untranslated region (Vandenbergh et al., 1992). Hypothetically, the 40bp sequence (and variations of this sequence) can be repeated three to eleven times.

The primer sequences used to amplify the polymorphic region of DAT1 was: forward, 5'-TGTGGTGTAGGGAACGGCCTGAG-3' (fluorescently labeled), and reverse, 5'-CTTCCTGGAGGTCACGGCTCAAGG-3'. These primer sequences resulted in the following fragment sizes: 320 (6-repeat allele), 360 (7-repeat allele), 400 (8-repeat allele), 440 (9-repeat allele), 480 (10-repeat allele), and 520 (11-repeat allele) base pairs (Add Health Biomarkers Team, no date).

Figure 5.2 Illustration of a chromosome

Short and Long Arms of a Chromosome

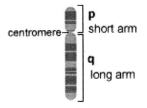

centromere —
p
short arm

q
long arm

http://www.ornl.gov/sci/techresources/Human_Genome/posters/chromosome/o
mim.shtml

Figure 5.3 Illustration of chromosome 5

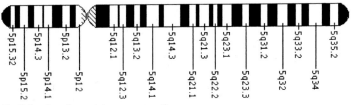

http://ghr.nlm.nih.gov/chromosome=5

Dopamine Receptor Polymorphism (DRD2).

The DRD2 gene (locus symbol: 1813; C32806T) maps to chromosome 11q23 and contains a polymorphic Taq1A restriction endonuclease site located in the 3' untranslated region (Figure 5.4). The A1 allele has a C to T substitution in the noncoding region of the gene. Researchers at the Institute for Behavioral Genetics used the Applied Biosystem's "Taqman© Assays by Design™ for SNP Genotyping Service" to develop a SNP assay. The primer and probe sequences used to amplify the DRD2 Taq1A polymorphism included: forward primer, 5'-GTGCAGCTCACTCCATCCT-3', reverse primer, 5'-

GCAACACAGCCATCCTCAAAG-3', probe 1, VIC-
CCTGCCT*T*GACCAGC-NFQMGB, probe 2, FAM-
CTGCCT*C*GACCAGC-NFQMGB. Probe 1 anneals to the "T" form at
the no restriction site (Taq1A-1) and represents the 304 base pair
fragment. Probe 2 anneals to the "C" form at the restriction site
(Taq1A-2) and represents the 178 base pair fragment (Add Health
Biomarkers Team, no date; Haberstick & Smolen, 2004).

Figure 5.4 Illustration of chromosome 11

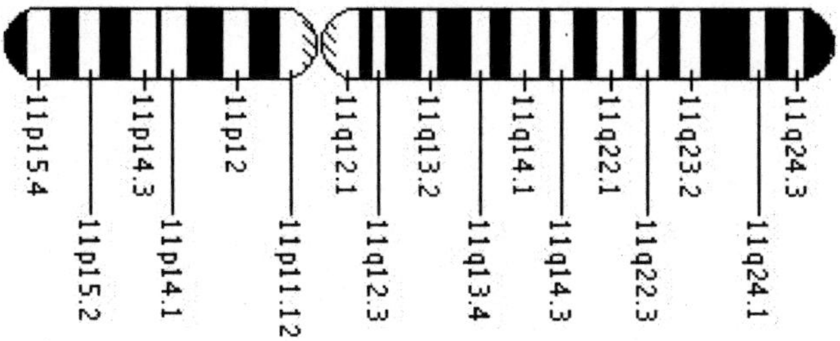

http://ghr.nlm.nih.gov/chromosome=11

Dopamine Receptor Polymorphism (DRD4).

The DRD4 gene maps to chromosome 11p15.5 and has a 48 base pair
variable number of tandem repeat (VNTR) polymorphism in the third
exon (Van Tol et al., 1992). The primer sequences included: forward,
5'-AGGACCCTCATGGCCTTG-3' (fluorescently labeled), and
reverse, 5'-GCGACTACGTGGTCTACTCG-3'. These primer
sequences resulted in the following PCR products: 379 (2-repeat
allele), 427 (3-repeat allele), 475 (4-repeat allele), 523 (5-repeat allele),
571 (6-repeat allele), 619 (7-repeat allele), 667 (8-repeat allele), 715 (9-
repeat allele), 763 (10-repeat allele), and 811 (11-repeat allele) base
pairs (Add Health Biomarkers Team, no date).

Serotonin Transporter Polymorphism (5HTTLPR).

The 5HTT gene maps to chromosome 17q11.1-17q12 and has a 44 base
pair insertion or deletion polymorphism in the 5' region (Heils et al.,
1996) (Figure 5.5). Researchers at the Institute for Behavioral Genetics

used a modified version of the assay described by Lesch et al. (1996) to genotype the 5HTTLPR polymorphism. The primer sequences used to amplify the 5HTTLPR polymorphism were: forward, 5'-GGCGTTGCCGCTCTGAATGC-3' (fluorescently labeled), and reverse, 5'- GAGGGACTGAGCTGGACAACCAC-3'. These primer sequences produced the PCR products of 484 (short allele) and 528 (long allele) base pairs (Add Health Biomarkers Team, no date).

Figure 5.5 Illustration of chromosome 17

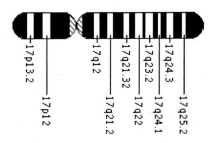

http://ghr.nlm.nih.gov/chromosome=17

Monoamine Oxidase Promoter A Polymorphism (MAOA).

The MAOA genetic marker maps to the X-chromosome at position Xp11.3-11.4 (Figure 5.6). It has a 30 base pair variable number of tandem repeats in the 5' regulatory section of the gene (Samochowiec et al., 1999). To genotype the MAOA polymorphism, researchers at the Institute for Behavioral Genetics used a modified version of the assay described by Sabol, Hu, and Hamer (1998). The primer sequences used to amplify the MAOA gene were: forward, 5'ACAGCCTGACCG-TGGAGAAG-3' (fluorescently labeled), and reverse, 5'-GAACGTGACGCTCCATTCGGA-3'. The touchdown PCR method was used to amplify the polymorphic region of MAOA (Don, Cox, Wainwright, Baker, & Mattick, 1991; Anchordoquy, McGeary, Liu, Krauter, & Smolen, 2003). The PCR method resulted in the following products: 291 (2-repeat allele), 321 (3-repeat allele), 336

(3.5-repeat allele), 351 (4-repeat allele), and 381 (5-repeat allele) base
pairs (Add Health Biomarkers Team, no date).

Figure 5.6 Illustration of the X chromosome

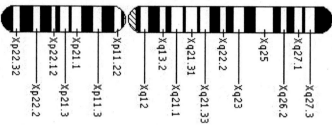

http://ghr.nlm.nih.gov/chromosome=X

Analytical Sample
The Add Health data are available in two different data sets: a publicly
released data set and restricted-use data set. The publicly released data
set contains information on one-half of the respondents in the core
sample and one-half of the respondents in the oversampled African
American sample. This procedure resulted in information being
available for 4,882 subjects from wave I to wave III. The publicly
released data set includes information from the youths' wave I in-
school survey, wave I and II in-home interview, wave I parent
questionnaire, the Picture Vocabulary Test, in-school social network,
wave III relationships, wave III pregnancies, and education data. While
the publicly released data includes information on a variety of topics, it
does not include data on the subjects' DNA markers or genetic
relatedness. Due to this consideration, I analyzed data from the
restricted-use data for the current study.

The restricted-use data includes information on subjects' in-school
network, friendship nominations, genetic relatedness (i.e., MZ twin, DZ
twin, full sibling, half sibling, and unrelated siblings), DNA analysis
and biospecimen results, and spatial analysis data. To obtain these
data, certified researchers must sign a contractual agreement with the
Carolina Population Center/University of North Carolina at Chapel
Hill. This contract describes how to securely store the data and who is
granted access to the data. This contract must also be approved and

signed by The Institutional Review Board—Social and Behavioral Sciences at the University of Cincinnati. Finally, one twin from each MZ twin pair was randomly removed from the analytical sample. A twin was removed from each MZ pair because MZ twins (theoretically) share 100 percent of their DNA. This means that the genetic data from each twin would be double counted if both twins were included in statistical analysis. Thus, the results from genetic markers could be biased, especially since MZ twins comprised a substantial proportion of the sibling subsample (48.9 percent). After removing one twin from each MZ twin pair, the final analytic sample consists of 2,403 subjects (female n= 1,246, male n= 1,157).

Measures
Measures of Abuse.

Feminist criminology has long hypothesized that victimization increases substantially the likelihood of criminal behavior and psychological dysfunction, especially among females (Belknap & Holsinger, 1998; Widom & Maxfield, 2001; Fitzgerald, 2002). Research has also suggested, however, that the effect of victimization on criminal behavior and psychological distress may vary by type of victimization (Brown, 1984; Coker et al., 2002; Widom & Ames, 1994; Kingree et al., 2003; Lang et al., 2004; Maxfield & Widom, 1996). Some studies, for example, have shown that neglect has a stronger effect on females' criminal behavior than physical abuse and sexual abuse (Widom & Ames, 1994; Kingree et al., 2003), while other studies have failed to replicate these results (Herrera & McCloskey, 2003). In addition, studies have revealed that childhood maltreatment and intimate partner violence may have different effects on females' psychological functioning (Lang et al., 2004). This difference in the effects of abuse may be due to timing of the abuse (Ireland et al., 2002) or context of abuse (Kruttschnitt & MacMillian, 2006). Regardless, these studies highlight the importance of differentiating between types of victimization when investigating the effects of victimization on psychological and behavioral outcomes.

In light of the above research, the current study uses five separate measures of victimization to test the abuse-crime hypothesis. The first measure, a retrospective measure of *childhood sexual victimization*, assesses whether subjects were sexually abused during childhood. Specifically, in wave III respondents were asked, "How often had one of your parents or other adult care-givers touched you in a sexual way, forced you to touch him or her in a sexual way, or forced you to have sexual relations"? Responses were measured as a dichotomous measure: 0= this never happened, 1= this happened one or more times. A frequency distribution showed that approximately 5 percent of the sample had been sexually victimized at least once by a parent during childhood.

A retrospective measure of *childhood neglect* was created from one variable that assessed how often the parent or caretaker did not take care of their basic physical needs (Bernstein, Fink, Handelsman, & Fotte, 1994; Bernstein, Ahluvalia, Pogge, & Handelsman, 1997). Subjects were asked during wave III how often their parents had not taken care of their basic needs any time prior to sixth grade. Responses were originally measured as an ordinal scale: 0= this never happened, 1= one time, 2= two times, 3= three to five times, 4= six to ten times, 5= more than ten times. However, due to limited variation in some of the categories, the current study coded the variable as: 0 = never, 1 = one to five times, and 2 = six or more times. This approach allowed for an adequate number of cases in each response category and for variation in the frequency of neglect.

Childhood physical abuse was retrospectively measured during wave III. Subjects were asked during wave III whether their parents or caregivers had slapped, hit, or kicked them. Simlar to the neglect measure, responses were measured as an ordinal scale: 0 = never, 1 = one to five times, and 2 = six or more times.

The third measure, a *violent victimization* index, assesses the frequency of serious physical victimization the subject experienced during the previous year. Respondents were asked in waves II to report how often someone had pulled a knife or gun on them, shot, stabbed, and jumped them during the past twelve months. Other studies that use the Add Health study have used the same violent victimization scale (Hagan & Foster, 2001; Russell & Joyner, 2001; Shaffer & Ruback, 2002; Boardman & Saint Onge, 2005; Beaver et al., 2007). Responses to these items were coded as: 0= never, 1= once, 2= more than once. Scores from the four questions were summed to form the violent victimization index (wave II α= .64). Due to the small number of cases experiencing more than one victimization event, the index was dichotomized so that 0 = did not experience any violent victimization events, and 1 = experienced at least one violent victimization event. Finally, an *intimate partner violence* scale measured the prevalence of minor verbal and physical abuse by romantic partners. During wave II, the subject was asked if romantic partners 1, 2, or 3 had ever insulted, sweared at, threatened with violence, pushed, or thrown something that could hurt him or her (0= No, 1= Yes). These items were drawn from the revised Conflict Tactics Scale (Straus, Hamby, Boney-McCoy, & Sugarman, 1996; Straus, 2004). Other studies that use the Add Health data have employed similar measures of intimate partner violence (Roberts & Klein, 2003; Kaestle & Halpern, 2005; Roberts, Auinger, & Klein, 2005). The responses for these fifteen variables (3 partners * 5 questions) were summed to form a limited count variable. Higher scores indicated that a subject was more likely to experience intimate partner violence (α= .61). However, inspection of a frequency distribution revealed that only a small percentage of cases experienced more than one form of intimate partner violence from one partner, and the measure was coded so that 0 = never experienced intimate partner violence from any partner, 1 = experienced at least one IPV incident from at least one partner, and 2 = experienced more than one incident (either from same partner or different partners).

Limitations of Abuse Measures.

There has been some discussion regarding the reliability and validity of retrospective measures of childhood abuse. Overall, research suggests that retrospective measures of childhood maltreatment generally underestimate the prevalence of childhood abuse (Fergusson, Horwood, & Woodward, 2000; Hardt & Rutter, 2004). For instance, Widom and Shepard's (1996) analysis of 726 individuals who were abused during childhood and 543 matched controls found that approximately 40 percent of individuals with officially recorded histories of childhood physical abuse (n= 110) did not report physical abuse during adulthood. Other studies have also concluded that retrospective measures of child abuse underestimate the actual prevalence of abuse (Widom & Morris, 1997; Brown, Craig, Harris, Handley, & Harvey, 2007). This underestimation of abuse may occur because subjects did not remember the abuse, they were too embarrassed to report the abuse, they did not define the behaviors as abusive, or they were trying to protect the abuser (Femina, Yeager, & Lewis, 1990).

Despite these limitations, there is some evidence that suggests retrospective measures of childhood abuse are moderately valid and reliable (Durrett, Trull, & Silk, 2004). These studies typically examine the reliability of retrospective measures by comparing self-reports of childhood abuse that were collected at two time points during adulthood. For instance, Hardt and colleague's (2006) analysis of 100 adult patients found that the reliabilities of severe sexual abuse (κ = .64) and regular harsh physical abuse (κ = .56) were moderate. Patients who reported sexual abuse were consistent in their reports of the age at which abuse happened and the frequency of abuse at both time periods. Dube and colleague's (2004) analysis of 658 subjects from the Adverse Childhood Experiences study found that estimates of childhood abuse from retrospective measures were moderately reliable across time periods. The reliabilities ranged from .51 to .66 for emotional abuse, .55 to .63 for physical abuse, and .57 to .69 for sexual abuse. Finally, Fergusson, Horwood, and Woodward (2000) reported that there was substantial measurement error in their retrospective measures of childhood physical and sexual abuse, yet this error did not attenuate the relationships between abuse and subsequent adjustment problems.

Widom and Morris's (1997) analyses of prospective data also suggest that measurement error in retrospective measures of abuse may not completely attenuate the associations between abuse and maladaptive outcomes. Their study found that only 16 percent of males and 64 percent of females with officially recorded cases of sexual abuse reported sexual abuse during follow-ups in adulthood. However, officially reported and self-reported measures of childhood sexual abuse significantly predicted suicide attempts and alcohol diagnosis later in adulthood for men and women. This research suggests that retrospective measures of child abuse may underestimate the prevalence of abuse (especially serious abuse), but this error may not significantly affect how these measures perform in statistical analysis.

Subsequent research, however, suggests that researchers may be more likely to find a relationship between abuse and maladaptive behaviors with a retrospective approach (such as the one used in this study), compared to a prospective approach. Widom and colleagues' (1999) later analyses revealed that retrospective, self-reported measures of childhood abuse had a stronger effect on drug abuse than official reports in a prospective approach. The authors also found that respondents who had an official report of abuse but who did not self report childhood abuse had the lowest reported prevalence of drug abuse. However, the prevalence of drug abuse did not significantly differ between those who self-reported abuse and who did not have an officially reported case, compared to those who self-reported abuse and who did have an officially reported case. One would expect a significant difference between these two groups if retrospective reports overestimated the relationship between abuse and maladaptive behaviors. Instead, Widom and colleagues' results suggest that there may be some response bias in self-report methods with respondents underestimating their problems (i.e., ever abused, abuse drugs).

The current measure of intimate partner violence may also be limited in scope and reliability. First, the measure may be limited because it is a self-report measure of intimate partner violence. Self-report measures of sensitive topics, such as intimate partner violence, may be biased due to subjects over or under inflating the prevalence and severity of an incident. However, studies have shown that the ASCII method of data collection minimizes the amount of error and unreliability in sensitive measures, such as intimate partner violence (Couper et al., 2003; Ghanem et al., 2005). Second, the current measure of intimate partner violence includes items that tap less serious forms of intimate partner violence. The measure primarily consists of items inquiring about verbal abuse and minor physical abuse. It may be that more serious forms of intimate partner violence have a stronger effect on females' antisocial behavior, than less serious forms.

Genetic Polymorphisms

The current study includes measures of five polymorphic genes (DAT1, DRD2, DRD4, 5HTTLPR, and MAOA). These genes are labeled as polymorphic because more than one variation or type of allele is available in the population. Behavioral genetics has shown that certain alleles or variations of each gene may place individuals at-risk for maladaptive outcomes (Plomin, 1990). Questions arise, however, when researchers discuss *which* alleles place one at-risk and how to code the alleles for analysis. Researchers have treated and coded alleles as dominant, recessive, co-dominant, and heterosis (Comings et al., 2000b). These strategies may assume that the same allele (i.e., A1) connotes different levels of genetic risk. For instance, if the A1 allele of DRD2 is conceptualized as the risk allele, researchers who assumed A1 is operating in a dominant fashion would code the variable as: 0 [A2/A2 genotype], 2 [A1/A2 genotype], and 2 [A1/A1 genotype]. Researchers assuming that the A1 allele is recessive would code the variable as: 0 [A2/A2 genotype], 0 [A1/A2 genotype], and 2 [A1/A1 genotype]. Different codings and assumptions about how genetic risk is operating could influence whether a researcher finds a significant or non-significant genetic effect.

For the purposes of the current study, the polymorphisms will be predominantly coded as co-dominant for correlational analyses. The co-dominant method has been employed in other genetic studies (Vaske et al., 2008), and the linear assumptions of codominant method are in line with the linearity assumptions of logistic and multinomial regression (i.e., logits are linear function of exogenous variables or genetic markers). All marginally significant gene-environment correlations, however, are investigated to determine whether heterotic coding methods (A1/A2 vs. A1/A1 & A2/A2) better capture the relationship between polymorphisms and victimization. The co-dominant method is not employed in the moderating analyses. The moderating analyses (G x E analyses) estimate a separate equation for each genotype, in order to explore whether non-linear gene X environment interaction effects are present.

Dopamine transporter polymorphism (DAT1)

The DAT1 gene has a 40 base pair variable number of tandem repeats (VNTR) polymorphism that is located in the 3' untranslated region of the gene (Haddley et al., 2008). Genotyping of the dopamine transporter gene (DAT1) resulted in six different PCR products: 320 (6-repeat allele), 360 (7-repeat allele), 400 (8-repeat allele), 440 (9-repeat allele), 480 (10-repeat allele), and 520 (11-repeat allele) base pairs (Add Health Biomarkers Team, no date). Respondents who did not carry a 9-repeat allele or 10-repeat allele were excluded from the sample (Hopfer et al., 2005; Beaver et al., 2007). The 480 base pairs product or 10-repeat allele has been linked to a variety of maladaptive behaviors (Rowe et al., 1998; Mill et al., 2005a); thus, the 10-repeat allele was considered a risk allele and received a score of "1." The 9-repeat allele was scored as a "0." The values of each allele were summed to create an overall risk measure, with the values representing the number of risk alleles. The genotypes were in Hardy Weinberg equilibrium for females ($\chi^2 = .05$, $p = .82$) and males ($\chi^2 = .07$, $p = .79$).

Dopamine receptor polymorphism (DRD2)

The DRD2 gene has a polymorphism at the TaqIA site that is located at 10kb downstream from exon 8 (Grandy et al., 1989). There are two different alleles that are available at this site: the A1 allele (304 base pairs) and A2 allele (178 base pairs). The A1 allele is considered the risk allele for various antisocial behaviors, including criminal behavior (Connor et al., 2002; Noble, 2003; Hopfer et al., 2005; Guo et al., 2007). In light of this evidence, the A2 allele was scored as "0" and the A1 allele was scored as "1." These values were summed together to form an overall risk measure for DRD2. Higher scores reflected a greater number of risk alleles. The genotypes were in Hardy Weinberg equilibrium for females ($\chi^2 = 2.55$, $p = .89$) and males ($\chi^2 = 2.19$, $p = .14$).

Dopamine receptor polymorphism (DRD4)

DRD4 gene has a functional polymorphism located in the third exon (Van Tol et al., 1992). This polymorphism is characterized by a 48 base pair variable number of tandem repeats that is repeated two to eleven times. More specifically, the PCR products included 379 (2-repeat allele), 427 (3-repeat allele), 475 (4-repeat allele), 523 (5-repeat allele), 571 (6-repeat allele), 619 (7-repeat allele), 667 (8-repeat allele), 715 (9-repeat allele), 763 (10-repeat allele), and 811 (11-repeat allele) base pairs (Add Health Biomarkers Team, no date). The 7-repeat allele is considered the risk allele for various maladaptive behaviors, including attention deficit disorder, alcohol abuse, and risk seeking behaviors (Asghari et al., 1995; Becker et al., 2005; Franke et al., 2000; Li et al., 2006). In line with prior research using the Add Health data, the current study assigned a score of "0" to all alleles that were less then 7-repeats (Hopfer et al., 2005; Beaver et al., 2007). Alleles that had seven or more repeats were assigned a score of "1." The values from both alleles were summed together, so that higher scores reflected a greater number of risk alleles. The genotypes were in Hardy Weinberg equilibrium for females ($\chi^2 = .03$, $p = .86$) and males ($\chi^2 = 2.68$, $p = .10$).

Serotonin transporter polymorphism (5HTTLPR)

The 5HTT gene has a functional insertion/deletion polymorphism that is located in the promoter region (Heils et al., 1996). There are two alleles available in the population: a short allele (484 base pairs) and a long allele (528 base pairs). Studies have shown that the short allele increases the risk of antisocial behaviors (Comings et al., 2000b; Haberstick et al., 2006; Lesch et al., 1996; Sen, Burmeister, & Ghosh, 2004), but numerous studies have found that the association does not hold for female subjects (Baca-Garcia et al., 2000; Brummett et al., 2003; Du et al., 2000; Flory et al., 1999; Gelernter et al., 1998). Following prior research using the Add Health data, the current study assigned a score of "0" to the long allele and a score of "1" to the short allele. These values were summed together to form an overall risk measure for 5HTTLPR. The genotypes were not in Hardy Weinberg equilibrium for females ($\chi^2 = 4.69$, $p = .03$) or males ($\chi^2 = 3.77$, $p = .05$).

Monoamine Oxidase A Promoter polymorphism (MAOA)

The MAOA gene has a 30 base pair variable number of tandem repeats in the promoter region (Samochowiec et al., 1999). The VNTR can be repeated two to five times. Typically, 2-repeat and 3-repeat alleles are considered low activity alleles, while high activity alleles consist of 3.5-repeat, 4-repeat, and 5-repeat alleles (Haberstick et al., 2005; Huizinga et al., 2006; Young et al., 2006). The low activity allele is considered the risk allele (Caspi et al., 2002; Ducci et al., 2006; Foley et al., 2004). In line with this research, the current study coded high activity alleles as "0" and low activity alleles as "1."

The MAOA gene is located on the X-chromosome. Since the number of X-chromosomes differs between genders, the number of

MAOA alleles will also differ across genders. Males only have one X-chromosome, so they will only have one MAOA allele. This means that males will either carry zero risk alleles or one risk allele. Females, on the other hand, have two X-chromosomes. Therefore, females can carry zero risk alleles, one risk allele, or two risk alleles. Caution must be used, however, in interpreting significant direct or interactive effects of MAOA for females since one X-chromosome is rendered inactive (Skuse, 2006). This suggests that findings regarding the heterozygote group (l/h) may be mixed and ambiguous since it is impossible to tell whether the low activity allele or the high activity allele is inactivated. Furthermore, the inactivation of X-chromosomes will vary across females and create a very heterogeneous group for heterozygous females. Due to these considerations, post-hoc analyses will primarily focus on comparing the two homozygous groups (l/l vs. h/h) for females. The genotypes were not in Hardy Weinberg equilibrium for females ($\chi^2 = 5.63$, $p = .02$) and males ($\chi^2 = 30.22$, $p < .001$).

Control Variables
  Age

Age is used as a control variable all subsequent analyses. The effects of age are controlled because previous research has shown that age has a significant effect on criminal behavior (Blumstein, Cohen, & Farrington, 1988; Farrington, 1986; Hirschi & Gottfredson, 1983). Age is measured as a continuous variable in wave II.

Property offending wave II

Property offending in wave II is included as a control variable in all analyses where property offending wave III is the endogenous variable. Property offending in wave II is an index of whether the subjects' had engaged in theft. Subjects were asked if they had taken something from a store without paying, driven a car without permission, stolen something more than $50, stolen something worth less than $50, and went into a house or building to steal something within the past 12 months. The response set for the five items was: 0= never, 1= at least once.. Responses were coded so that higher scores reflected greater property offending in wave II ($\alpha = .68$).

Violent offending wave II

Violent offending in wave II is included as a control variable in analyses where violent offending in wave III is regressed on exogenous variables. Respondents were asked how often they had carried or used a weapon, gotten into a physical fight, and caused serious injury to another person during a fight. The seven items were recoded into dichotomous measures (0= No, 1= Yes) and summed to form a composite scale of violent offending in wave II (α= .63).

Alcohol abuse wave II

Alcohol abuse during wave II is assessed with nine questions that inquired about how often they had experienced negative or harmful consequences from consuming alcohol. The response set for the nine questions was: 0= never, 1= once, 2= twice, 3= three to four times, and 4= five or more times. The nine items were summed to form a composite scale of serious alcohol problems in wave II. The responses from the nine items were summed into a composite scale of alcohol abuse, where higher scores reflected higher levels of abuse (α= .85).

Frequency of marijuana use wave II

Frequency of marijuana use in wave II is included in analyses where wave III frequency of marijuana use is the endogenous variable. During wave II, respondents were asked how many times they had tried or used marijuana in the past 30 days. Frequency of marijuana use is a continuous measure that ranges from 0 to 30, where 30 represents 30 or more times using marijuana in the past 30 days.

Dependent Variables

The current study uses four dependent variables to examine the biosocial pathways to offending for females and males. The dependent variables are property offending, violent criminal behavior, alcohol abuse, and frequency of marijuana use in wave III. Property offenses and substance abuse were chosen as outcomes because they capture the antisocial behaviors that are most common among females, relative to other offense types (Steffensmeier, 1993; Belknap & Holsinger, 1998). The current study also included a measure of violent criminal behavior because very little is known about females' pathway into violent offending (Steffensmeier & Allan, 1996).

Property offending

During wave III, respondents were asked whether they engaged in six different criminal behaviors that may have resulted in profit or obtaining property during the past 12 months. These behaviors included steal something worth more/less than $50, going into a building or house to steal something, using someone else's credit card without their knowledge, receiving stolen property, and deliberately writing a bad check. The measures were recoded into dichotomous items (0= No, 1= Yes). The responses to the six items were summed into a composite measure of property offending in wave III (α= .63).

Violent offending

Respondents were asked seven questions regarding their violent criminal behavior within the previous twelve months. These behaviors included using a weapon, fighting, and causing serious harm to others during a fight. The measures were recoded into dichotomous items (0= No, 1= Yes), and then summed to form an index of violent criminal behavior. Higher scores on the scale reflected greater prevalence of violent offending (α= .60).

Alcohol abuse

The alcohol abuse scale includes eight items that inquire about the negative effects of using alcohol. The negative consequences resulting from alcohol use included problems at work or school, problems with friends, problems with their dating partner, being hung over, being sick to one's stomach, getting into a physical fight, and placing oneself in a sexual situation that they later regretted. The response set for the eight items measuring serious alcohol problems was: 0= never, 1= once, 2= twice, 3= three or four times, and 4= five or more times. These responses were summed to form a measure of alcohol related problems. Higher scores reflected higher levels of alcohol abuse (α = .76).

Frequency of marijuana use

Respondents were asked during wave III how many times they had used marijuana within the past 30 days. This was a continuous measure of marijuana use. The variable was coded so that it ranges from 0 to 30, where 30 represented 30 or more times in the past 30 days. Marijuana was chosen as an outcome (rather than an alternative type of drug) due to the extremely low prevalence of other drug types (i.e., cocaine, methamphetamines).

Table 5.1. Descriptive statistics of analytic sample

	Female	Male
Sexually abused (Yes)	5.7%	4.4%
Neglected		
1-5 times	6.2%	12.1%
6+ times	3.2%	4.7%
Physically abused		
1-5 times	20.1%	21.7%
6+ times	8.0%	8.8%
Violently victimized	6.0%	18.9%
Intimate partner victim		
One incident	10.1%	10.4%
More than one incident	8.9%	8.3%
DAT1		
10R/9R	33.3%	34.5%
10R/10R	62.1%	60.6%
DRD2		
A1/A2	37.1%	37.3%
A1/A1	8.0%	7.9%
DRD4		
>7R/<7R	34.4%	31.0%
>7R/>7R	5.1%	5.0%
5HTTLPR		
Short/Long	45.5%	46.7%
Short/Short	18.9%	21.0%
MAOA		
H/H	38.2%	
L/L	17.3%	
L		41.8%
African American	18.9%	17.3%
Hispanic	14.2%	15.5%

Table 5.1. Descriptive statistics cont.

	Females		Males	
	Mean	SD	Mean	SD
Violent offending wave 2	0.21	0.61	0.51	1.08
Violent offending wave 3	0.08	0.41	0.33	0.79
Property offending wave 2	0.40	0.88	0.50	0.99
Property offending wave 3	0.14	0.55	0.28	0.75
Alcohol abuse wave 2	1.31	3.11	1.77	3.96
Alcohol abuse wave 3	1.85	3.15	3.04	4.28
Frequency of marijuana use wave 2	0.84	3.68	1.51	5.60
Frequency of marijuana use wave 3	1.38	5.17	3.42	8.46
Age	16.45	1.67	16.53	1.70

Analytical Plan

The current investigation examines the interplay of genetic markers and victimization in the etiology of adulthood criminal behavior and adulthood substance use. To explore these issues, the analyses investigate two types of gene-environment effects: (1) indirect effects of a gene on environment (gene-environment correlation or G → E), and (2) a gene-environment interaction (GxE → antisocial behavior). First, zero order correlations will be used to preliminarily investigate the presence of gene-environment correlations. Any significant gene-victimization correlations will be subject to subsequent regression analyses. Multinomial regression will be used for ordinal level variables (i.e., childhood physical abuse and childhood neglect), while logistic regression will be used for any dichotomous variable (i.e., childhood sexual abuse, violent victimization, and inimate partner violence). Age and race will be entered as control variables in the equations. Huber/White variance estimates will be used in both analyses due to the nesting of siblings within the same household (Rogers, 1993). Regression models will be estimated separately for each genetic marker (DAT1, DRD2, DRD4, 5HTTLPR, and MAOA). In addition, these analyses (and subsequent analyses) will be conducted separately for males (n= 1,157) and females (n= 1,246). A difference of coefficients test will be used to examine whether genetic effects on abuse vary across gender (Clogg, Petkova, & Haritou, 1995).

Research question one: **Are dopaminergic, serotonergic, and monoamine oxidase A polymorphisms related to youths' levels of childhood neglect, childhood physical abuse, adolescent violent victimization and adolescent intimate partner violence (i.e., gene-environment correlations)?**

Research question two: **Do the gene-environment correlations vary by gender?**

Techniques of estimating the gene X environment interactions.

Second, regression models will be used to examine whether genetic markers moderate the effects of abuse on property offending, violent offending, alcohol abuse, and the frequency of marijuana use. The current analyses investigate whether genetic markers condition the effects of victimization on antisocial behavior by: (1) regressing antisocial behavior on a victimization measure for each separate genotype, and (2) using a difference of coefficients test to examine whether the effect of victimization on antisocial behavior varies by genotype. For example, an analysis of the effect of neglect on property offending across DRD2 genotypes (A2/A2, A1/A2, and A2/A2) would generate three separate regression models, one for each genotype. This approach may be beneficial to some gene X environment interaction studies because: (1) it avoids the problem of collinearity between product terms and first order predictors; and (2) it allows for identifying interactions that are not bilinear.

Traditionally, researchers have investigated gene X environment interactions by creating a product term from measures that were dummy coded, in deviation regressor form/effect coding, or mean centered. These approaches, however, either have empirical or theoretical limitations. For instance, collinearity between the product term $(X1*Z)$ and a first order predictor $(X1)$ may be quite common when researchers use a product term with dummy coded or deviation regressor coding. Caspi, Hariri, Holmes, Uher, & Moffitt (2010) recently argued that researchers will have collinearity between interaction terms and first order predictors when the frequency of exposure to the "risky" environment is less than 50 percent and when the prevalence of a minor allele is less than 50 percent. Since victimization is a relatively rare event (< 50 percent in many cases), it was expected that there would be collinearity between the product term and first order predictor in models that used dummy coding and deviation regressor coding. Exploration of these methods revealed that there was moderate to severe collinearity between the first order predictors and interaction terms. Correlations between the first order predictor variables and interaction variable ranged from -.20 to -.80, and correlations between first order regression coefficients and the interaction coefficient(s) ranged from .30 to .95. Also, it was common to find 'beta-bounce' or the signs of first order coefficients flipping in the opposite direction (i.e., + to -) when the interaction term was included into the analyses. The shift in the coefficients combined with strong correlations between coefficients suggests that dummy coding and deviation regressor coding is not appropriate for the current study.

As a way to skirt around the collinearity issue, researchers have also tried to mean center the first order predictors prior to creating the interaction term (Vaske et al., 2008). This technique does reduce the correlations between first order predictors and product terms to an acceptable level, thus alleviating the problem of collinearity. Mean centering, however, is not theoretically appropriate for ordinal level variables, such as genotypes. When a model includes the mean centered first order predictors (X1 and X2) and a product term from these centered variables (X1*X2), one would interpret the effect of X1 on Y as the effect of X1 on Y when X2 is at its mean. Theoretically, the mean of an ordinal level variable is not interpretable; thus, the interpretation of a genetic regression coefficient and the coefficient of an ordinal level environmental variable are complicated by mean centering. One may argue that the first order predictors are not relevant in moderation analysis (Baron & Kenny, 1986), but as will be shown later on, a multiplicative interaction term (created with mean centered categorical variables) may produce predicted values that are quite different than the predicted values found with other interaction techniques.

In light of the empirical and theoretical limitations of previous techniques, the current study sought to use a method that minimized the previous limitations. The current study investigates the effects of victimization on antisocial behavior across each genotype, and uses a difference of coefficients test to examine whether the effect is significantly stronger for one genotype versus another (Baron & Kenny, 1986). This method does sacrifice the ability to examine the 'main' effects of genetic polymorphisms on antisocial behavior. The current study, however, is focused on whether the effects of victimization on antisocial behavior vary across genotypes rather than the effect of a genetic marker on antisocial behavior, and thus the moderating effect of the genetic polymorphism is the key focus of the analyses rather than the main effect of the polymorphism (Rutter & Pickles, 1991). This method avoids the problem of collinearity between first order predictors and interaction term, since an interaction term is never formally entered into the model.

Further, this method allows researchers to test alternative interaction effects, while interaction product terms only allow one to test bilinear interaction effects (Jaccard & Turrisi, 2003). Bilinear interaction terms assume that the difference in slopes is the same across levels of the moderator variable, while it may be plausible that the differences in victimization slopes vary in size by genotype. For instance, a bilinear interaction would occur if there was a .4 unit (b_3 = .4) difference in the victimization-offending slope for the A2/A2 DRD2 genotype (i.e., b = 1.20) compared to the victimization-offending slope for the A1/A2 DRD2 genotype (i.e., b = .80), and if there was a .4 unit difference in the victimization-offending slope for the A1/A2 genotype compared to the slope for the A1/A1 genotype (b = .40). It is plausible, however, that alternative interactions occur in gene-environment interactions. Given the varied nature of genetic expression (i.e., dominant, recessive, heterotic) (Comings et al., 2000b), it is likely that there may be a greater difference between victimization-offending slopes as one compares individuals with the A2/A2 genotype (b = 1.20) and individuals with the A1/A2 genotype (b = .50, .7 unit difference), than when one compares A1/A2 individuals to A1/A1 individuals (i.e., b = .40, .1 unit difference) (if the A1 had a dominant effect). Other types of results may also emerge if recessive or heterotic effects are operating.

In light of these considerations, the current study conducted some preliminary analyses to examine whether the results and predicted values would differ whether one used interaction terms from mean centered variables or separate models for the genotypes with differences of coefficients tests. The candidate interaction is between DRD2 and childhood sexual abuse on the frequency of marijuana use in adulthood for all males and females. The first step was to examine the observed average levels of marijuana use for each category/cell of the interaction in the data (Figure 5.7). The next step was to estimate the negative binomial regression models in STATA 9.1 with Huber/White variance estimates with the two techniques. First, the results from the model with the mean centered variables revealed that the frequency of marijuana use was not a function of DRD2 (b = -.130, p = .206), childhood sexual abuse (b = .326, p = .191), or the interaction between DRD2 and childhood sexual abuse (b = -.179, p = .714). The interaction coefficient suggests a .179 difference in the abuse slopes across DRD2 genotypes. The predicted values from this model are plotted in Figure 5.8. It should be noted that the results and adjusted values were similar when analyses were re-ran with only the interaction term (i.e., did not include first order predictors).

Figure 5.7. Plotted mean levels of marijuana use by DRD2 genotype and childhood sexual abuse for the full sample

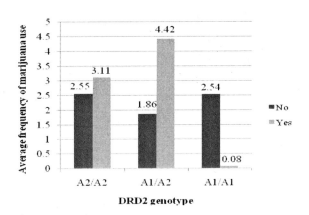

Figure 5.8. Predicted values of marijuana use from negative binomial regression with interaction term from mean centered predictors

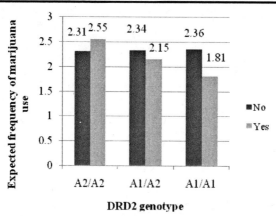

Second, the effect of childhood sexual abuse on marijuana use was estimated separately for each DRD2 genotype. The results revealed that childhood sexual abuse was not related to marijuana use for the A2/A2 genotype ($b = .196$, $p = .562$), but it was related to marijuana use for the A1/A2 ($b = .860$, $p = .019$) and A1/A1 genotypes ($b = -3.418$, $p = .001$). As can be seen, there is more than a .179 unit difference in the abuse slopes across genotypes. Differences of coefficients tests reveal that the coefficient for sexual abuse does not differ between A2/A2 and A1/A2 genotypes ($z = 1.33$), but there are significant differences in coefficients between A1/A2 and A1/A1 genotypes ($z = 4.03$) and between A2/A2 and A1/A1 genotypes ($z = 3.45$); thus, suggesting a significant interaction effect. The predicted values from the three regression models are ploted in Figure 5.9.

If one compares the plotted values and the results from the regression models to the observed mean values of marijuana use in Figure 5.7, it can be seen that the 'difference of coefficients tests' regression models appear to fit the data better than the regression model with the interaction term (i.e., predicted values closer to observed values). In light of the theoretical and empirical considerations, the current study examines whether there is a presence of gene X environment interactions in the data by separately estimating the effects of victimization on antisocial behavior for each genotype, and comparing the coefficients with a difference of coefficients test.

Figure 5.9. Predicted values of marijuana use from negative binomial regression with differences of coefficients tests for separate analyses by genotype

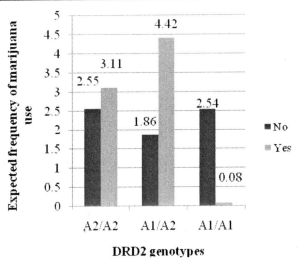

Techniques used in the current study.
The current study estimates the effect of victimization on antisocial behavior for each genotype of a genetic polymorphism, for females and males separately, and uses a difference of coefficients test to test whether the effects statistically vary across genotypes. This method allows one to examine: (1) whether victimization has an effect on antisocial behavior for each genotype (i.e., simple main effects); and (2) whether the effect of victimization on antisocial behavior is statistically different for different genotypes (i.e., interaction effects) (Jaccard & Turrisi, 2003). The simple main effect, in this study, allows

one to examine the difference in antisocial behavior between abused and non-abused respondents for all individuals who have a certain genotype. That is, the analyses can address the question, "Within a genotype, do abused individuals have a different level of antisocial behavior than non-abused individuals?" A simple main effect will be present when the victimization regression coefficient is statistically significant for a genotype. Examination of the simple main effects may suggest that an interaction effect is operating.

An interaction effect may be operating if one simple main effect for one genotype is statistically significant or in the opposite direction of the simple main effect for another genotype. In interaction analyses, the researcher is arguing that the effect of X on Y varies across categories of a third variable (Z). This concept of statistical interaction is similar to the concept of gene X environment interaction in this study. The current study hypothesizes that the effect of victimization on antisocial behavior will vary by genotype. For instance, it is expected that there will be a statistically significant relationship between victimization and antisocial behavior among individuals with high "genetic risk" (i.e., S/S 5HTTLPR genotype), but there will not be a statistically significant relationship between victimization and antisocial behavior among individuals with low "genetic risk" (i.e., L/L 5HTTLPR genotype). That is, there will be a large difference in the expected levels of antisocial behavior for victimized and non-victimized individuals in the high "genetic risk" category, while there may be a smaller difference in antisocial behavior levels between victimized and non-victimized in the low "genetic risk" category. These analyses may suggest whether some individuals are more sensitive to the effects of victimization (i.e., larger difference in antisocial behavior between victimized and non-victimized). Comparison of the simple main effects may indicate an interaction effect, but the differences in the simple main effects may reflect error and must be statistically analyzed.

In the current study, the simple main effects are statistically compared with a difference of coefficients test (Clogg et al., 1995). A difference of coefficients test is used to examine whether a genotype conditions the effect of victimization on antisocial behavior. For instance, the current analyses use the coefficients tests to compare the coefficients for childhood sexual abuse on violent offending for males with the A2/A2, A1/A2, and A1/A1 genotype. A significant difference of coefficients test ($z \geq 1.96$) implies a significant gene X environment interaction.

A difference of coefficients test is also used to examine whether gender conditions the effect of victimization on antisocial behavior within a genotype. An example of this test is used in comparing the effect of childhood physical abuse on violent offending for females with the A2/A2 genotype and males with the A2/A2 genotype. A significant difference of coefficients test implies that males and females respond differently to victimization, even if they share the same genotype (i.e., "genetic risk").

Negative binomial regression is used in the current study because the measures of property offending, violent offending, serious alcohol problems, and frequency of marijuana use are overdispersed ($\overline{X}_{property}= .21$, $s_{property}= .65$, skew $= 4.19$; $\overline{X}_{viol\ offend}= .20$, $s_{viol\ offend}= .63$, skew $= 4.03$; $\overline{X}_{alc\ aubse}= 2.42$, $s_{alc\ prob}= 3.78$, skew $= 2.19$; $\overline{X}_{marij}= 2.36$, $s_{marij}= 7.02$, skew $= 3.22$). Huber/White variance estimates will again be used due to the nesting of siblings within families. Regression models are calculated using STATA 9.0, and coefficients are considered statistically significant if $p \leq .05$. Negative binomial models will be estimated separately by gender, and all regression analyses control for the effects of age, ethnicity, and prior offending/alcohol abuse/marijuana use.

It should be noted that the following analyses are considered preliminary analyses. Inspection of Table 5.2 shows that many of the joint categories of the interaction contain fewer than 10 cases. The small number of cases in an interaction category may produce unstable results, which can often evidence itself in the form of extremely large coefficients ($b = \pm 10.00$). Further, the small number of cases can mean that many of the analyses are underpowered, and that the probability of making a Type II error is significantly higher, especially for small effect sizes.

Research question three: Do dopaminergic, serotonergic, and monoamine oxidase A polymorphisms moderate the effects childhood neglect, childhood sexual abuse, childhood physical

abuse, adolescent violent victimization, and adolescent intimate partner violence on a wide range of antisocial behaviors?

Research question four: **Do the moderating effects of dopaminergic, serotonergic, and monoamine oxidase A polymorphisms vary by gender?**

Table 5.2. Number of cases in interaction categories

Childhood sexual abuse

	Females			Males		
	9R/9R	10R/9R	10R/10R	9R/9R	10R/9R	10R/10R
No	51 (94.4)	373 (95.2)	689 (94.1)	53 (98.1)	351 (97.8)	599 (94.5)
Yes	3 (5.6)	19 (4.8)	43 (5.9)	1 (1.9%)	8 (2.2)	35 (5.5)
	A2/A2	A1/A2	A1/A1	A2/A2	A1/A2	A1/A1
No	625 (93.8)	429 (95.1)	91 (93.8)	568 (95.6)	388 (96.0)	82 (93.2)
Yes	41 (6.2)	22 (4.9)	6 (6.2)	26 (4.4)	16 (4.0)	6 (6.8)
	<7R/<7R	>7R/<7R	>7R/>7R	<7R/<7R	>7R/<7R	>7R/>7R
No	689 (94.4)	395 (94.0)	61 (96.8)	667 (95.8)	323 (95.3)	50 (94.3)
Yes	41 (5.6)	25 (6.0)	2 (3.2)	29 (4.2)	16 (4.7)	3 (5.7)
	L/L	S/L	S/S	L/L	S/L	S/S
No	404 (93.1)	522 (95.3)	215 (94.7)	331 (93.8)	491 (96.7)	220 (96.1)
Yes	30 (6.9)	26 (4.7)	12 (5.3)	22 (6.2)	17 (3.3)	9 (3.9)
	High/High	Low/High	Low/Low	High	Low	
No	433 (94.7)	504 (94.0)	200 (94.8)	605 (96.5)	429 (94.7)	
Yes	24 (5.3)	32 (6.0)	11 (5.2)	22 (3.5)	24 (5.3)	

Table 5.2. Number of cases in interaction categories cont.

Childhood neglect

	Females			Males		
	9R/9R	10R/9R	10R/10R	9R/9R	10R/9R	10R/10R
Never	50 (92.6)	359 (90.9)	666 (90.6)	50 (94.3)	302 (84.4)	510 (81.9)
1-5 times	4 (7.4)	22 (5.6)	46 (6.3)	2 (3.8)	41 (11.5)	79 (12.7)
6+ times	0 (0)	14 (3.5)	23 (3.1)	1 (1.9)	15 (4.2)	34 (5.5)
	A2/A2	A1/A2	A1/A1	A2/A2	A1/A2	A1/A1
Never	611 (90.9)	407 (90.0)	86 (89.6)	492 (83.5)	329 (83.3)	70 (80.5)
1-5 times	40 (6.0)	29 (6.4)	8 (8.3)	65 (11.0)	49 (12.4)	16 (18.4)
6+ times	21 (3.1)	16 (3.5)	2 (2.1)	32 (5.4)	17 (4.3)	1 (1.1)
	≤7R/<7R	>7R/<7R	>7R/>7R	≤7R/<7R	>7R/<7R	>7R/>7R
Never	667 (90.6)	380 (90.3)	57 (91.9)	582 (84.1)	265 (81.0)	44 (83.0)
1-5 times	46 (6.3)	27 (6.4)	3 (4.8)	80 (11.6)	45 (13.8)	5 (9.4)
6+ times	23 (3.1)	14 (3.3)	2 (3.2)	30 (4.3)	17 (5.2)	4 (7.5)
	L/L	S/L	S/S	L/L	S/L	S/S
Never	405 (92.9)	495 (90)	200 (87.3)	282 (81)	426 (85.4)	185 (81.1)
1-5 times	19 (4.4)	43 (7.8)	14 (6.1)	54 (15.5)	48 (9.6)	29 (12.7)
6+ times	12 (2.8)	12 (2.2)	15 (6.6)	12 (3.4)	25 (5.0)	14 (6.1)
	High/High	Low/High	Low/Low	High	Low	
Never	422 (91.7)	490 (91.1)	185 (87.3)	522 (84.6)	364 (81.1)	
1-5 times	25 (5.4)	29 (5.4)	21 (9.9)	67 (10.9)	63 (14.0)	
6+ times	13 (2.8)	19 (3.5)	6 (2.8)	28 (4.5)	22 (4.9)	

Table 5.2. Number of cases in interaction categories cont.

Childhood physical abuse

	Females			Males		
	9R/9R	10R/9R	10R/10R	9R/9R	10R/9R	10R/10R
Never	39 (70.9)	278 (71.6)	529 (72.9)	38 (70.4)	253 (70.3)	429 (69.0)
1-5 times	10 (18.2)	83 (21.4)	138 (19.0)	10 (18.5)	77 (21.4)	139 (22.3)
6+ times	6 (10.9)	27 (7.0)	59 (8.1)	6 (11.1)	30 (8.3)	54 (8.7)
	A2/A2	A1/A2	A1/A1	A2/A2	A1/A2	A1/A1
Never	478 (72.5)	325 (72.2)	63 (65.6)	413 (70.7)	274 (68.3)	59 (67.0)
1-5 times	125 (19.4)	94 (20.9)	21 (21.9)	124 (21.2)	84 (20.9)	24 (27.3)
6+ times	53 (8.0)	31 (6.9)	12 (12.5)	47 (8.0)	43 (10.7)	5 (5.7)
	<7R/<7R	>7R/<7R	>7R/>7R	<7R/<7R	>7R/<7R	>7R/>7R
Never	530 (72.6)	294 (71.4)	42 (67.7)	471 (68.3)	237 (71.6)	38 (71.7)
1-5 times	143 (19.6)	86 (20.9)	13 (21.0)	153 (22.2)	67 (20.2)	13 (24.5)
6+ times	57 (7.8)	32 (7.8)	7 (11.3)	66 (9.6)	27 (8.2)	2 (3.8)
	L/L	S/L	S/S	L/L	S/L	S/S
Never	307 (71.7)	407 (74.5)	150 (66.4)	240 (69.0)	367 (73.0)	140 (61.9)
1-5 times	90 (21.0)	102 (18.7)	50 (22.1)	79 (22.7)	102 (20.3)	54 (23.9)
6+ times	31 (7.2)	37 (6.8)	26 (11.5)	29 (8.3)	34 (6.8)	32 (14.2)
	High/High	Low/High	Low/Low	High	Low	
Never	332 (73.3)	386 (72.4)	145 (69.4)	424 (68.4)	318 (71.1)	
1-5 times	91 (20.1)	103 (19.3)	43 (20.6)	132 (21.3)	100 (22.4)	
6+ times	30 (6.6)	44 (8.3)	21 (10.0)	64 (10.3)	29 (6.5)	

Table 5.2. Number of cases in interaction categories cont.

Violent victimization

	Females			Males		
	9R/9R	10R/9R	10R/10R	9R/9R	10R/9R	10R/10R
None	48 (92.3)	352 (93.4)	674 (94.5)	50 (90.9)	274 (76.5)	515 (83.1)
1+ events	4 (7.7)	25 (6.6)	39 (5.5)	5 (9.1)	84 (23.5)	105 (16.9)
	A2/A2	A1/A2	A1/A1	A2/A2	A1/A2	A1/A1
None	603 (93.9)	414 (94.7)	86 (90.5)	496 (84.4)	305 (76.4)	68 (80.0)
1+ events	39 (6.1)	23 (5.3)	9 (9.5)	92 (15.6)	94 (23.6)	17 (20.0)
	<7R/<7R	>7R/<7R	>7R/>7R	<7R/<7R	>7R/<7R	>7R/>7R
None	677 (94.7)	374 (93.3)	51 (89.5)	569 (81.6)	256 (79.8)	42 (79.2)
1+ events	38 (5.3)	27 (6.7)	6 (10.5)	128 (18.4)	65 (20.2)	11 (20.8)
	L/L	S/L	S/S	L/L	S/L	S/S
None	392 (95.1)	505 (93.9)	204 (92.7)	272 (79.5)	421 (83.0)	177 (78.7)
1+ events	20 (4.9)	33 (6.1)	16 (7.3)	70 (20.5)	86 (17.0)	48 (21.3)
	High/High	Low/High	Low/Low	High	Low	
None	414 (93.2)	491 (94.6)	190 (94.1)	496 (80.5)	369 (82.2)	
1+ events	30 (6.8)	28 (5.4)	12 (5.9)	120 (19.5)	80 (17.8)	

162 Genes and Abuse as Causes of Offending

Table 5.2. Number of cases in interaction categories cont.

Intimate partner victimization

	Females			Males		
	9R/9R	10R/9R	10R/10R	9R/9R	10R/9R	10R/10R
Never	44 (84.6)	307 (81.6)	570 (79.8)	45 (81.8)	282 (79.4)	508 (82.1)
Once	5 (9.6)	32 (8.5)	80 (11.2)	6 (10.9)	43 (12.1)	58 (9.4)
1+ times	3 (5.8)	37 (9.8)	64 (9.0)	4 (7.3)	30 (8.5)	53 (8.6)
	A2/A2	A1/A2	A1/A1	A2/A2	A1/A2	A1/A1
Never	521 (81.3)	358 (81.9)	72 (75)	478 (81.6)	318 (79.9)	74 (87.1)
Once	67 (10.5)	38 (8.7)	14 (14.6)	59 (10.1)	43 (10.8)	8 (9.4)
1+ times	53 (8.3)	41 (9.4)	10 (10.4)	49 (8.4)	37 (9.3)	3 (3.5)
	<7R/<7R	>7R/<7R	>7R/>7R	<7R/<7R	>7R/<7R	>7R/>7R
Never	583 (81.4)	319 (79.8)	47 (82.5)	571 (82.4)	257 (79.8)	42 (79.2)
Once	73 (10.2)	39 (9.8)	7 (12.3)	70 (10.1)	35 (10.9)	6 (11.3)
1+ times	60 (8.4)	42 (10.5)	3 (5.3)	52 (7.5)	30 (9.3)	5 (9.4)
	L/L	S/L	S/S	L/L	S/L	S/S
Never	326 (79.1)	442 (82.2)	180 (81.8)	271 (79.2)	420 (83.2)	179 (79.9)
Once	48 (11.7)	46 (8.6)	23 (10.5)	42 (12.3)	49 (9.7)	21 (9.4)
1+ times	38 (9.2)	50 (9.3)	17 (7.7)	29 (8.5)	36 (7.1)	24 (10.7)
	High/High	Low/High	Low/Low	High	Low	
Never	364 (81.8)	410 (79.2)	169 (83.7)	500 (81.2)	366 (82.1)	
Once	41 (9.2)	58 (11.2)	19 (9.4)	62 (10.1)	48 (10.8)	
1+ times	40 (9.0)	50 (9.7)	14 (6.9)	54 (8.8)	32 (7.2)	

CHAPTER SIX

Findings

Introduction

The current chapter will empirically address whether genetic polymorphisms are correlated with higher rates of victimization, and whether genetic polymorphisms moderate the effects of victimization on antisocial behavior. This chapter will be divided into three sections. The first section will describe the bivariate relationships between the independent variables and dependent variables. The bivariate relationships will be assessed through t-tests, chi-square tests, and zero order correlations. This section will focus on whether there are gender differences in any of the independent and dependent variables. In addition, this section will focus on the heterogeneity of responses to victimization. That is, the analyses will explore what percentage of abused or victimized subjects engage in crime or abuse substances.

The second section will present the findings from the gene-environment correlations analyses. The gene-environment correlation analyses will reveal whether the five genetic polymorphisms correspond to greater exposure to criminogenic environments or events. That is, the five genetic polymorphisms may indirect lead to criminal behavior because they increase the likelihood that an individual may be neglected, physically abused, violently victimized, or a victim of intimate partner violence.

The last section will describe the results from the gene X victimization analyses. These analyses will help address whether the five genetic polymorphisms explain why some abused (i.e., sexual, physical, and neglect) and victimized (i.e., violently victimized and intimate partner violence) individuals engage in criminal behaviors,

163

while other victims refrain from offending. Four measures of criminal behavior are included in the analyses: property offending, violent offending, alcohol abuse, and frequency of marijuana use. In light of the evidence that males and females may respond differently to victimization (Widom, 1989a), separate analyses are estimated for males and females.

Bivariate Analyses

The bivariate associations between the independent and dependent variables are examined with t-tests, chi-square tests, and zero order correlations. T-tests show that males, on average, have higher levels of violent offending in wave 2 ($t = 7.67$, $p < .001$) and wave 3 ($t = 9.34$, $p < .001$), property offending in wave 2 ($t = 2.54$, $p = .011$) and wave 3 ($t = 5.18$, $p < .001$), alcohol abuse in wave 2 ($t = 3.05$, $p = .002$) and wave 3 ($t = 7.66$, $p < .001$), and frequency of marijuana use in wave 2 ($t = 3.27$, $p = .001$) and wave 3 ($t = 7.07$, $p < .001$). Males are also more likely to be neglected during childhood ($\chi^2 = 28.55$, $p < .001$) and violently victimized during adolescence ($\chi^2 = 87.02$, $p < .001$). There are no significant gender differences in the prevalence of childhood sexual abuse ($\chi^2 = 1.99$, $p = .158$), childhood physical abuse ($\chi^2 = 1.62$, $p = .444$), or adolescent intimate partner violence ($\chi^2 = .337$, $p = .845$). Finally, there are no gender differences in the prevalence of DAT1 ($\chi^2 = .59$, $p = .743$), DRD2 ($\chi^2 = .005$, $p = .997$), DRD4 ($\chi^2 = 3.39$, $p = .183$), or 5HTTLPR ($\chi^2 = 3.44$, $p = .179$) genotypes.

Table 6.1 displays the percentage of victimized and abused individuals who do not go on to engage in crime or engage in substance abuse. As shown in the table, a substantial proportion of females and males who are abused or neglected during childhood do not go on to engage in crime or abuse alcohol or marijuana. Approximately 15 to 30 percent of females who are sexually abused, severely physically abused (i.e., six or more times), or severely neglected (i.e., six or more times) engage in violent crime, engage in property crime, report severe alcohol abuse (+1 SD above the mean), or use marijuana during adolescence or early adulthood. This suggests that 70 to 85 percent of abused females *do not* engage in antisocial behaviors later on in life. The percentage of females who are violently victimized who engage in antisocial behavior in adolescence is higher than the percentage of females who experience childhood abuse. This may reflect the fact that many victims are often engaging in criminal behavior, and vice versa. Finally, the table shows that approximately 8 to 40 percent of females who are repeat victims of intimate partner violence engage in crime or substance use during adolescence or adulthood.

A similar pattern is found for males, but males are less resilient to the effects of abuse and victimization than females. Approximately 15 to 40 percent of males who experience abuse (physical or sexual) or neglect during childhood engage in crime or substance use during adolescence or adulthood. This is higher than the percentages for females (15 to 30 percent). Also, a substantial percentage of males who are violently victimized in adolescence are also engaging in violent criminal behavior (68 percent) and property offending (47.5 percent) in adolescence. Again, this may reflect the overlap in the victim-offender relationship. Finally, approximately 60-80 percent of males who are victimized by an intimate partner *do not* engage in antisocial behavior during adolescence or adulthood.

Zero order correlations are displayed in Tables 6.2 and Tables 6.3 for females and males, respectively. As shown in the tables, childhood sexual abuse (X1), childhood physical abuse (X2), and childhood neglect (X3) are significantly associated with violent (X11) and property offending (X12) in adulthood for females and males. Only intimate partner violence (X5) is associated with alcohol abuse (X13) for females, while alcohol abuse for males is associated with childhood physical abuse (X2), violent victimization (X4), and intimate partner violence (X5). Marijuana use is significantly associated with violent victimization (X4) and intimate partner violence (X5) for females and males.

Table 6.2 also reveals that DAT1 is related to adult alcohol abuse (r = -.09), DRD4 is significantly related to adult marijuana use (r = .06), MAOA is related to adult property offending (r = .06), and 5HTTLPR is related to adult alcohol abuse (r = .05) for females. Post-hoc analyses reveal that alcohol abuse is highest among females with the 9R/9R DAT1 genotype (relative to 9R/10R and 10R/10R) and females with the short/long or short/short 5HTTLPR genotype (relative to long/long 5HTTLPR genotype). The average level of marijuana use is highest among females with the 7R>/7R> genotype, compared to females with the <7R/<7R and <7R/>7R genotype.

Table 6.1. Percentage of abused or victimized subjects who engage in violent crime, engage in property crime, exhibit signs of severe alcohol abuse, and who use marijuana

Female

	% viol off (wave 2)	% viol off (wave 3)	% prop off (wave 2)	% prop off (wave 3)	% alc ab (wave 2)	% alc ab (wave 3)	% mari (wave 2)	% mari (wave 3)
Sexually abused	19.4%	13.4%	31.1%	23.2%	12.9%	11.6%	21.3%	21.7%
Physically abused	29.1%	9.6%	23.3%	16.7%	16.9%	10.4%	17.2%	19.8%
Neglected	15.8%	12.8%	15.8%	15.4%	7.9%	7.7%	26.3%	12.8%
Violently victimized	59.2%	14.5%	42.3%	12.7%	27.1%	11.4%	29.0%	22.5%
Intimate partner victim	22.9%	7.9%	40.4%	14.4%	27.6%	21.9%	31.7%	22.1%

Male

	% viol off (wave 2)	% viol off (wave 3)	% prop off (wave 2)	% prop off (wave 3)	% alc ab (wave 2)	% alc ab (wave 3)	% mari (wave 2)	% mari (wave 3)
Sexually abused	41.9%	48.9%	31.1%	31.9%	19.6%	27.7%	22.2%	31.2%
Physically abused	35.3%	21.5%	32.9%	21.1%	18.8%	21.3%	16.7%	30.5%
Neglected	15.6%	26.0%	26.7%	20.0%	11.1%	11.8%	8.9%	29.4%
Violently victimized	68.0%	28.6%	47.5%	18.8%	17.0%	18.4%	30.4%	32.5%
Intimate partner victim	39.8%	30.7%	43.2%	17.0%	25.8%	23.9%	22.9%	37.5%

Table 6.2. Zero order correlations for females

	X1	X2	X3	X4	X5	X6	X7	X8	X9	X10	X11	X12	X13	X14	X15	X16	X17
X1	1.000																
X2	**.198**	1.000															
X3	**.241**	**.148**	1.000														
X4	.019	**.103**	**.078**	1.000													
X5	**.061**	.054	.006	.049	1.000												
X6	.017	-.010	.014	-.028	.021	1.000											
X7	-.015	.030	.010	.017	.028	.036	1.000										
X8	-.010	.024	.001	.048	.011	-.020	.015	1.000									
X9	-.032	.042	**.074**	.037	-.026	-.033	.020	-.056	1.000								
X10	.033	.040	.036	-.017	-.012	.041	**.084**	-.021	.017	1.000							
X11	**.077**	**.101**	**.134**	**.087**	-.001	.003	.011	.023	-.017	.044	1.000						
X12	**.132**	**.131**	**.095**	.002	**.075**	-.029	-.024	-.012	.032	**.063**	**.300**	1.000					
X13	.006	.051	-.036	-.008	**.090**	-**.092**	-.050	-.010	**.056**	.041	**.108**	**.162**	1.000				
X14	.038	**.057**	.044	**.078**	**.070**	-.007	-.036	**.068**	.004	.050	**.122**	**.172**	**.242**	1.000			
X15	.054	.040	-.014	-.024	**.100**	.054	.018	-.040	**.086**	.042	-.014	-.037	-.038	-.033	1.000		
X16	.018	-.007	.054	.001	-**.061**	**.067**	**.105**	**.083**	-**.230**	**.158**	**.116**	.055	-**.152**	.009	-**.061**	1.000	
X17	.055	**.086**	.048	**.113**	.003	.005	**.144**	**.082**	**.101**	.012	-.011	.046	-.050	-.008	.043	-**.197**	1.000

Table 6.3. Zero order correlations for males

	X1	X2	X3	X4	X5	X6	X7	X8	X9	X10	X11	X12	X13	X14	X15	X16	X17
X1	1.000																
X2	**.249**	1.000															
X3	**.328**	**.212**	1.000														
X4	.031	**.121**	.028	1.000													
X5	.044	.048	.041	**.103**	1.000												
X6	**.077**	.006	.065	-.025	-.011	1.000											
X7	.017	.025	-.009	**.076**	-.019	-.011	1.000										
X8	.018	-.042	.035	.023	.034	.010	**-.074**	1.000									
X9	-.047	-.058	.013	.001	.002	.038	-.009	**-.062**	1.000								
X10	.044	-.051	.038	-.021	-.021	**.090**	.011	.020	**-.062**	1.000							
X11	**.241**	**.134**	**.187**	**.131**	.054	.036	.025	-.004	-.015	-.003	1.000						
X12	**.139**	**.093**	**.096**	.019	.029	.019	-.039	-.009	-.012	-.041	**.330**	1.000					
X13	.036	**.163**	.052	**.085**	**.117**	.019	-.020	-.036	-.006	**-.100**	**.296**	**.344**	1.000				
X14	.037	.059	.034	**.098**	**.103**	.037	-.034	.042	-.057	.039	**.233**	**.195**	**.251**	1.000			
X15	-.040	-.002	-.053	.030	**.094**	.039	.018	.008	.014	.031	**-.119**	**-.102**	-.020	**-.080**	1.000		
X16	.036	.014	**.113**	.043	.016	.030	**.095**	**.067**	**-.197**	**.165**	.058	.030	**-.128**	.005	-.032	1.000	
X17	.009	.060	.031	**.088**	-.012	.020	**.190**	**.073**	**.124**	.013	-.037	-.045	-.057	-.026	.042	**-.196**	1.000

Legend for Tables 6.2 and 6.3:

X1 = Sexual abuse, X2 = Physical Abuse, X3 = Neglect, X4 = Violent victimization, X5 = IPV, X6 = DAT1, X7 = DRD2, X8 = DRD4, X9 = 5HTTLPR, X10 = MAOA, X11 = Viol offending (W3), X12 = Prop offending (W3), X13 = Alc abuse (W3), X14 = Mari use (W3), X15 = Age, X16 = African American, X17 = Hispanic.

Finally, females who are homozygous for the low activity allele report higher levels of property offending than females who are homozygous for the high activity allele. For males, the high activity allele is associated with higher levels of alcohol abuse than the low activity allele. The zero order correlations suggest a number of gene-environment correlations for females and males. For females, there is a positive correlation between 5HTTLPR and childhood neglect ($r = .074$). Cross-tab analyses reveal that females who are homozygous for the short allele are approximately three times more likely to be neglected (6.6 percent) than females who were not homozygous for the short allele (2.8 percent long/long, 2.2 percent short/long). For males, it appears that DAT1 is associated with childhood neglect and DRD2 is associated with violent victimization. Males who carry one or more copies of the 10R allele are more likely to experience childhood neglect than males who are homozygous for the 9R allele. Finally, violent victimization is more prevalent among males with the A2/A1 genotype (23.6 percent) than males with the A1/A1 (20 percent) or A2/A2 genotypes (15.6 percent). The heterozygous genotype seems to be the risk allele in terms of violent victimization for males. Subsequent gene-environment correlation analyses with DRD2 and violent victimization recodes DRD2 (0 = A1/A1 and A2/A2 genotype, 1 = A2/A1 genotype). The strength of these gene-environment correlations are further examined with regression models that account for age, race, and the nesting of siblings within households.

Gene-Environment Correlations
The zero order correlations suggest three gene-environment correlations: (1) 5HTTLPR and childhood neglect for females; (2) DAT1 and childhood neglect for males; and (3) DRD2 and violent victimization for males. In this section, the gene-environment correlations are further investigated with multinomial and logistic regression. Further, this section investigates whether these three gene-environment correlations significantly vary by gender.

Table 6.4 reveals that serotonergic and dopaminergic genetic polymorphisms help distinguish between individuals who are neglected and violently victimized, from those who are not. Females who carried short 5HTTLPR alleles are more likely to report experiencing six or more incidents of neglect (compared to zero incidents). For males, DAT1 helps distinguish between males who experienced 1 to 5 incidents from males that experienced zero incidents of neglect. Finally, the odds of violent victimization are significantly higher for males who carry the A2/A1 genotype, compared to males with the A1/A1 and A2/A2 genotypes. A difference of coefficients test shows that the effect of DRD2 on violent victimization is significantly stronger for males (z = -2.49); thus, males who have the A2/A1 genotype are more likely to be violently victimized than females with the A2/A1 genotype. Gender does not condition the 5HTTLPR-neglect or DAT1-neglect gene-environment correlations.

Summary of Gene-Environment Correlations
The results reveal that the five genetic polymorphisms do not have a consistent effect on neglect, physical abuse, violent victimization, and intimate partner violence. This is in line with previous research that has failed to find a relationship between genetic polymorphisms and abuse/victimization (Haberstick et al., 2005; Kim-Cohen et al., 2006; Surtees et al., 2006). However, there are three significant gene-environment correlations: (1) 5HTTLPR on neglect for females, (2) DAT1 on neglect for males, and (3) DRD2 on violent victimization for males. That is, females who carry one or more copies of the short 5HTTLPR allele are more likely to be neglected than females who do not carry the allele. Males who carry one or more copies of the 10R allele report higher levels of childhood neglect, and males with the A1/A2 genotype report higher levels of violent victimization (than males with the A1/A1 and A2/A2 genotypes). The effect of DRD2 on violent victimization is significantly stronger for males than females. While these coefficients are significant, these significant effects may have occurred by chance alone, especially for females. It was expected that out of 25 analyses, one coefficient would be significant for each gender (25 analyses * .05 = 1.25 significant effect for females or males). Thus, future research will need to revisit these relationships to examine whether the effects are real or statistical artifacts.

Table 6.4. Gene-environment correlations, accounting for age and ethnicity

	Females	Males	
	_b_	_b_	_z_
5HTTLPR on Neglect			
1-5 experiences	.197	-.130	1.47
	(.165)	(.150)	
6+ experiences	.715**	.319	1.15
	(.275)	(.206)	
DAT1 on Neglect	_b_	_b_	_z_
1-5 experiences	.047	.332*	-1.00
	(.230)	(.167)	
6+ experiences	.053	.478	-1.12
	(.253)	(.281)	
DRD2 on Violent Victimization	_b_	_b_	_z_
A1/A2 genotype	-0.349	.435**	-2.49**
	(0.269)	(.162)	

Gene X Abuse Interactions
The next set of analyses examine whether genetic polymorphisms moderate the effects of sexual abuse, physical abuse, neglect, violent victimization, and intimate partner violence on the four criminal behavior outcomes. The findings will be presented by offense and by abuse type for females and males. That is, the effect of genetic polymorphisms X sexual abuse on property offending for females and males will be presented, followed by the effect of genetic polymorphisms X physical abuse on property offending for females and males, and so forth.

Violent offending.

Childhood Sexual Abuse.

Table 6.5 shows the effects of childhood sexual abuse on violent offending by DAT1, DRD2, DRD4, 5HTTLPR, and MAOA for females and males. Overall, the results suggest that DRD2 and 5HTTLPR moderate the effects of childhood sexual abuse on violent offending for males. These interactions, however, do not appear to be significantly stronger for males.

The first panel displays the results for sexual abuse by DAT1 genotypes for females and males. As shown in the panel, childhood sexual abuse is negatively associated with violent offending for females and males with the 9R/9R genotype. The power for the 9R/9R models, however, cannot be computed and thus it is likely that the large negative coefficients are a statistical artifact. Sexually abused males with the 10R/9R and 10R/10R genotypes are more likely to engage in violent offending than non-abused males with the 10R/9R and 10R/10R genotypes. These models are adequately powered (power = 1.00), and a difference of coefficients test suggests that the sexual abuse coefficients do not vary by 10R/9R and 10R/10R genotypes ($z = 1.35$); thus, there is not a statistically significant interaction for males.

The results indicate an interaction between DRD2 and childhood sexual abuse for males, but not for females. As shown in Figure 6.1, sexually abused males who have the A2/A2 and A1/A2 genotypes are expected to have higher rates of violent offending than sexually abused males who have the A1/A1 genotype. Differences of coefficients tests reveal that there are significant differences between the coefficients for A1/A2 vs. A1/A1 ($z = 2.37$) and A2/A2 vs. A1/A1 ($z = 2.25$) for males, but there is not a difference between A2/A2 and A1/A2 ($z = -.042$). This finding suggests that carrying one or more A2 alleles may increase males' sensitivity to the criminogenic effects of sexual abuse.

Figure 6.1. DRD2 X childhood sexual abuse on violent offending for males

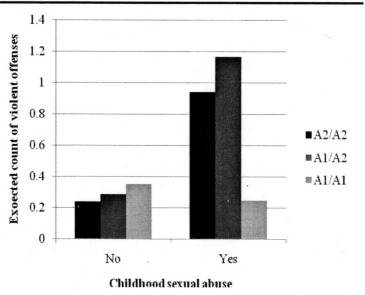

The results for DRD4 and childhood sexual abuse are unstable for the >7R/<7R genotype for females, and the >7R/>7R genotype for females and males (i.e., statistical power cannot be computed, small number of cases in the interaction cells). A difference of coefficients test shows that the childhood sexual abuse coefficients for the <7R/<7R and >7R/<7R genotypes for males do not significantly differ ($z = .532$); thus, DRD4 does not moderate the effects of childhood sexual abuse on violent offending for males and the interaction cannot be explored for females due to instability in the data.

Regression analyses suggest that there is an interaction between 5HTTLPR and childhood sexual abuse on violent offending for males. The long allele seems to amplify the criminogenic effects of childhood sexual abuse for males, while the short allele seems to act as a protective factor. Childhood sexual abuse increases violent offending for S/L males (z = 4.03) and L/L (z = 4.90) males (relative to the S/S genotype), while childhood sexual abuse is associated with lower levels of violent offending for S/S males (Figure 6.2). Sexual abuse does not significantly influence violent offending for any of the 5HTTLPR genotypes for females.

Finally, differences of coefficients tests reveal that MAOA does not condition the effects of childhood sexual abuse on violent offending for females or males. As indicated by the large negative coefficient, the effect of childhood sexual abuse is not stable for the H/H female model, and thus the significant effect should not be interpreted. A comparison of the L/L coefficient for females and L coefficient for males suggests that there is not a significant difference between these coefficients (z = .51), and thus the low activity allele does not have a gender specific effect for sexually abused males and females.

Childhood Neglect.

The results in Table 6.6 displays results on whether the polymorphisms moderate the effects of childhood neglect on violent offending. Overall, the results suggest that the polymorphisms do not condition the effects of childhood neglect. The difference of coefficients tests reveal that DAT1, DRD2, and DRD4 genotypes do not moderate the effects of childhood neglect for males, and the female models suffer from low power issues. Further, there are no significant differences in the coefficients for the L/L, S/L, or S/S genotypes for females or males. Finally, the effect of childhood neglect did not significantly vary by MAOA genotypes for either females or males. These results suggest that the genetic polymorphisms do not condition the effects of childhood neglect on violent offending.

Figure 6.2. 5HTTLPR X childhood sexual abuse on violent offending for males

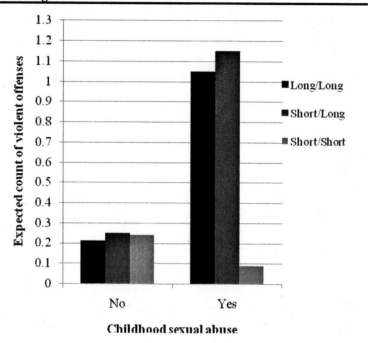

Table 6.5. Genetic moderation of childhood sexual abuse on violent offending for females and males

	Females			Males		
DAT1	9R/9R	10R/9R	10R/10R	9R/9R	10R/9R	10R/10R
Childhood sexual abuse	-14.69*** (1.16)	.574 (.747)	.247 (.619)	-16.061*** (1.331)	1.871*** (.445)	1.116*** (.334)
DRD2	A2/A2	A1/A2	A1/A1	A2/A2	A1/A2	A1/A1
Childhood sexual abuse	.903 (.609)	.665 (.568)	.127 (.943)	1.384***[a] (.427)	1.408***[b] (.368)	-.363 (.647)
DRD4	<7R/<7R	>7R/<7R	>7R/>7R	<7R/<7R	>7R/<7R	>7R/>7R
Childhood sexual abuse	.981* (.428)	-17.127*** (.489)	-16.298*** (1.219)	1.178** (.375)	1.484*** (.436)	-16.523*** (1.097)
5HTTLPR	L/L	S/L	S/S	L/L	S/L	S/S
Childhood sexual abuse	.480 (.667)	.060 (1.129)	1.097 (.744)	1.601*** (.320)	1.499*** (.447)	-.946*[c,d,e] (.409)
MAOA	H/H	L/H	L/L	H	L	
Childhood sexual abuse	-13.570*** (.362)	.741 (.540)	.755 (.792)	.888 (.485)	1.230** (.457)	

a. A2/A2 significantly differs from A1/A1 for males.; b. A1/A2 significantly differs from A1/A1 for males.; c. L/L coefficient differs from S/S coefficient for males.; d. S/L coefficient differs from S/S coefficient for males.; e. S/S coefficient for males differs S/S coefficient for females.

Table 6.6. Genetic moderation of childhood neglect on violent offending for females and males

	Females			Males		
DAT1	9R/9R	10R/9R	10R/10R	9R/9R	10R/9R	10R/10R
Childhood neglect	2.638*** (.805)	.540 (.413)	.702** (.272)	-13.899*** (1.127)	.382 (.295)	.661*** (.140)
DRD2	A2/A2	A1/A2	A1/A1	A2/A2	A1/A2	A1/A1
Childhood neglect	1.280*** (.300)	.488 (.310)	-15.347*** (.610)	.493** (.183)	.829*** (.168)	.609 (.534)
DRD4	<7R/<7R	>7R/<7R	>7R/>7R	<7R/<7R	>7R/<7R	>7R/>7R
Childhood neglect	.797** (.270)	.553 (.416)	1.845 (1.047)	.573*** (.148)	.807*** (.241)	.646 (.454)
5HTTLPR	L/L	S/L	S/S	L/L	S/L	S/S
Childhood neglect	.997* (.424)	.662 (.343)	.501 (.382)	.649** (.250)	.651*** (.181)	.630** (.230)
MAOA	H/H	L/H	L/L	H	L	
Childhood neglect	.466 (.499)	.439 (.367)	1.269*** (.341)	.571*** (.164)	.598** (.204)	

Table 6.7. Genetic moderation of childhood physical abuse on violent offending for females and males

	Females			Males		
DAT1	9R/9R	10R/9R	10R/10R	9R/9R	10R/9R	10R/10R
Childhood physical abuse	-1.584	.948**	.575**	.964*	.383	.478***
	(.873)	(.339)	(.211)	(.419)	(.206)	(.139)
DRD2	A2/A2	A1/A2	A1/A1	A2/A2	A1/A2	A1/A1
Childhood physical abuse	.840***[a]	.643*[b]	-1.004*	.403*[c]	.597***[d]	-.465
	(.268)	(.292)	(.409)	(.162)	(.157)	(.381)
DRD4	<7R/<7R	>7R/<7R	>7R/>7R	<7R/<7R	>7R/<7R	>7R/>7R
Childhood physical abuse	.664***[e]	.782**[f]	-1.409	.380**	.384	1.003
	(.229)	(.279)	(.788)	(.133)	(.198)	(.549)
5HTTLPR	L/L	S/L	S/S	L/L	S/L	S/S
Childhood physical abuse	.063	.986***[g]	.500	.657***	.331	.358
	(.292)	(.326)	(.362)	(.188)	(.183)	(.224)
MAOA	H/H	L/H	L/L	H	L	
Childhood physical abuse	-.059	.636**	1.012**[h]	.364**	.395	
	(.388)	(.235)	(.365)	(.128)	(.206)	

a. A2/A2 coefficient differs from the A1/A1 coefficient for females.; b. A1/A2 coefficient differs from the A1/A1 coefficient for females.; c. A2/A2 coefficient differs from A1/A1 coefficient for males.; d. A1/A2 coefficient differs from A1/A1 coefficient for males.; e. <7R/<7R coefficient differs from >7R/<7R coefficient for females.; f. >7R/<7R coefficient differs from >7R/>7R coefficient for females.; g. S/L coefficient differs from L/L coefficient for females.; h. L/L coefficient differs from H/H coefficient for females.

Childhood physical abuse.

Table 6.7 displays the effects of childhood physical abuse on violent offending across genotypes for females and males. The results suggest that there may be non-linear interactions between childhood physical abuse and DRD2, 5HTTLPR, and MAOA for females. For females, the childhood physical abuse coefficients for the A2/A2 genotype and A1/A2 genotype are significantly higher than the A1/A1 genotype (z vs. A2/A2 = 3.77, z vs. A1/A2 genotype = 3.27), but the coefficient for A2/A2 genotype does not differ from the A1/A2 genotype (z = .49). As suggested in Figure 6.3, females who carry one or more copies of the A2 allele may be more sensitive to the criminogenic effects of physical abuse than females who do not carry the A2 allele (A1/A1 genotype). For males, a similar pattern emerges; there are significant differences in the physical abuse coefficients for the A2/A2 vs. the A1/A1 genotypes (z = 2.09) and differences in A1/A2 vs. A1/A1 (z = 2.57), but no significant differences between A2/A2 and A1/A2 genotypes (z = .85). Physically abused males with one or more copies of the A2 allele expected to engage in more violent offending than physically abused males with two copies of the A1 allele. Difference of coefficients tests reveal that gender does not condition the interaction between DRD2 and physical abuse on violent offending; thus, the interaction is not gender specific.

It does not appear that there is a significant interaction between DRD4 and physical abuse on violent offending for females or males. There are no significant differences in the physical abuse coefficients for the <7R/<7R and >7R/<7R genotypes for females or males. Further, the >7R/>7R models are underpowered (power = ~ 50 percent, very small number of cases) and the effects should be cautiously interpreted.

Table 6.7 and Figure 6.4 show that physical abuse is related to violent offending for females with the S/L genotype, but not for females with the L/L (z = 2.10) or S/S genotype. Severely physically abused females (6+ times) who have the S/L genotype are expected to have higher rates of violent offending than severely physically abused females with the L/L and S/S genotypes. Results reveal that the effect of physical abuse on violent offending does not significantly vary across the 5HTTLPR genotypes for males. Further, the effect of physical abuse on violent offending does not differ for S/L females and S/L males, and suggesting that S/L females are not significantly more sensitive to the effects of physical abuse than S/L males.

Figure 6.3. DRD2 X childhood physical abuse on violent offending for males and females

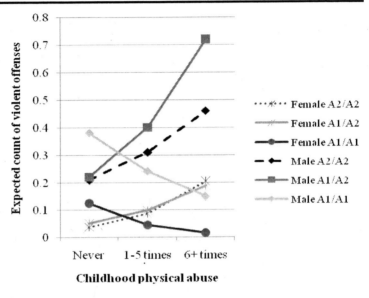

Finally, MAOA moderates the effect of physical abuse on violent offending for females, but not males. Childhood physical abuse has a significant effect on violent offending for L/L females, but not H/H females, and this difference is statistically significant ($z = 2.01$). Physically abused females with the L/L genotype have higher expected rates of violent offending than physically abused females with the H/H genotype (Figure 6.5). There are no significant differences in the physical abuse coefficients for high activity males versus low activity males, and no differences between low activity males and L/L genotype females. Thus, while there is an interaction effect for females but not males, this effect is not significantly stronger for females.

Figure 6.4. 5HTTLPR X childhood physical abuse on violent offending for females

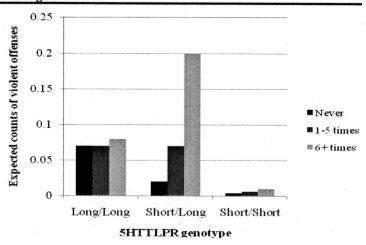

Figure 6.5. MAOA X childhood physical abuse on violent offending for females

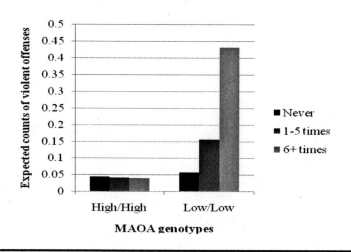

Violent victimization.

Table 6.8 shows that the genetic polymorphisms, overall, do not moderate the effects of violent victimization on violent offending for females and males.

Intimate partner violence.

Table 6.9 reveals that the genetic polymorphisms do not interact with intimate partner violence to influence violent offending for females or males. The differences of coefficients tests reveal that there are no significant differences in the effects of intimate partner violence across genotypes (i.e., A2/A2 vs. A1/A2 for females). The 9R/9R and the A1/A1 models for females can not be estimated or are unstable (i.e., low power, large negative coefficient), respectively.

Property offending.

Childhood sexual abuse.

Table 6.10 displays the effects of childhood sexual abuse on property offending across the DAT1, DRD2, DRD4, 5HTTLPR, and MAOA genotypes for females and males. While the table shows that childhood sexual abuse is significant for some genotypes but not others, differences of coefficients tests reveal that the effect of childhood sexual abuse does not significantly vary across the genotypes. Thus,the genetic polymorphisms do not moderate the effects of childhood sexual abuse on property offending for either females or males.

Childhood neglect.

Table 6.11 reveals that DRD2 moderates the effects of childhood neglect on property offending for females, and 5HTTLPR X childhood neglect to influence property offending for males. Childhood neglect is significant for females with the A2/A2 genotype—but not for females with the A1/A2 or A1/A1 genotype—and the difference of coefficients tests reveals that the coefficient for the A2/A2 genotype is significantly different than the coefficient for A1/A2 genotype ($z = 2.26$).

Table 6.8. Genetic moderation of violent victimization on violent offending for females and males

	Females			Males		
DAT1	9R/9R	10R/9R	10R/10R	9R/9R	10R/9R	10R/10R
Violent victimization	Not converge	.727 (.798)	.518 (.654)	-2.136 (1.542)	.396 (.318)	.226 (.259)
DRD2	A2/A2	A1/A2	A1/A1	A2/A2	A1/A2	A1/A1
Violent victimization	1.999*** (.496)	.529 (.901)	-18.032*** (2.106)	-.131 (.267)	.540 (.293)	.084 (.578)
DRD4	<7R/<7R	>7R/<7R	>7R/>7R	<7R/<7R	>7R/<7R	>7R/>7R
Violent victimization	1.072 (.624)	.884 (.690)	2.561** (.808)	-.095 (.250)	.710* (.340)	-.358 (.805)
5HTTLPR	L/L	S/L	S/S	L/L	S/L	S/S
Violent victimization	1.415* (.653)	.730 (.738)	.876 (.813)	.036 (.347)	.336 (.271)	.115 (.379)
MAOA	H/H	L/H	L/L	H	L	
Violent victimization	1.978*** (.605)	.266 (.676)	.121 (1.110)	.108 (.237)	.237 (.310)	

Table 6.9. Genetic moderation of intimate partner violence on violent offending for females and males

	Females			Males		
DAT1	9R/9R	10R/9R	10R/10R	9R/9R	10R/9R	10R/10R
Intimate partner violence	-16.334*** (1.067)	.161 (.379)	.121 (.254)	-.383 (.911)	.246 (.184)	.230 (.140)
DRD2	A2/A2	A1/A2	A1/A1	A2/A2	A1/A2	A1/A1
Intimate partner violence	-.069 (.373)	.051 (.297)	.413 (.351)	.271 (.153)	.260 (.164)	-.005 (.445)
DRD4	<7R/<7R	>7R/<7R	>7R/>7R	<7R/<7R	>7R/<7R	>7R/>7R
Intimate partner violence	.345 (.231)	-.396 (.508)	-15.518*** (.891)	.181 (.144)	.301 (.180)	.684 (.553)
5HTTLPR	L/L	S/L	S/S	L/L	S/L	S/S
Intimate partner violence	-.107 (.356)	.174 (.317)	.231 (.436)	.227 (.204)	.305* (.144)	.089 (.218)
MAOA	H/H	L/H	L/L	H	L	
Intimate partner violence	.082 (.442)	.321 (.283)	-.164 (.506)	.274* (.130)	.078 (.188)	

Table 6.10. Genetic moderation of childhood sexual abuse on property offending for females and males

	Females			Males		
DAT1	9R/9R	10R/9R	10R/10R	9R/9R	10R/9R	10R/10R
Childhood sexual abuse	1.054 (.811)	1.185* (.514)	.922* (.457)	-14.899*** (1.224)	.975 (.700)	1.108** (.388)
DRD2	A2/A2	A1/A2	A1/A1	A2/A2	A1/A2	A1/A1
Childhood sexual abuse	1.388*** (.420)	.858 (.700)	.678 (1.091)	.585 (.377)	1.869*** (.463)	-14.833*** (.747)
DRD4	≤7R/<7R	>7R/<7R	>7R/>7R	≤7R/<7R	>7R/<7R	>7R/>7R
Childhood sexual abuse	.990* (.411)	.576 (.704)	4.201** (1.429)	1.249*** (.336)	.531 (.936)	-19.093*** (1.484)
5HTTLPR	L/L	S/L	S/S	L/L	S/L	S/S
Childhood sexual abuse	1.644** (.575)	.249 (.651)	1.246* (.323)	.686 (.363)	1.644*** (.513)	.471 (1.384)
MAOA	H/H	L/H	L/L	H	L	
Childhood sexual abuse	.602 (.643)	.486 (.447)	1.675** (.580)	.379 (.527)	1.133* (.452)	

a. A1/A2 coefficient differs from A2/A2 coefficient for males.

Table 6.11. Genetic moderation of childhood neglect on property offending for females and males

	Females			Males		
DAT1	9R/9R	10R/9R	10R/10R	9R/9R	10R/9R	10R/10R
Childhood neglect	.385 (.973)	.692* (.291)	.299 (.284)	-14.916*** (.930)	.006 (.259)	.306 (.213)
DRD2	A2/A2	A1/A2	A1/A1	A2/A2	A1/A2	A1/A1
Childhood neglect	.893*** (.246)	-.623 (.624)	-.011 (.544)	-.044 (.184)	.557* (.247)	.871 (.743)
DRD4	<7R/<7R	>7R/<7R	>7R/>7R	<7R/<7R	>7R/<7R	>7R/>7R
Childhood neglect	.298 (.275)	.590* (.294)	15.550*** (.973)	.205 (.184)	.465 (.282)	-21.138*** (.958)
5HTTLPR	L/L	S/L	S/S	L/L	S/L	S/S
Childhood neglect	-.315 (.545)	.495* (.252)	.479 (.311)	-.269 (.252)	.607** (.223)	.059 (.330)
MAOA	H/H	L/H	L/L	H	L	
Childhood neglect	.159 (.331)	.338 (.315)	.689* (.303)	.001 (.209)	.306 (.219)	

a. A1/A1 coefficient differs from A1/A2 coefficient for females; b. A2/A2 coefficient for females differs from A2/A2 coefficient for males; c. L/L coefficient differs from S/L coefficient for males.

Figure 6.6. DRD2 X childhood neglect on property offending for females

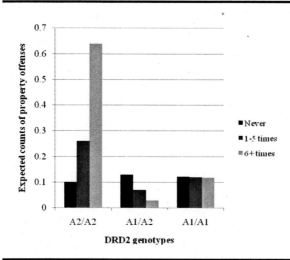

Figure 6.7. DRD2 X childhood neglect on property offending for females and males

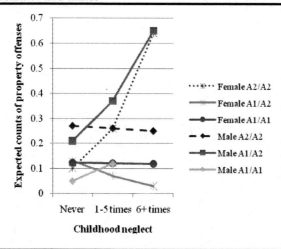

As shown in Figure 6.6, females with the A2/A2 genotype who report six or more incidents of childhood neglect are expected to engage in more property offending than females with the A2/A2 genotype who do not report being neglected. Further, neglected females with the A2/A2 genotype are expected to have higher rates of property offending than neglected females with the A1/A2 and A2/A2 genotype.

A difference of coefficients test also reveals that gender conditions the effects of childhood neglect on property offending for individuals with the A2/A2 genotype (z = 3.05). As shown in Figure 6.7, the expected rates of property offending are approximately two times higher for A2/A2 females who experience six or more incidents of neglect, compared to the rates for A2/A2 males who experience six or more incidents of neglect. Thus, it is expected that females with the A2/A2 genotype may be more sensitive to the criminogenic effects of severe neglect than males with the A2/A2 genotype.

Table 6.11 also reveals a significant interaction between 5HTTLPR and neglect on property offending for males. Childhood neglect has a stronger effect on property offending for males with the S/L genotype, compared to males with the L/L genotype (z = 2.60). As shown in Figure 6.8, severe neglect (i.e., six or more incidents) has the greatest effect on property offending for males with the S/L genotype. Otherwise, males with different levels of "genetic risk" and "environmental risk" are comparable in terms of property offending. For instance, the expected level of property offending is comparable for males with the S/S genotype who never experienced neglect to males with the L/L genotype who experienced moderate (i.e., 1-5 times) to severe neglect (i.e., 6+ times). It is important to note that there are no gender differences in the effects of neglect on property offending across 5HTTLPR genotypes.

Childhood physical abuse.

Table 6.12 shows that the genetic polymorphisms, overall, do not moderate the effects of childhood physical abuse on property offending for females or males. One significant interaction, however, does emerge from the analyses: MAOA X childhood physical abuse on property offending for females. Childhood physical abuse has an effect on property offending for L/L females, but not for H/H females, and these coefficients are statistically different ($z = 2.57$). Figure 6.9 shows that physically abused females who have the L/L genotype are expected to have higher rates of property offending than physically abused females with the H/H genotype and L/L females who are not physically abused.

Figure 6.8. 5HTTLPR X childhood neglect on property offending for males

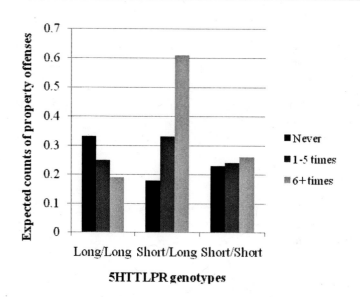

Figure 6.9. MAOA X childhood physical abuse on property offending for females

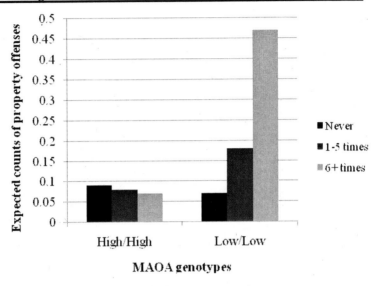

Table 6.12. Genetic moderation of childhood physical abuse on property offending for females and males

	Females			Males		
DAT1	9R/9R	10R/9R	10R/10R	9R/9R	10R/9R	10R/10R
Childhood physical abuse	.821* (.343)	.486 (.292)	.607*** (.179)	.551 (.579)	.420* (.187)	.277 (.160)
DRD2	A2/A2	A1/A2	A1/A1	A2/A2	A1/A2	A1/A1
Childhood physical abuse	.643** (.213)	.623** (.222)	.424 (.251)	.446** (.144)	.180 (.188)	-.205 (.687)
DRD4	<7R/<7R	>7R/<7R	>7R/>7R	<7R/<7R	>7R/<7R	>7R/>7R
Childhood physical abuse	.528** (.185)	.641* (.270)	1.184 (.651)	.327* (.142)	.262 (.217)	No converge
5HTTLPR	L/L	S/L	S/S	L/L	S/L	S/S
Childhood physical abuse	.476 (.303)	.743*** (.189)	.510 (.311)	.143 (.185)	.540** (.199)	.213 (.250)
MAOA	H/H	L/H	L/L	H	L	
Childhood physical abuse	-.145 (.282)	.752*** (.203)	.923** (.305)	.187 (.141)	.473* (.215)	

a. L/L coefficient differs from H/H coefficient for females.

Violent victimization.

Table 6.13 shows that the genetic polymorphisms do not condition the effects of violent victimization on property offending for females or males. The only significant coefficients are those that are unstable and are calculated from a small number of cases in the interaction categories.

Intimate partner violence.

In line with the previous analyses, Table 6.14 shows that the genetic polymorphisms, overall, do not moderate the effects of intimate partner violence on property offending for females or males. There is, however, one significant interaction: DRD4 X intimate partner violence on property offending for females. Intimate partner violence is significantly related to property offending for females with the <7R/<7R genotype, but it is not related to property offending for females with the >7R/<7R genotype. These coefficients are statistically different ($z = 2.09$), indicating an interaction effect. The coefficient for the >7R/>7R genotype is unstable and should not be interpreted. As shown in Figure 6.10, females with the <7R/<7R genotype who experience one more incidents of intimate partner violence are expected to have higher levels of property offending than females who have the >7R/<7R genotype who experience intimate partner violence. Further, the expected rate of property offending is higher among <7R/<7R females who experience multiple intimate partner violence incidents than <7R/<7R females who do not experience intimate partner violence. Thus, it is the combination of the <7R/<7R genotype and intimate partner victimization that increases the risk of property offending for females. It is important to note that the intimate partner violence coefficient is significantly stronger for <7R/<7R females than <7R/<7R males; therefore, females with the <7R/<7R genotype are more sensitive to the criminogenic effects of intimate partner violence than males with the <7R/<7R genotype.

Table 6.13. Genetic moderation of violent victimization on property offending for females and males

	Females			Males		
DAT1	9R/9R	10R/9R	10R/10R	9R/9R	10R/9R	10R/10R
Violent victimization	.128 (.993)	-.061 (.552)	-.041 (.584)	-16.619*** (.778)	-.129 (.290)	.012 (.325)
DRD2	A2/A2	A1/A2	A1/A1	A2/A2	A1/A2	A1/A1
Violent victimization	.145 (.528)	-.709 (.789)	1.075 (.739)	.099 (.229)	-.245 (.357)	-17.378*** (.934)
DRD4	<7R/<7R	>7R/<7R	>7R/>7R	<7R/<7R	>7R/<7R	>7R/>7R
Violent victimization	.180 (.416)	-.848 (.591)	-15.194*** (.845)	-.214 (.238)	-.015 (.434)	.130 (.943)
5HTTLPR	L/L	S/L	S/S	L/L	S/L	S/S
Violent victimization	-1.102 (1.259)	.287 (.440)	-.863 (.732)	-.194 (.264)	-.230 (.443)	-.065 (.416)
MAOA	H/H	L/H	L/L	H	L	
Violent victimization	.301 (.508)	-.564 (.647)	-.073 (.883)	-.196 (.254)	-.447 (.314)	

Table 6.14. Genetic moderation of intimate partner victimization on property offending for females and males

DAT1

	Females			Males		
	9R/9R	10R/9R	10R/10R	9R/9R	10R/9R	10R/10R
Intimate partner violence	-16.060*** (.570)	.441 (.243)	.244 (.218)	-15.923*** (.641)	.349 (.181)	-.015 (.230)

DRD2

	Females			Males		
	A2/A2	A1/A2	A1/A1	A2/A2	A1/A2	A1/A1
Intimate partner violence	.359 (.227)	.313 (.248)	-.460 (.607)	.231 (.143)	-.209 (.319)	.706 (.698)

DRD4

	Females			Males		
	<7R/<7R	>7R/<7R	>7R/>7R	<7R/<7R	>7R/<7R	>7R/>7R
Intimate partner violence	.550**a, b (.178)	-.184 (.302)	-15.333*** (.652)	-.020 (.168)	.243 (.247)	-.054 (.211)

5HTTLPR

	Females			Males		
	L/L	S/L	S/S	L/L	S/L	S/S
Intimate partner violence	.300 (.330)	.276 (.198)	.509 (.359)	.243 (.176)	-.019 (.278)	-.071 (.287)

MAOA

	Females			Males	
	H/H	L/H	L/L	H	L
Intimate partner violence	.273 (.228)	.294 (.246)	.456 (.318)	.086 (.160)	-.189 (.219)

a. <7R/<7R coefficient differs from >7R/<7R coefficient for females.; b. <7R/<7R coefficient for females differs from <7R/<7R coefficient for males.

Figure 6.10. DRD4 X intimate partner violence on property offending for females and males

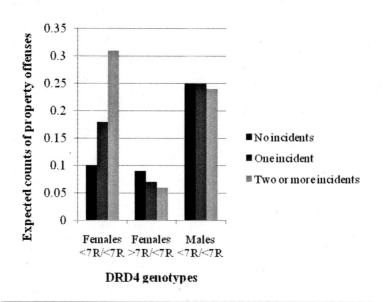

Alcohol abuse.

Childhood sexual abuse.

Table 6.15 reveals that DRD2, DRD4, 5HTTLPR, and MAOA do not condition the effects of childhood sexual abuse on alcohol abuse for females and males. It does appear that the effects of sexual abuse vary by DAT1 genotypes for females and males. It should be noted, however, that these effects may be unstable and unreliable. Only three females reported sexual abuse and carried the 9R/9R genotype and only one male was sexually abused and had the 9R/9R genotype.

Table 6.15. Genetic moderation of childhood sexual abuse on alcohol abuse for females and males

	Females			Males		
DAT1	9R/9R	10R/9R	10R/10R	9R/9R	10R/9R	10R/10R
Childhood sexual abuse	.909*** (.250)	.152 (.327)	-.374 (.261)	1.040** (.404)	.818 (.505)	.030 (.296)
DRD2	A2/A2	A1/A2	A1/A1	A2/A2	A1/A2	A1/A1
Childhood sexual abuse	-.210 (.253)	.081 (.353)	.242 (.704)	.112 (.234)	.214 (.463)	-.130 (.704)
DRD4	<7R/<7R	>7R/<7R	>7R/>7R	<7R/<7R	>7R/<7R	>7R/>7R
Childhood sexual abuse	-.267 (.271)	.130 (.316)	.704 (.430)	.314 (.287)	-.352 (.479)	-.013 (.429)
5HTTLPR	L/L	S/L	S/S	L/L	S/L	S/S
Childhood sexual abuse	.179 (.313)	-.517 (.315)	.163 (.408)	.365 (.342)	.195 (.398)	-.443 (.443)
MAOA	H/H	L/H	L/L	H	L	
Childhood sexual abuse	-.038 (.416)	.026 (.261)	-.703 (.472)	-.044 (.312)	.423 (.324)	

a. 9R/9R coefficient differs from 10R/9R coefficient for females.; b. 9R/9R coefficient differs from 10R/10R coefficient for females.

Childhood neglect.

Table 6.16 reveals that DRD2 and 5HTTLPR moderate the effects of childhood neglect on alcohol abuse for males, while 5HTTLPR and MAOA condition the effects of neglect on alcohol abuse for females. Childhood neglect is associated with alcohol abuse among males with the A1/A2 genotype, but not for males with the A2/A2 or A1/A1 genotypes. Differences of coefficients tests show that the neglect coefficient for the A1/A2 genotype is significantly different than the neglect coefficient for the A2/A2 genotype for males ($z = 3.68$). Figure 6.11 shows that severely neglected males with the A1/A2 genotype are expected to have higher levels of alcohol abuse than severely neglected males with the A2/A2 genotype. Further, the effect of neglect on alcohol abuse is significantly stronger for males with the A1/A2 genotype than females with the A1/A2 genotype ($z = 2.91$).

Figure 6.11. DRD2 X childhood neglect on alcohol abuse for males and females

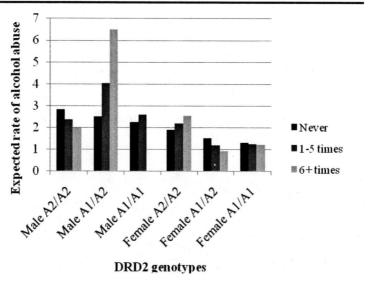

It also appears that DRD4 moderates the effects of neglect on alcohol abuse for males. The effect of childhood neglect on alcohol abuse is significantly stronger for males with the <7R/<7R genotype than for males with the >7R/>7R genotype (z = 2.97). It should be noted, however, that only nine respondents experienced any neglect and carried the >7R/>7R genotype, and that the <7R/<7R neglect coefficient did not significantly differ from the neglect coefficient for the <7R/>7R genotype (z = 1.39). Thus, the statistically significant difference of coefficients test could reflect an actual statistical interaction or it could be a statistical artifact. The current study errs on the conservative side and concludes this effect is more likely to reflect a statistical artifact rather than a real interaction effect.

Figure 6.12. 5HTTLPR X childhood neglect on alcohol abuse for females and males

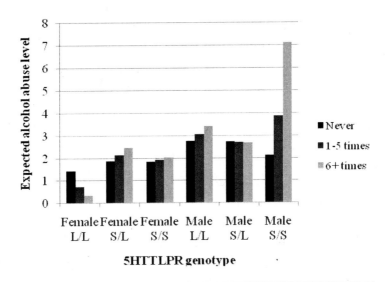

The results also reveal a significant interaction between 5HTTLPR and childhood neglect on alcohol abuse for females and males. Childhood neglect has a significantly stronger effect on alcohol abuse for L/L females compared to S/L females ($z = 2.08$), and it appears that the L/L genotype acts as a protective factor. Females with the L/L genotype who are severely neglected have a lower expected level of alcohol abuse than L/L females who were never neglected (Figure 6.12). Further, the protective effect of the L/L genotype is significantly stronger for females than for males ($z = 2.10$). For males, childhood neglect has a stronger effect on individuals with the S/S genotype than the S/L ($z = 2.55$) and L/L genotypes ($z = 1.96$). Severely neglected males who are homozygous for the S allele have expected levels of alcohol abuse that are two to three times higher than the expected levels for severely neglected males with the L/L and S/L genotypes (Figure 6.12).

Finally, childhood neglect has a stronger effect on alcohol abuse for H/H females compared to L/L females ($z = 2.80$). As shown in Figure 6.13, the H/H genotype acts as a protective factor for females. Females with the H/H genotype who are severely neglected have a lower predicted level of alcohol abuse than H/H females who are not neglected. A difference of coefficients test also reveals that the protective effect of the H allele is significantly stronger for females than males ($z = 3.06$).

Childhood physical abuse.

Table 6.17 shows that the genetic polymorphisms, overall, do not moderate the effects of childhood physical abuse on alcohol abuse. There is, however, a significant interaction between MAOA and childhood physical abuse for females. Childhood physical abuse has a significantly stronger effect on alcohol abuse for L/L females than H/H females ($z = 2.39$). Physcially abused females with the L/L genotype have a higher expected level of alcohol abuse than physically abused females with the H/H genotype (Figure 6.14). Further, the predicted level of alcohol abuse is higher among L/L females who experience some physical abuse compared to L/L females who did not experience any physical abuse.

Table 6.16. Genetic moderation of childhood neglect on alcohol abuse for females and males

	Females			Males		
DAT1	9R/9R	10R/9R	10R/10R	9R/9R	10R/9R	10R/10R
Childhood neglect	-.332 (.559)	-.350 (.242)	.233 (.225)	.715 (1.052)	.176 (.249)	.111 (.120)
DRD2	A2/A2	A1/A2	A1/A1	A2/A2	A1/A2	A1/A1
Childhood neglect	.146 (.227)	-.233 (.199)	-.034 (.639)	-.179 (.110)	.472***a, b (.138)	.145 (.512)
DRD4	<7R/<7R	>7R/<7R	>7R/>7R	<7R/<7R	>7R/<7R	>7R/>7R
Childhood neglect	-.257 (.180)	.238 (.310)	1.028* (.418)	.287**c (.110)	-.040 (.207)	-.392 (.200)
5HTTLPR	L/L	S/L	S/S	L/L	S/L	S/S
Childhood neglect	-.682*d, e (.333)	.138 (.210)	.045 (.293)	.104 (.169)	-.008 (.143)	.608**f (.194)
MAOA	H/H	L/H	L/L	H	L	
Childhood neglect	-.573*g, h (.232)	-.003 (.196)	.628 (.360)	.225 (.118)	.112 (.162)	

a. A1/A2 coefficient differs from A2/A2 coefficient for males.; b. A1/A2 coefficient for males differs from A1/A2 coefficient for females.; c. <7R/<7R coefficient differs from >7R/<7R coefficient for males.; d. L/L coefficient differs from S/L coefficient for females.; e. L/L coefficient for females differs from L/L coefficient for males.; f. S/S coefficient differs from S/L coefficient for males.; g. H/H coefficient differs from L/L coefficient for females.; h. H/H coefficient for females differs from H coefficient for males.

Table 6.17. Genetic moderation of childhood physical abuse on alcohol abuse for females and males

DAT1	Females			Males		
	9R/9R	10R/9R	10R/10R	9R/9R	10R/9R	10R/10R
Childhood physical abuse	.305 (.267)	.188 (.145)	.169 (.119)	-.184 (.264)	.303** (.113)	.292** (.092)

DRD2	Females			Males		
	A2/A2	A1/A2	A1/A1	A2/A2	A1/A2	A1/A1
Childhood physical abuse	.220* (.107)	.062 (.155)	-.169 (.218)	.295*** (.091)	.219 (.112)	.470 (.315)

DRD4	Females			Males		
	<7R/<7R	>7R/<7R	>7R/>7R	<7R/<7R	>7R/<7R	>7R/>7R
Childhood physical abuse	.047 (.105)	.360* (.151)	.149 (.438)	.320*** (.084)	.162 (.123)	.008 (.242)

5HTTLPR	Females			Males		
	L/L	S/L	S/S	L/L	S/L	S/S
Childhood physical abuse	.102 (.119)	.116 (.148)	.343 (.186)	.392** (.133)	.299** (.094)	.225 (.151)

MAOA	Females			Males	
	H/H	L/H	L/L	H	L
Childhood physical abuse	.053 (.118)	-.022 (.121)	.576**[a] (.184)	.201* (.082)	.345** (.124)

a. L/L coefficient differs from H/H coefficient for females.

Figure 6.13. MAOA X childhood neglect on alcohol abuse for females

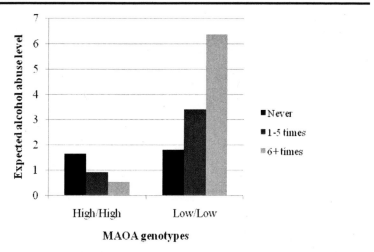

Figure 6.14. MAOA X childhood physical abuse on alcohol abuse for females

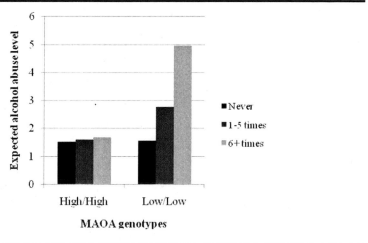

Violent victimization.

Table 6.18 reveals that the effect of violent victimization on alcohol abuse does not significantly vary across genotypes for females or males. These findings indicate that DAT1, DRD2, DRD4, 5HTTLPR, and MAOA do not interact with violent victimization to influence alcohol abuse for either females or males in adulthood.

Intimate partner violence.

As shown in Table 6.19, intimate partner violence has a stronger effect on alcohol abuse for females with the A1/A1 genotype, compared to females with the A2/A2 ($z = 2.09$) and A1/A2 genotypes ($z = 2.90$). Plotting the results suggests that it is the dual hazards of intimate partner violence and the A1/A1 genotype that increase the risk of alcohol abuse for females. Females who are homozygous for the A1 allele and who have experienced two or more incidents of intimate partner violence have the highest expected level of alcohol abuse, compared to A2/A2 females with two or more IPV incidents and A1/A1 females who did not experience intimate partner violence (Figure 6.15).

Figure 6.15. DRD2 X intimate partner violence on alcohol abuse for females

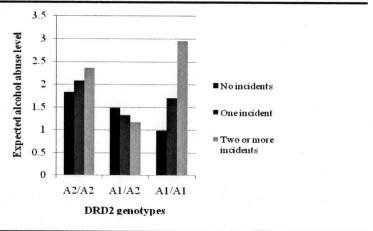

Table 6.18. Genetic moderation of violent victimization on alcohol abuse for females and males

	Females			Males		
DAT1	9R/9R	10R/9R	10R/10R	9R/9R	10R/9R	10R/10R
Violent victimization	-.574 (.795)	.116 (.329)	-.488 (.329)	-.255 (.561)	.154 (.170)	.262 (.157)
DRD2	A2/A2	A1/A2	A1/A1	A2/A2	A1/A2	A1/A1
Violent victimization	-.043 (.270)	-.904 (.469)	.378 (.751)	.315 (.162)	-.008 (.171)	.400 (.418)
DRD4	<7R/<7R	>7R/<7R	>7R/>7R	<7R/<7R	>7R/<7R	>7R/>7R
Violent victimization	-.252 (.296)	-.119 (.419)	-.116 (.573)	.242 (.136)	.099 (.204)	.269 (.449)
5HTTLPR	L/L	S/L	S/S	L/L	S/L	S/S
Violent victimization	-.043 (.382)	-.425 (.342)	.202 (.642)	.366 (.197)	.212 (.148)	.020 (.281)
MAOA	H/H	L/H	L/L	H	L	
Violent victimization	-.278 (.360)	.098 (.365)	-.437 (.562)	.144 (.147)	.283 (.169)	

Table 6.19. Genetic moderation of intimate partner victimization on alcohol abuse for females and males

	Females			Males		
DAT1	9R/9R	10R/9R	10R/10R	9R/9R	10R/9R	10R/10R
Intimate partner violence	-.103 (.338)	.111 (.106)	.132 (.087)	.365 (.293)	.200* (.101)	.115 (.095)
DRD2	A2/A2	A1/A2	A1/A1	A2/A2	A1/A2	A1/A1
Intimate partner violence	.127 (.084)	-.117 (.138)	.547***[a,b] (.182)	.198* (.088)	.093 (.102)	.060 (.384)
DRD4	<7R/<7R	>7R/<7R	>7R/>7R	<7R/<7R	>7R/<7R	>7R/>7R
Intimate partner violence	.176* (.083)	-.029 (.112)	-.064 (.321)	.216** (.082)	.090 (.131)	-.158 (.291)
5HTTLPR	L/L	S/L	S/S	L/L	S/L	S/S
Intimate partner violence	.212 (.124)	.094 (.087)	.062 (.199)	.263*[c] (.110)	.152 (.103)	-.150 (.142)
MAOA	H/H	L/H	L/L	H	L	
Intimate partner violence	.256* (.113)	.086 (.096)	-.161 (.184)	.153 (.083)	.133 (.117)	

a. A1/A1 coefficient differs from A1/A2 coefficient for females.; b. A1/A1 coefficient differs from A2/A2 coefficient for females; c. L/L coefficient differs from S/S coefficient for males.

Frequency of marijuana.

Childhood sexual abuse.

Table 6.20 reveals that DAT1, 5HTTLPR, and MAOA moderate the effects of childhood sexual abuse on the frequency of marijuana use for females. Childhood sexual abuse has a stronger negative effect on marijuana use for females with the 10R/10R genotype than for females with the 10R/9R genotype (z = 2.49). As shown in Figure 6.16, sexually abused females with the 10R/10R have a lower expected frequency of marijuana use than sexually abused females with the 10R/9R genotype and non-sexually abused females with the 10R/10R genotype; thus, the 10R/10R genotype appears to act as a protective factor for females. It should be noted that the 9R/9R genotype model is unstable and should be interpreted with caution.

Figure 6.16. DAT1 X childhood sexual abuse on frequency of marijuana use for females

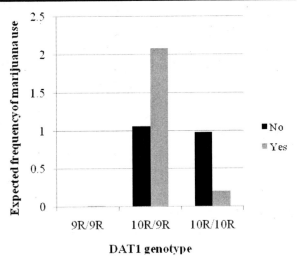

Table 6.20 also shows that the L/L genotype of 5HTTLPR acts as a protective factor against the effects of childhood sexual abuse on

marijuana use for females. Sexually abused females with the L/L genotype have a lower predicted frequency of marijuana use than sexually abused females with the S/L or S/S genotypes (Figure 6.17).

Finally, MAOA moderates the effects of childhood sexual abuse on marijuana use for females. Childhood sexual abuse has a stronger (negative) effect on marijuana use among females with the low activity/low activity genotype than for females with the high activity/high activity genotype ($z = 3.25$). The expected frequency of marijuana use is significantly lower among sexually abused females with the L/L genotype than among sexually abused females with the H/H genotype and among non-sexually abused females with the L/L genotype (Figure 6.18). A difference of coefficients test also reveals that the protective effect of the L allele is significantly stronger for females compared to males ($z = 3.87$).

Figure 6.17. 5HTTLPR X childhood sexual abuse on frequency of marijuana use for females

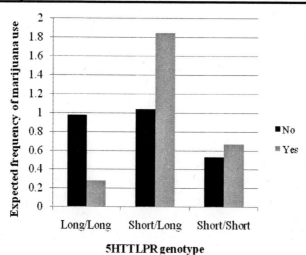

Figure 6.18. MAOA X childhood sexual abuse on frequency of marijuana use for females

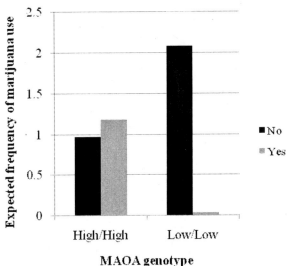

Childhood neglect.

Table 6.21 reveals that DRD2, 5HTTLPR, and MAOA polymorphisms condition the effects of childhood neglect on the frequency of marijuana use for females. Childhood neglect is associated with a higher frequency of marijuana use among females with the A2/A2 genotype more so than among females with the A1/A2 (z = 2.70). Severely neglected females with the A2/A2 genotype are expected to use marijuana more frequently than severely neglected females with the A1/A2 genotype and A1/A1 genotype (Figure 6.19).

Table 6.20. Genetic moderation of childhood sexual abuse on frequency of marijuana use for females and males

	Females			Males		
DAT1	9R/9R	10R/9R	10R/10R	9R/9R	10R/9R	10R/10R
Childhood sexual abuse	1.988*** (.594)	.676 (.680)	-1.580***a, b (.473)	-18.901*** (1.347)	.518 (.835)	-.148 (.477)
DRD2	A2/A2	A1/A2	A1/A1	A2/A2	A1/A2	A1/A1
Childhood sexual abuse	-.461 (.768)	1.265* (.590)	.559 (1.359)	.610 (.584)	.837 (.493)	-16.749*** (.523)
DRD4	<7R/<7R	>7R/<7R	>7R/>7R	<7R/<7R	>7R/<7R	>7R/>7R
Childhood sexual abuse	-.043 (.640)	.285 (.736)	-17.450*** (1.722)	.504 (.484)	.265 (.762)	-4.339*** (.981)
5HTTLPR	L/L	S/L	S/S	L/L	S/L	S/S
Childhood sexual abuse	-1.246*c (.628)	.572 (.651)	.235 (.953)	.470 (.634)	.667 (.577)	-.073 (1.072)
MAOA	H/H	L/H	L/L	H	L	
Childhood sexual abuse	.190 (.937)	.501 (.583)	-3.763***d, e (.770)	.417 (.656)	.030 (.605)	

a. 10R/10R coefficient differs from 9R/9R coefficient for females.; b. 10R/10R coefficient differs from 10R/9R coefficient for females.; c. L/L coefficient differs from S/L coefficient for females.; d. L/L coefficient differs from H/H coefficient for females.; e. L/L coefficient for females differs from L coefficient for males.

Figure 6.19. DRD2 X childhood neglect on frequency of marijuana use for females

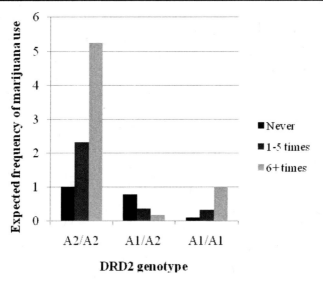

5HTTLPR also moderates the effect of neglect on adulthood marijuana use for females. Differences of coefficients tests reveal that the effect of childhood neglect on marijuana use is significantly different for the L/L genotype vs. the S/L genotype for females (z = 2.37), and for the L/L genotype compared to the S/S genotype for females (z = 3.29). The L/L genotype appears to have a protective effect for females, while the S/S genotype seems to increase females' sensitivity to neglect. Severely neglected females with the L/L genotype are expected to use marijuana less frequently (expected count = .05) than severely neglected females with the S/L (EC = 2.51) and S/S genotype (EC = 15.09) (Figure 6.20). Differences of coefficients tests also reveal that neglect has a stronger effect on marijuana use for S/S females compared to S/S males (z = 2.41), and L/L females more so than L/L males (z = 2.24). This latter finding suggests that gender conditions the interaction between 5HTTLPR and neglect on adulthood marijuana use.

Finally, the results suggest that MAOA conditions the effect of neglect on marijuana use for females. Neglect has a stronger effect on marijuana use for females with the L/L genotype compared to females with the H/H genotype ($z = 2.80$). As shown in Figure 6.21, the expected frequency of marijuana use is significantly higher among severely neglected females with the low/low activity MAOA genotype, compared to severely neglected females with the high/high activity genotype and non-neglected females with the low/low activity genotype. A difference of coefficients test also reveals that the neglect coefficient for L/L females is significantly different than that for L males ($z = 2.06$), suggesting that females with the L/L are more sensitive to the effects of neglect than L males.

Figure 6.20. 5HTTLPR X childhood neglect on frequency of marijuana use for females and males

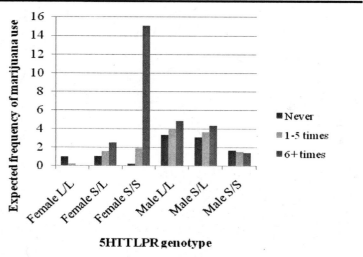

Table 6.21. Genetic moderation of childhood neglect on frequency of marijuana use for females and males

	Females			Males		
DAT1	9R/9R	10R/9R	10R/10R	9R/9R	10R/9R	10R/10R
Childhood neglect	no converg	1.004 (.585)	.047 (.365)	.335 (1.488)	.216 (.279)	-.019 (.176)
DRD2	A2/A2	A1/A2	A1/A1	A2/A2	A1/A2	A1/A1
Childhood neglect	.815* (.380)	-.719 (.420)	1.110 (.915)	.095 (.228)	.126 (.235)	.450 (.633)
DRD4	<7R/<7R	>7R/<7R	>7R/>7R	<7R/<7R	>7R/<7R	>7R/>7R
Childhood neglect	.273 (.593)	1.079** (.400)	3.702 (2.265)	.197 (.191)	-.001 (.306)	.529 (.808)
5HTTLPR	L/L	S/L	S/S	L/L	S/L	S/S
Childhood neglect	-1.447* (.644)	.443 (.465)	2.081* (.855)	.186 (.339)	.163 (.212)	-.073 (.255)
MAOA	H/H	L/H	L/L	H	L	
Childhood neglect	-.921 (.505)	.412 (.530)	.893* (.404)	.218 (.258)	-.067 (.228)	

a. A2/A2 coefficient differs from A1/A2 coefficient for females.; b. L/L coefficient differs from S/L coefficient for females.; c. L/L coefficient differs from S/S coefficient for females.; d. L/L coefficient differs from L/L coefficient for males.; e. S/S coefficient for females differs from S/S coefficient for males.; f. L/L coefficient differs from H/H coefficient for females.; g. L/L coefficient differs from L coefficient for males.

Figure 6.21. MAOA X childhood neglect on frequency of marijuana use for females

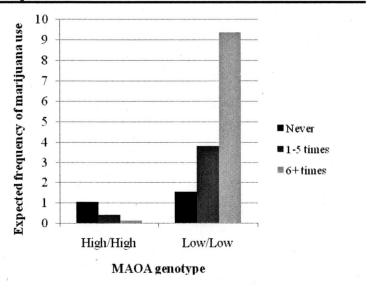

Childhood physical abuse.

Table 6.22 reveals whether the genetic polymorphisms interact with physical abuse to influence marijuana use for females and males. It appears that DAT1 moderates physical abuse on marijuana use for females. However, the 9R/9R genotype model is statistically unstable and there is not a significant difference in the physical abuse coefficient for 10R/9R and 10R/10R genotypes.

The results do suggest that 5HTTLPR interacts with childhood physical abuse for both females and males. Childhood physical abuse has a significantly stronger influence on marijuana use for S/S females than L/L females ($z = 2.27$), and for S/S males than S/L males ($z = 2.27$). As shown in Figure 6.22, females and males with the S/S genotype who are severely abused are more likely to frequently use marijuana than S/S females and males who do not experience physical abuse. Further, severely physically abused S/S females are expected to

use marijuana more frequently than severely abused L/L females.
There is a non-significant difference in the physical abuse coefficients
between S/S females and S/S males, suggested that gender does not
condition the effect of abuse on marijuana use for that genotype.

**Figure 6.22. 5HTTLPR X childhood physical abuse on frequency of
marijuana use for females**

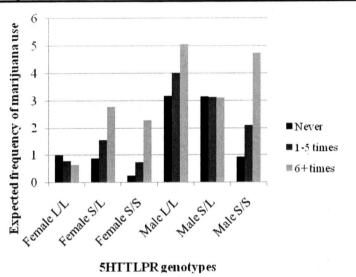

Table 6.22. Genetic moderation of childhood physical abuse on frequency of marijuana use for females and males

Females

DAT1	9R/9R	10R/9R	10R/10R
Childhood physical abuse	-.881* (.435)	.744*[a] (.337)	.067 (.263)
DRD2	A2/A2	A1/A2	A1/A1
Childhood physical abuse	.410 (.275)	-.067 (.327)	-.459 (.471)
DRD4	<7R/<7R	>7R/<7R	>7R/>7R
Childhood physical abuse	.338 (.303)	.611 (.345)	-2.933*** (.697)
5HTTLPR	L/L	S/L	S/S
Childhood physical abuse	-.220 (.336)	.576 (.320)	1.128*[b] (.488)
MAOA	H/H	L/H	L/L
Childhood physical abuse	-.531 (.289)	.609* (.308)	.409 (.438)

Males

DAT1	9R/9R	10R/9R	10R/10R
Childhood physical abuse	-.089 (1.077)	.037 (.238)	.291 (.186)
DRD2	A2/A2	A1/A2	A1/A1
Childhood physical abuse	.052 (.197)	.368 (.232)	.964 (.592)
DRD4	<7R/<7R	>7R/<7R	>7R/>7R
Childhood physical abuse	.144 (.179)	.137 (.244)	-1.576*** (.492)
5HTTLPR	L/L	S/L	S/S
Childhood physical abuse	.231 (.235)	-.006 (.207)	.810**[c] (.292)
MAOA	H	L	
Childhood physical abuse	.295 (.195)	.121 (.257)	

a. 10R/9R coefficient differs from 9R/9R coefficient for females.; b. S/S coefficient differs from L/L coefficient for females.; c. S/S coefficient differs from S/L coefficient for males.

Violent Victimization.

Table 6.23 shows that DRD2 conditions the effects of violent victimization on marijuana use for males, while MAOA moderates violent victimization on marijuana use for females. Violent victimization has a stronger effect on marijuana use for males with the A1/A1 genotype than males with the A1/A2 genotype ($z = 2.66$) and males with the A2/A2 genotype ($z = 2.43$). Violently victimized males with the A1/A1 genotype have an expected frequency of marijuana use that is significantly higher than violently victimized males with the A1/A2 or A2/A2 genotypes, or non-victimized males with the A1/A1 genotype (Figure 6.24). The effect is not gender specific.

MAOA interacts with violent victimization to influence marijuana use for females. Violent victimization has a stronger effect on marijuana use for H/H females than L/L females ($z = 3.55$). As shown in Figure 6.24, violently victimized females with the H/H genotype are expected to use marijuana more frequently than violently victimized females with the L/L genotype and non-victimized females with the H/H genotype. A difference of coefficients test also reveals that violent victimization has a stronger influence on marijuana use for females with the H/H genotype than males with the H allele ($z = 3.04$).

Figure 6.23. DRD2 X violent victimization on frequency of marijuana use for males

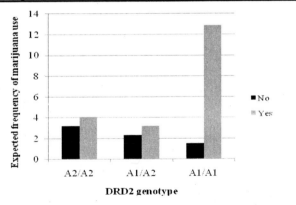

Table 6.23. Genetic moderation of violent victimization on frequency of marijuana use for females and males

	Females			Males		
DAT1	9R/9R	10R/9R	10R/10R	9R/9R	10R/9R	10R/10R
Violent victimization	1.780 (1.023)	-.242 (.771)	.759 (.466)	-20.999** (6.780)	.670* (.326)	.351 (.300)
DRD2	A2/A2	A1/A2	A1/A1	A2/A2	A1/A2	A1/A1
Violent victimization	.479 (.472)	2.118* (.982)	.809 (.824)	.240 (.282)	.326 (.359)	2.139****[a,b] (.653)
DRD4	<7R/<7R	>7R/<7R	>7R/>7R	<7R/<7R	>7R/<7R	>7R/>7R
Violent victimization	.041 (.459)	-.319 (.726)	1.998 (1.039)	.199 (.289)	.820* (.354)	.053 (.702)
5HTTLPR	L/L	S/L	S/S	L/L	S/L	S/S
Violent victimization	-.129 (.945)	1.125* (.508)	.019 (1.292)	.026 (.354)	.859*** (.286)	.339 (.611)
MAOA	H/H	L/H	L/L	H	L	
Violent victimization	3.598****[c,d] (.912)	-1.967** (.747)	-.961 (.900)	.646 (.330)	.405 (.287)	

a. A1/A1 coefficient differs from A1/A2 coefficient for males.; b. A1/A1 coefficient differs from A2/A2 coefficient for males.; c. H/H coefficient differs from L/L coefficient for females; d. H/H coefficient differs from H coefficient for males.

Figure 6.24. MAOA X violent victimization on frequency of
marijuana use for females

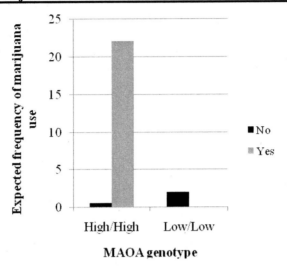

Intimate Partner Violence.

The final set of analyses examines whether the genetic polymorphisms
moderate the effects of intimate partner violence on marijuana use for
females and males. Table 6.24 shows that 5HTTLPR interacts with
intimate partner violence to influence marijuana use for females.
Intimate partner violence has a stronger effect on marijuana use for
females with the S/S genotype than females with the L/L genotype (z =
2.11). Figure 6.25 shows that females who have experienced multiple
intimate partner victimization incidents and who have the S/S genotype
are expected to use marijuana more frequently in adulthood (relative to
adolescence) than repeat IPV female victims with the L/L or S/L
genotypes, and non-victimized females with the S/S genotype.

Figure 6.25. 5HTTLPR X intimate partner violence on frequency of marijuana use for females

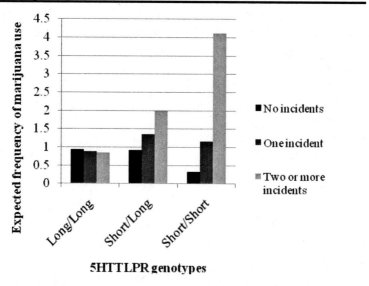

Table 6.24. Genetic moderation of intimate partner violence on frequency of marijuana use for females and males

	Females			Males		
DAT1	9R/9R	10R/9R	10R/10R	9R/9R	10R/9R	10R/10R
Intimate partner violence	-18.317*** (.943)	.303 (.432)	.420 (.233)	-1.314 (1.251)	.389* (.188)	.308 (.169)
DRD2	A2/A2	A1/A2	A1/A1	A2/A2	A1/A2	A1/A1
Intimate partner violence	.302 (.252)	.375 (.409)	.657 (.533)	.536*** (.167)	.012 (.222)	.979* (.499)
DRD4	<7R/<7R	>7R/<7R	>7R/>7R	<7R/<7R	>7R/<7R	>7R/>7R
Intimate partner violence	.508 (.283)	.114 (.344)	1.341 (.939)	.396* (.169)	.252 (.208)	.584 (.840)
5HTTLPR	L/L	S/L	S/S	L/L	S/L	S/S
Intimate partner violence	-.045 (.313)	.379 (.255)	1.262*[a] (.533)	.508* (.235)	.322 (.214)	.528* (.269)
MAOA	H/H	L/H	L/L	H	L	
Intimate partner violence	.438 (.287)	.666* (.290)	-.282 (.490)	.405* (.181)	.226 (.182)	

a. S/S coefficient differs from L/L coefficient for females.

Table 6.25. Summary of gene X victimization interactions

Violent offending

Violent offending	Females					Males				
	DAT1	DRD2	DRD4	5HTTLPR	MAOA	DAT1	DRD2	DRD4	5HTTLPR	MAOA
Sexual abuse		X					X		X	
Neglect										
Physical abuse				X	X		X			
Violent victimization										
IPV										

Property offending

Property offending	Females					Males				
	DAT1	DRD2	DRD4	5HTTLPR	MAOA	DAT1	DRD2	DRD4	5HTTLPR	MAOA
Sexual abuse										
Neglect		X							X	
Physical abuse					X					
Violent victimization										
IPV			X							

Alcohol abuse

Alcohol abuse	Females					Males				
	DAT1	DRD2	DRD4	5HTTLPR	MAOA	DAT1	DRD2	DRD4	5HTTLPR	MAOA
Sexual abuse							X		X	
Neglect				X	X					
Physical abuse					X					
Violent victimization										
IPV		X								

Table 6.25. Summary of gene X victimization interactions cont.

Marijuana use	Females					Males				
	DAT1	DRD2	DRD4	5HTTLPR	MAOA	DAT1	DRD2	DRD4	5HTTLPR	MAOA
Sexual abuse	X			X	X					
Neglect		X		X	X					
Physical abuse				X					X	
Violent victimization					X		X			
IPV				X						

Take home messages

- Overall, youths appear to be moderately resilient to the criminogenic effects of victimization. Results showed that approximately 60-80 percent of victimized individuals do not engage in violent crime, engage in property crime, severely abuse alcohol, or use marijuana.
- There was evidence of three gene-environment correlations. Results revealed that females with the short 5HTTLPR allele and males with the 10R DAT1 allele reported higher levels of neglect than females with the long 5HTTLPR and males with the 9R DAT1 allele, respectively. Males with the A1/A2 genotype were more likely to be violently victimized than males with the A2/A2 genotype, males with the A1/A1 genotype, and females with the A1/A2 genotype.
- Genetic polymorphisms do appear to moderate the effects of victimization on criminal behavior and substance use (Table 6.25). Regression models revealed 27 significant gene X environment interactions (8 males, 19 female), and these 27 interactions are more than what would be expected by chance alone (200 regression models * .05 = 10 significant interactions).

CHAPTER SEVEN

Conclusion

Criminological research has shown that victimization is an important risk factor for antisocial and criminal behavior, especially for females (Chesney-Lind, 1986; Singer, 1986). Further, many studies have shown that victimization is not randomly distributed across individuals and that certain victimized individuals do not go on to engage in crime. While researchers have typically used sociological and socio-psychological perspectives to explain these findings, it may be argued that biological and genetically informed explanations can be applied to the findings. The purpose of this study was to examine whether genetic polymorphisms were related to the likelihood of victimization, and whether genetic factors could explain variation in individuals' responses to victimization. Furthermore, given the literature showing gender differences in the effects of abuse and genetic polymorphisms on behavior, the current study explored whether the indirect and interactive effects of the genetic polymorphisms varied by gender. The results suggest that genetic polymorphisms may explain both individual differences in the likelihood of victimization and differential responses to victimization. Further, gender appears to condition these relationships. Each of these ideas will be separately discussed in the following sections.

Gene-environment correlations and gender
The current study revealed three significant gene-environment correlations: (1) 5HTTLPR on neglect for females, (2) DAT1 on neglect for males, and (3) DRD2 on violent victimization for males. Females who carried one or more copies of the short allele were more

likely to report severe childhood neglect (i.e., six or more incidents) than females who did not carry the short allele. Similarly, males who carried one or more copies of the 10R allele were more likely to report moderate neglect (i.e., one to five incidents) than males who did not carry the 10R allele. Finally, males with the A1/A2 genotype were more likely to report violent victimization than males with the A1/A1 genotype or A2/A2 genotype. The effect was significantly stronger for males, suggesting that males with the A1/A2 genotype were more likely to be violently victimized than females with the A1/A2 genotype.

There are two at least two explanations for these significant findings: (1) they are 'real' effects, or (2) they are artifacts of the data. It could be likely that these effects are 'real'. Results from behavioral genetic studies suggest that genetics explain a moderate percentage of variance in childhood abuse and adolescent victimization. A recent study of the Add Health twins revealed that genetic factors explain 24 percent of the variance in neglect, with genetic factors accounting for 32 percent and 3 percent of the variance in neglect for females and males, respectively (Schultz-Heik et al., 2009). Another study of Add Health revealed that genetics explained 39 percent of the variance in violent victimization (Vaske, Boisvert, & Wright, forthcoming). Thus, it appears that genetics are important to explaining differences in the prevalence of victimization.

Assuming the effects are real, the results suggest that passive or evocative gene-environment correlations may be operating. If a passive gene-environment correlation is at work, parents may be passing along these "genetic risks" (i.e., short 5HTTLPR allele, 10R DAT1 allele) to their offspring and they may be creating a lack luster environment that does not foster their child's development (due to the parents' own "genetic risks" or propensities for antisocial behavior). Thus, there is a correlation between the "genetic risk" factor and neglect because parents are providing both the "genetic risk" and the environmental risk (i.e., neglect). This may be a plausible explanation because studies have shown that neglect is more prevalent among parents who engage in criminal behavior and substance use (Wolock & Magura, 1996), and many of these antisocial behaviors are genetically mediated.

An evocative gene-environment correlation may also be at work. If an evocative gene-environment correlation is at play, children may be eliciting negative reactions from parents due to their own 'bad' behavior. The notion of a "child effect" suggests that childrens' misbehavior may cause their parents to behave in negative ways, such as becoming physically abusive or withdrawing from the relationship. From the current results, it may be hypothesized that females and males may be at-risk for neglect because they are engaging in unattractive behaviors (i.e., depression, disruptive behaviors) that stem from their low serotonin activity (as proxied by the short 5HTTLPR allele for females) or low dopamine activity (as proxied by the 10R allele for males). Thus, the genetic polymorphisms may lead to lower levels of serotonin and dopamine, which increases the likelihood of antisocial behavior and subsequently leads to a parent withdrawing from the parent-child relationship and neglecting their children. A similar explanation may apply to the DRD2-violent victimization association for males. Males with the A1/A2 genotype may experience low levels of dopamine activity, as such they engage in risky behaviors (i.e., verbal threats, stealing, physical assault) that may provoke others to attack them. This is merely one explanation for this effect and it is pertinent that future research explore the neurobiological and social mechanisms underlying these relationships.

A second explanation for these findings is that they are statistical or methodological artifacts. There were 20 empirical gene-environment correlation tests (5 polymorphisms X 4 measures of victimization (excluding sexual abuse) = 20 tests), and it was expected that one coefficient would be significant by chance alone (20 * .05 = 1). While three coefficients were significant and this is larger than one coefficient expected by chance alone, this is not drastically larger than one. If sexual abuse was included in the analyses, one would expect 2.5 coefficients to be significant by chance alone, which is barely less than the three significant coefficients. Future research should attempt to replicate the current findings in order to examine the reliability of these genetic effects. It could also be argued that the genetic effects on neglect are a methodological artifact. Individuals with the short allele or 10R allele may be at-risk for neuroticism, and they may be more likely to recall or exaggerate the negative aspects of their childhood than individuals who do not have a genetic propensity for neuroticism. Thus, the genetic polymorphisms may be related to the respondents' reporting behavior, more so than the criminogenic situations themselves (i.e., neglect). The results also revealed that males with the A1/A2 genotype were significantly more likely to be violently victimized than females with the A1/A2 genotype. The explanation for this gendered effect is not readily clear, since the functional consequences of the A1/A2 genotype for males (compared to females) is currently not known. It may be hypothesized that males with the A1/A2 genotype are more likely to engage in behaviors that provoke physical attacks than females with the A1/A2 genotype. For instance, perhaps males with the A1/A2 genotype are more likely to be suspicious of others and automatically act on their anger (which may evoke physical assaults from others), while females with the A1/A2 genotype are characterized by depressive symptoms (which may cause others to avoid them). This is one potential explanation for the association between DRD2 and violent victimization for males, but it is likely that there are numerous other processes connecting DRD2 and victimization.

Gene X victimization interactions and gender
The current study revealed a number of gene X victimization interactions for males and females. The sheer number of interactions (27) suggests that genetic polymorphisms may moderate or condition the effects of victimization on criminal behavior and substance use. Individuals with a certain genotype may be more sensitive to the criminogenic effects of abuse and victimization than individuals with other genotypes. Thus, the current study supports the use of a biosocial explanation for why victimization may lead to higher levels of criminal behavior and substance use.

The results also show that genetic factors may act as a risk enhancer or a protective factor. For a number of interactions, a genotype acted as a protective factor, in that victimized individuals who carried that genotype had a lower predicted rate of offending or substance use than victimized individuals without that genotype and non-victimized individuals with that genotype. For instance, sexually abused males who carried the S/S 5HTTLPR genotype were expected to have lower rates of adulthood violent offending (relative to their levels of adolescent violent offending) than sexually abused males with the L/L and S/L genotypes, and non-sexually abused males with the S/S genotype. This finding, and others, suggests that genetic factors may enhance or mask the effects of victimization on offending.

There were a number of patterns concerning: (a) the types of victimization that are frequently moderated, (b) the types of outcomes gene X victimization effects influenced, (c) the types of polymorphisms that condition the effects of victimization, and (d) the moderating effect of gender in gene X victimization interactions. First, the results reveal that forms of childhood maltreatment were moderated more frequently than forms of adolescent victimization. Out of the 27 significant interactions, 22 of the interactions (82 percent) involved either childhood sexual abuse, neglect, or physical abuse. This result calls into question whether childhood victimization is truly moderated more frequently than adolescent victimization, or whether the measurement differences between childhood abuse and adolescent victimization are driving the results. Based on the results, it may be hypothesized that genetic factors are more important for determining long-term psychological and behavioral consequences of childhood victimization, more so than the consequences of adolescent victimization. This hypothesis rests on assumptions regarding the timing of abuse and the timing of genetic effects. Studies have shown that childhood victimization may impact brain structures (i.e., hippocampus), but these effects may not emerge until adulthood, while adolescent victimization has immediate impact on brain structures in adolescence (Andersen & Teicher, 2008). Similarly, genetic effects may be more evident during adulthood than adolescence (Guo et al., 2007b). These findings suggest that some effects of childhood maltreatment may not emerge until adulthood, and it is then during adulthood that genetic factors moderate these effects. One potential way to explore this idea would be to estimate a linear growth curve model of antisocial behavior from childhood to middle adulthood for each of the interaction categories. If the effects of maltreatment are lagged and they may be more important for one genetic group (versus another group), then one would expect to see a substantial increase antisocial behavior from adolescence to adulthood for one interaction category (i.e., abused individuals with S/S genotype), while there may be little to no change in antisocial behavior for another interaction category (i.e., abused individuals with L/L genotype). In terms of the specific types of victimization, neglect was the most frequent form of victimization involved in the gene X victimization interactions (i.e., 9 interactions), followed by childhood physical abuse (8 interactions) and sexual abuse (5 interactions). These differences, however, are not substantial and thus it may not be argued that one specific form of victimization is more likely to be moderated than other forms of victimization. Instead, the results point to the timing of abuse as relevant to the interaction process, rather than the specific type of abuse.

Second, the results indicate that genetic polymorphisms may moderate the effects of victimization on substance use, more so than on criminal behavior. Approximately two-thirds of the interactions included alcohol abuse or marijuana use as the endogenous variable. While these findings are highly preliminary, it may be hypothesized that a biosocial model involving victimization may better explain differences in substance use than differences in criminal behavior. The previous gene X victimization interaction literature does not show a preference for substance use over criminal behavior. However, it is important to note that gene X victimization/stressful life interactions are consistently related to psychological correlates of substance use (i.e., depression, PTSD, anxiety) than to antisocial behavior. It may be likely, therefore, that substance use is more of an organic process that is more sensitive to the neurobiological consequences of victimization and genetic polymorphisms than criminal behavior. This hypothesis is based on very preliminary findings and should be empirically evaluated before adopted by researchers.

Third, the analyses reveal a number of patterns concerning the specific polymorphisms that frequently condition the effects of victimization on antisocial behavior. DRD2 and 5HTTLPR are the most frequent polymorphisms that moderate the effects of victimization on antisocial behavior for females and males. Approximately one-third of the significant gene X victimization interactions for females and males include either DRD2 or 5HTTLPR. Further, MAOA is involved in approximately 36 percent (n = 7) of the significant gene X victimization interactions for females (N = 19), suggesting that MAOA is an important moderator for females (more so than males). These findings suggest that DRD2, 5HTTLPR, and MAOA may be more important for determining psychological and behavioral responses to victimization, than the DAT1 and DRD4 polymorphisms. It should be noted, however, that many of the models involving DAT1 and DRD4 were seriously underpowered, and the null results for DAT1 and DRD4 may reflect a Type II error more so than a 'real' effect. Many of the significant differences of coefficients tests for DAT1 and DRD4 were not considered due to a very small number of cases falling into the interaction categories. The current data, therefore, provide preliminary evidence that DRD2, 5HTTLPR, and MAOA are more relevant for gene X victimization interactions (than DAT1 and DRD4), but this should be empirically evaluated with higher powered studies.

Finally, the results suggest that genetic polymorphisms moderate the effects of victimization on antisocial behavior more so for females than for males. Out of the 27 significant interactions, 19 (or 70 percent) were significant for females and only 8 were significant for males. This pattern of results suggests that the effects of victimization are more likely to be genetically moderated for females than males. For males, it appears that the victimization measures have more of a "main" effect than an interaction effect; there are multiple significant simple main effects, but not significant differences of coefficients tests comparing thos e main effects. Further, males appear to be less resilient to the effects of victimization than females, suggesting that males' likelihood of offending is increased with only the environmental risk (i.e., victimization). For females, it appears that they are more resilient to the effects of victimization than males, and that victimization by itself does not exponentially increase their level of criminal behavior and substance use as they move from adolescence into adulthood. Instead, following the dual hazards hypothesis, females' risk of offending is exponentially increased when they carry a certain genotype and they are victimized. Thus, victimization may increase females' risk of offending, but it is genetic factors that exacerbate the criminogenic effects of victimization and that push female victims to increase their level of offending in adulthood.

While there is more significant gene X victimization interactions for females than males, one cannot conclude from those tests that females are more sensitive to the intersection of genetic risk and victimization than males. Instead, one would have to review the differences of coefficients tests that examined whether victimization had a stronger effect on offending for males and females with the same genotype. A review of the differences of coefficients tests reveals that gender conditions twelve gene X victimization interactions, with two coefficients having a stronger effect for males and 10 coefficients having a significantly stronger effect for females. This finding suggests that there may be something about the female gender that enhances the risk and protective effects of the genetic polymorphisms, especially 5HTTLPR and MAOA.

In regards to 5HTTLPR, it may be argued that the female gender (Young et al., 2007), 5HTTLPR (McCormack et al., 2009), and victimization all individually contribute to higher HPA axis activity (Champagne & Curley, 2008), and so the synergism of these three risk factors may lead to exponentially higher levels of HPA hyperactivity. For instance, non-human primate studies have found 5HTTLPR interacts with maternal separation to influence HPA axis reactivity among females, but notamong males. Barr et al. (2004) found that maternally separated female rhesus monkeys with the short allele had higher levels of ACTH and lower levels of cortisol in response to stress than maternally separated males with the short allele, maternally separated females with the L/L genotype, and non-maternally separated females with the short allele. In regards to MAOA, it may be hypothesized that MAOA escaped inactivation for a significant number of females in the sample, and thus these females may have experienced a double dose of "genetic risk" or protective effects (i.e., L/L) while males did not since they only have one X chromosome (i.e., L). These are plausible explanations for these effects, but the neurobiological mechanisms underlying these relationships extend past the current data.

Before moving into the limitations of the current study, it is important to touch on one last issue. The current study revealed that gene X victimization interactions are rarely bilinear in nature. Instead, the differences in victimization slopes varied across genotypes. For example, the difference in the sexual abuse-violent offending slopes for

A2/A2 males compared to A1/A2 males is .024, compared to a difference of 1.771 in the sexual abuse-violent offending slope for A1/A2 males relative to A1/A1 males. This interaction may not have emerged if the current study used a multiplicative interaction term, since interaction terms assume a bilinear interaction effect. While the current study's methods of estimating interactions may consider alternative and complex forms of interaction (that may better approximate the observed effects from the raw data), the parsimony of interactions is lost with the complexity of the results. Reviewing the interactions for DRD2 for females, it can be seen that the A1/A1 genotype exacerbates the harmful effects of victimization for some analyses (i.e., alcohol abuse), while the A2 alleles increase the criminogenic effects of victimization for other analyses (i.e., violent offending, property offending, and marijuana use). Thus, the current results may be less theoretically and empirically biased than interaction terms from mean centered first order predictors, but the method produces a messy set of results may be difficult to interpret. At the current time, it is suggested that research continue to investigate interactions with this method (and other methods), and then conduct a meta-analysis to examine whether there are larger patterns to the data.

Limitations
The current preliminary results suggest that genetic factors moderate the effects of childhood abuse and adolescent victimization on antisocial behaviors for males and females. While this contributes to the current criminological and molecular genetic literature, there are at least six limitations that must be considered when interpreting the current findings. First, the genetic subsample of the Add Health is a non-probability sample. This suggests that the sample may not be representative of the larger population. This is a real possibility, especially since the 5HTTLPR and MAOA genotypes deviated from Hardy Weinberg equilibrium. In light of this limitation, as well as others, it is important to note that these findings are preliminary and they need to be further investigated.

Second, the 5HTTLPR polymorphism was genotyped as a bi-allelic polymorphism, but recent research shows that the polymorphism may be tri-allelic (Nakamura, Ueno, Sano, & Tanabe, 2000; Hu et al.,

2006). The alleles are L_A, L_G, and S, with the L_G allele having similar functional consequences as the S allele. The operationalization of the 5HTTLPR as biallelic may mask important relationships. Under the biallelic coding, differences between the L/L and L/S (and S/S) may appear smaller than they actually are when a L_G allele is merely classified as an "L" allele, but it behaves as an S allele.

The third limitation is that the reliability of the childhood abuse and adolescent victimization measures may be questionable. The current dissertation used retrospective measures of childhood abuse and neglect. Yet, previous research has shown that retrospective measures of childhood abuse may underestimate the prevalence and frequency of abuse (Brown et al., 2007; Widom & Shepard, 1996). This underestimation of abuse may lead to null results. Studies have shown, however, that while retrospective measures introduce measurement error into statistical models, this measurement error is not large enough to significantly attenuate relationships (Fergusson et al., 2000; Widom & Brown, 1997). This pattern of results was also found in the current study; the retrospective measures of childhood abuse and neglect were significantly related to criminal behavior and substance abuse.

The current study's findings may also be limited by the moderate reliabilities of adolescent violent victimization (alpha = .64) and adolescent intimate partner violence (alpha = .61). The reliabilities for the intimate partner violence scale are somewhat lower than reliabilities of similar scales (alpha around .70 to .90) used in other studies (Straus, 2004). However, the current study's intimate partner violence scale primarily consists of items that measure psychological aggression. This subscale of the Revised Conflict Tactics Scale typically evidences the lowest reliability estimates (Straus, 2004), thus it is not surprising that the reliability of the current measure is moderate. Aside from the questionable reliability of the adolescent victimization scales, it should also be noted that these scales ignore the context in which victimization occurs. That is, victims may not be passively receiving verbal threats or physical assaults, but they may also be precipitating their victimization by acting out against the "perpetrator" first.

The fourth limitation is that the current study did not control for a number of relevant criminological variables, such as neighborhood disorder, social bonds, low self-control, or delinquent peers. Without including these measures into the models, the models may be misspecified and the observed relationships may be spurious.

Fifth, many of the significant gene X victimization interactions must be cautiously interpreted due to the small number of subjects falling into the interaction categories (i.e., homozygous for the risk allele and victimized). The small cell counts can create statistical instability, especially in negative binomial models. It would be pertinent for future research to investigate the statistical reliability of the gene X victimization effects found in the current study.

Finally, the current study only included measures of five genetic polymorphisms. As discussed in Chapter 3, however, many phenotypes are polygenic, meaning that multiple genetic polymorphisms work additively and multiplicatively to increase the likelihood of antisocial behavior. The null main effects of the genetic polymorphisms may be attributed to this limitation. Future research that investigates the link between genetic factors and antisocial behaviors should either use the multiple candidate gene approach (Comings et al., 2000a, 2000b) or the genome wide association approach to capture the polygenic nature of antisocial behavior (Uhl et al., 2008).

Conclusion
Traditional criminology has implicated victimization as a risk factor for antisocial behavior. The link between victimization and antisocial behavior was often couched in sociological or socio-psychological explanations. This relationship, however, may be explained by perspectives from numerous disciplines, including perspectives from molecular genetics and biological sciences. For instance, individuals who have a genetic propensity towards antisocial behavior may be more likely to be victimized than individuals who do not have this genetic propensity. Further, genetic factors may explain why some abused individuals go on to commit crime, while other abused individuals do not. That is, genetic risk factors may exacerbate the effects of victimization on cognitive functioning and behavioral regulation, which in turn increases the risk of antisocial behavior. The current dissertation provides support for these hypotheses, and it shows that these effects may vary by gender.

While traditional criminologists have been reluctant to include genetic factors into their explanations of offending, biological and genetic factors can enrich our understanding of antisocial behavior in a number of ways. These factors may explain individual variation in responses to victimization, and help explain how exposure to certain environments varies across individuals. Further, at the neurobiological level, these factors can help researchers understand the processes that underlie individuals' responses to victimization. Thus, biological and genetic factors may help researchers understand the mechanisms underlying relationships that are commonly found in the victimization literature.

In closing, biological and genetic factors should be viewed as one component of a larger process leading up to criminal behavior. These factors have the capability to enhance our understanding of human behavior, especially in regards to how responses to environmental stimuli vary across individuals. Without including these elements into our theories of antisocial behavior, we are potentially overlooking key processes that promote the development and maintenance of antisocial behavior. Further, we may be promoting sociological interventions that are neurobiologically counterintuitive. It is recommended that future research continue to examine the genetic and biological correlates of crime, as well as investigating whether these factors can be integrated into traditional criminological theories.

Appendix

Independent Variables

Abuse and Victimization

Childhood sexual abuse: By the time you started 6th grade:
1. How often had one of your parents or other adult-caregivers touched you in a sexual way, forced you to touch him or her in a sexual way, or forced you to have sexual relations?

Childhood neglect: By the time you started 6th grade:
1. How often had your parents or other adult care-givers not taken care of your basic needs such as keeping you clean or providing food or clothing?

Childhood physical abuse: By the time you started 6th grade:
1. How often had your parents or other adult care-givers slapped, hit, or kicked you?

Violent victimization wave II: During the past 12 months, how often did each of the following things happen:
1. Someone pulled a knife or gun on you.
2. Someone shot you.
3. Someone cut or stabbed you.
4. You were jumped.

Intimate partner violence:
1. Did (first romantic partner's initials) call you names, insult you, or treat you disrespectfully?
2. Did (first romantic partner's initials) swear at you?
3. Did (first romantic partner's initials) threaten you with violence?
4. Did (first romantic partner's initials) push or shove you?
5. Did (first romantic partner's initials) throw something at you that could hurt you?
6. Did (second romantic partner's initials) call you names, insult you, or treat you disrespectfully?

237

7. Did (second romantic partner's initials) swear at you?
8. Did (second romantic partner's initials) threaten you with violence?
9. Did (second romantic partner's initials) push or shove you?
10. Did (second romantic partner's initials) throw something at you that could hurt you?
11. Did (third romantic partner's initials) call you names, insult you, or treat you disrespectfully?
12. Did (third romantic partner's initials) swear at you?
13. Did (third romantic partner's initials) threaten you with violence?
14. Did (third romantic partner's initials) push or shove you?
15. Did (third romantic partner's initials) throw something at you that could hurt you?

Control variables

Age in wave II

Property offending wave II: In the past 12 months, how often did you:

1. Take something from a store without paying for it?
2. Drive a car without its owner's permission?
3. Steal something worth more than $50?
4. Go into a house or building to steal something?
5. Steal something worth less than $50?

Violent offending wave II: In the past 12 months, how often did you:

1. Use or threaten to use a weapon to get something from someone?
2. Take part in a fight where a group of your friends was against another group?
3. Pulled a knife or gun on someone?
4. Shot or stabbed someone?
5. Used a weapon in a fight?
6. Get into a physical fight in which you were injured and had to be treated by a doctor or nurse?
7. Hurt someone badly enough to need bandages or care from a doctor or nurse?

Alcohol abuse wave II: Over the past 12 months, how many times has each of the following happened?

1. Alcohol related problems
   a. You got into trouble with you parents because you had been drinking.
   b. You had problems at school or with school work because you had been drinking.

    c.   You had problems with your friends because you had been drinking.

    d.   You had problems with someone you were dating because you had been drinking.

    e.   You did something you later regretted because you had been drinking.

    f.   Were hung over?

    g.   Were you sick to your stomach or threw up after drinking?

    h.   Did you get into a sexual situation that you later regretted because you had been drinking?

    i.   Did you get into a physical fight because you had been drinking?

Frequency of marijuana use wave II

1. During the past 30 days, how many times did you use marijuana?

Dependent Variables

Property offending wave III: In the past 12 months, how often did you:

1. Steal something worth more than $50?
2. Go into a house or building to steal something?
3. Steal something worth less than $50?
4. Buy, sell, or hold stolen property?
5. Use someone else's credit card, bank card, or automatic teller card without their permission or knowledge?
6. Deliberately write a bad check?

Violent offending wave III: In the past 12 months, how often did you:

1. Use or threaten to use a weapon to get something from someone?
2. Take part in a physical fight where a group of your friends was against another group?
3. Use a weapon in a fight?
4. Take part in a physical fight in which you were so badly injured that you were treated by a doctor or nurse?
5. Hurt someone badly enough in a physical fight that he or she needed care from a doctor or nurse?
6. Pull a knife or gun on someone?
7. Shot or stabbed someone?

Alcohol abuse wave III: Over the past 12 months, how many times has each of the following happened?

1. Alcohol related problems

    a.   You had problems at school or work because you had been drinking.

b. You had problems with your friends because you had been drinking.

c. You had problems with someone you were dating because you had been drinking.

d. Were you hung over?

e. Were you sick to your stomach or threw up after drinking?

f. Did you get into a sexual situation that you later regretted because you had been drinking?

g. Did you get into a physical fight because you had been drinking?

h. Were drunk at school or work?

Frequency of marijuana use wave III

1. During the past 30 days, how many times did you use marijuana?

References

Aceves, M. J., & Cookston, J. T. (2007). Violent victimization, aggression, and parent-adolescent relations: Quality parenting as a buffer for violently victimized youth. *Journal of Youth and Adolescence, 36*(5), 635-647.

Add Health Biomarker Team. (no date). *Biomarkers in wave III of the Add Health Study.* Chapel Hill, NC: Population Center, University of North Carolina at Chapel Hill.

Aguirre, A. J., Apiquián, R., Fresán, A., & Cruz-Fuentes, C. (2007). Association analysis of exon III and exon I polymorphisms of the dopamine D4 receptor locus in Mexican psychotic patients. *Psychiatry Research, 153*(3), 209-215.

Allele Frequency Database (ALFRED). (2006). The allele frequency database: A resource of gene frequency data on human populations supported by the U.S. national science foundation.

Amadéo, S., Abbar, M., Fourcade, M. L., Waksman, G., Leroux, M. G., Madec, A.,...Mallet, J. (1993). D2 dopamine receptor gene and alcoholism. *Journal of Psychiatric Research, 27*(2), 173-179.

Amadéo, S., Noble, E. P., Fourcade-Amadéo, M. L., Tetaria, C., Brugiroux, M. F., Nicolas, L.,...Mallet, J. (2000). D2 dopamine receptor and alcohol dehydrogenase 2 genes with Polynesian alcoholics: Association of D2 dopamine receptor and alcohol dehydrogenase 2 genes with polynesian alcoholics. *European Psychiatry, 15*(2), 97-102.

Amin, Z., Canli, T., & Epperson, C. N. (2005). Effect of estrogen-serotonin interactions on mood and cognition. *Behavioral and Cognitive Neuroscience Reviews, 4*(1), 43-58.

Anchordoquy, H. C., McGeary, C., Liu, L., Krauter, K. S., & Smolen, A. (2003). Genotyping of three candidate genes after whole-genome

preamplification of DNA collected from buccal cells. *Behavior Genetics,*
     33(1), 73-78.

Andersen, S. L., Rutstein, M., Benzo, J. M., Hostetter, J. C., & Teicher, M. H.
     (1997). Sex differences in dopamine receptor overproduction and
     elimination. *NeuroReport, 8,* 1495-1498.

Andersen, S. L., Lyss, P. J., Dumont, N. L., & Teicher, M. H. (1999). Enduring
     neurochemical effects of early maternal separation on limbic structures.
     Annals New York Academy of Sciences, 877, 756-759.

Andersen, S. L., & Teicher, M. H. (2000). Sex differences in dopamine
     receptors and their relevance to ADHD. *Neuroscience and Biobehavioral
     Reviews, 24*(1), 137-141.

Andersen, S. L., Thompson, A. P., Krenzel, E., & Teicher, M. H. (2002).
     Pubertal changes in gonadal hormones do not underlie adolescent
     dopamine receptor overproduction. *Psychoneuroendocrinology, 27,* 683-
     691.

Andersen, S. L., Tomada, A., Vincow, E. S., Valente, E., Polcari, A., &
     Teicher, M. H. (2008). Preliminary evidence for sensitive periods in the
     effect of childhood sexual abuse on regional brain development. *Journal
     of Neuropsychiatry & Clinical Neurosciences, 20,* 292-301.

Andersen, S. L, & Teicher, M. H. (2009). Desperately driven and no brakes:
     Developmental stress exposure and subsequent risk for substance abuse.
     Neuroscience and Biobehavioral Reviews, 33, 516-524.

Arcos-Burgos, M., Castellanos, F. X., Konecki, D., Lopera, F., Pineda, D.,
     Palacio, J. D.,…Muenke, M. (2004). Pedigree disequilibrium test (PDT)
     replicates association and linkage between DRD4 and ADHD in
     multigenerational and extended pedigrees from a genetic isolate.
     Molecular Psychiatry, 9, 252-259.

Arinami, T., Itokawa, M., Komiyama, T., Mitsushio, H., Mori, H., Mifune,
     H.,…Toru, M. (1993). Association between severity of alcoholism and
     the A1 allele of the dopamine D2 receptor gene TaqI A RFLP in
     Japanese. *Biological Psychiatry, 33*(2), 108-114.

Asberg, M., Thoren, P., Traskman, L., Bertilsson, L., & Ringberger, V. (1976).
     " Serotonin depression"--a biochemical subgroup within the affective
     disorders? *Science, 191*(4226), 478-480.

Asberg, M. (1997). The evidence from cerebrospinal fluid studies. *Annals of
     the New York Academy of Sciences, 836,* 158-181.

Asghari, V., Schoots, O., van Kats, S., Ohara, K., Jovanovic, V., Guan, H. C.,...Van Tol, H. H. M. (1994). Dopamine D4 receptor repeat: Analysis of different native and mutant forms of the human and rat genes. *Molecular Pharmacology, 46*(2), 364-373.

Asghari, V., Sanyal, S., Buchwaldt, S., Paterson, A., Jovanovic, V., & Van Tol, H. H. M. (1995). Modulation of intracellular cyclic AMP levels by different human dopamine D4 receptor variants. *Journal of Neurochemistry, 65*(3), 1157-1165.

Avishai-Eliner, S., Hatalski, C. G., Tabachnik, E., Eghbal-Ahmadi, M., & Baram, T. Z. (1999). Differential regulation of glucocorticoid receptor messenger RNA (GR-mRNA) by maternal deprivation in immature rat hypothalamus and limbic regions. *Developmental Brain Research, 114,* 265-268.

Baca-Garcia, E., Vaquero, C., Diaz-Sastre, C., Saiz-Ruiz, J., Fernandez-Piqueras, J., & de Leon, J. (2002). A gender-specific association between the serotonin transporter gene and suicide attempts. *Neuropsychopharmacology, 26*(5), 692-695.

Bakker, S. C., van der Meulen, E.M., Oteman, N., Schelleman, H., Pearson, P. L., Buitelaar, J. K.,...Sinke, R. J. (2005). DAT 1, DRD 4, and DRD 5 polymorphisms are not associated with ADHD in Dutch families. *American Journal of Medical Genetics Part B Neuropsychiatric Genetics, 132*(1), 50-52.

Bainbridge, D. (2003). *The X in Sex: How the X chromosome controls our lives.* Cambridge, MA: Harvard University Press.

Baron, R. M., & Kenny, D. A. (1986). The moderator-mediator variable distinction in social psychological research: Conceptual, strategic, and statistical considerations. *Journal of Personality and Social Psychology, 51(6),* 1173-1182.

Barr, C. L., Wigg, K. G., Bloom, S., Schachar, R., Tannock, R., Roberts, W., Kennedy, J. L. (2000). Further evidence from haplotype analysis for linkage of the dopamine D4 receptor gene and attention-deficit hyperactivity disorder. *American Journal of Medical Genetics, 96*(3), 262-267.

Barr, C. L., Xu, C., Kroft, J., Feng, Y., Wigg, K., Zai, G.,...Kennedy, J. L. (2001). Haplotype study of three polymorphisms at the dopamine transporter locus confirm linkage to attention-deficit hyperactivity disorder. *Biological Psychiatry, 49,* 333-339.

Baskin, D. R., & Sommers, I. B. (1998). *Casualties of community disorder: Women's careers in violent crime.* Boulder, CO: Westview Press.

Bau, C. H. D., Almeida, S., Costa, F. T., Garcia, C. E. D., Elias, E. P., Ponso, A. C.,...Hutz,, M. H. (2001). DRD4 and DAT1 as modifying genes in alcoholism: Interaction with novelty seeking on level of alcohol consumption. *Molecular Psychiatry, 6,* 7-9.

Beaver, K. M., & Wright, J. P. (2005). Biosocial development and delinquent involvement. *Youth Violence and Juvenile Justice, 3*(2), 168-192.

Beaver, K. M., & Wright, J. P. (2007). A child effects explanation for the association between family risk and involvement in an antisocial lifestyle. *Journal of Adolescent Research, 22*(6), 640-664.

Beaver, K. M., Wright, J. P., DeLisi, M., Walsh, A., Vaughn, M. G., Boisvert, D.,...Vaske, J. (2007). A gene X gene interaction between DRD2 and DRD4 is associated with conduct disorder and antisocial behavior in males. *Behavior and Brain Functions, 3,* 30.

Beaver, K. M., Wright, J. P., DeLisi, M., Daigle, L. E., Swatt, M. L., & Gibson, C. L. (2007). Evidence of a gene X environment interaction in the creation of victimization: Results from a longitudinal sample of adolescents. *International Journal of Offender Therapy and Comparative Criminology, 51*(6), 620-645.

Beaver, K. M. (2008a). The interaction between genetic risk and childhood sexual abuse in the prediction of adolescent violent behavior. *Sexual Abuse: A Journal of Research and Treatment, 20,* 426-443.

Beaver, K. M. (2008b). Molecular genetics and crime. In A. Walsh, & K. M. Beaver (Eds.), *Biosocial criminology: New directions in theory and research* (pp. 50-72). New York: Routledge.

Becker, J. B. (1999). Gender differences in dopaminergic function in striatum and nucleus accumbens. *Pharmacol Biochem Behav, 64*(4), 803-812.

Becker, K., Laucht, M., El-Faddagh, M., & Schmidt, M. H. (2005). The dopamine D4 receptor gene exon III polymorphism is associated with novelty seeking in 15-year-old males from a high-risk community sample. *Journal of Neural Transmission, 112*(6), 847-858.

Beitchman, J. H., Davidge, K. M., Kennedy, J. L., Atkinson, L., Lee, V., Shapiro, S.,...Douglas, L. (2003). The serotonin transporter gene in aggressive children with and without ADHD and nonaggressive matched controls. *Annals of the New York Academy of Sciences, 1008*(1), 248-251.

Beitchman, J. H., Mik, H. M., Ehtesham, S., Douglas, L., & Kennedy, J. L. (2004). MAOA and persistent, pervasive childhood aggression. *Molecular Psychiatry, 9*(6), 546-547.

Belknap, J., & Holsinger, K. (1998). An overview of delinquent girls: How theory and practice have failed and the need for innovative change. In R. T. Zaplin (Ed.), *Female offenders: Critical perspectives and effective interventions* Jones & Bartlett Publishers.

Belknap, J., & Holsinger, K. (2006). The gendered nature of risk factors for delinquency. *Feminist Criminology, 1*(1), 48-71.

Bengel, D., Murphy, D. L., Andrews, A. M., Wichems, C. H., Feltner, D., Heils, A.,…Lesch, K. P. (1998). Altered brain serotonin homeostasis and locomotor insensitivity to 3, 4-methylenedioxymethamphetamine ("Ecstasy") in serotonin transporter-deficient mice. *Molecular Pharmacology, 53*(4), 649-655.

Berggren, U. L. F., Fahlke, C., Aronsson, E., Karanti, A., Eriksson, M., Blennow, K. A. J.,…Balldin, J. (2006). The DRD2 A1 allele is associated with alcohol dependence although its effect size is small. *Alcohol and Alcoholism, 41*(5), 479-487.

Bernstein, D.P., Fink, L., Handelsman, L., & Fotte, J. (1994). Initial reliability and validity of a new retrospective measure of child abuse and neglect. *American Journal of Psychiatry, 151(8)*, 1132-1136.

Bernstein, D.P., Ahluvalia, T., Pogge, D., & Handelsman, L. (1997). Validity of the Childhood Trauma Questionnaire in an adolescent psychiatric population. *Journal of the American Academy of Child & Adolescent Psychiatry, 36(3)*, 340-348.

Bethea, C. L., Mirkes, S. J., Su, A., & Michelson, D. (2002). Effects of oral estrogen, raloxifene and arzoxifene on gene expression in serotonin neurons of macaques. *Psychoneuroendocrinology, 27*(4), 431-445.

Beyer, C., Pilgrim, C., & Reisert, I. (1991). Dopamine content and metabolism in mesencephalic and diencephalic cell cultures: Sex differences and effects of sex steroids. *Journal of Neuroscience, 11*(5), 1325-1333.

Billig, J. P., Hershberger, S. L., Iacono, W. G., & McGue, M. (1996). Life events and personality in late adolescence: Genetic and environmental relations. *Behavior Genetics, 26*(6), 543-554.

Biver, F., Lotstra, F., Monclus, M., Wikler, D., Damhaut, P., Mendlewicz, J.,…Goldman, S. (1996). Sex difference in 5HT2 receptor in the living human brain. *Neuroscience Letters, 204*(1-2), 25-28.

Bloom, B., Owen, B., & Covington, S. (2003). *Gender-responsive strategies: Research, practice, and guiding principles for women offenders.* Washington, DC: National Institute of Corrections.

Blum, K., Noble, E. P., Sheridan, P. J., Finley, 0., Montgomery, A., Ritchie, T.,...Nogami, H. (1991). Association of the A1 allele of the D2 dopamine receptor gene with severe alcoholism. *Alcohol, 8,* 409-416.

Blum, K., Cull, J. G., Braverman, E., & Comings, D. E. (1996). Reward deficiency syndrome. *American Scientist, 84,* 132-139.

Blum, K., Braverman, E.R., Holder, J.M., Lubar, J.F., Monastra, V.J., Miller, D.,...Comings, D.E. (2000). Reward deficiency syndrome: A biogenetic model for the diagnosis and treatment of impulsive, addictive, and compulsive behaviors. *Journal of Psychoactive Drugs, 32,* 1-112.

Blumstein, A., Cohen, J., & Farrington, D. P. (1988). Criminal career research: Its value for criminology. *Criminology, 26*(1), 1-35.

Boardman, J. D., & Saint Onge, J. (2005). Neighborhoods and adolescent development. *Children, Youth, and Environments, 15*(1), 138-164.

Brendgen, M., Boivin, M., Vitaro, F., Girard, A., Dionne, G., & Pérusse, D. (2008). Gene–environment interaction between peer victimization and child aggression. *Development and Psychopathology, 20*(02), 455-471.

Brezina, T. (1998). Adolescent maltreatment and delinquency: The question of intervening processes. *Journal of Research in Crime and Delinquency, 35,* 71-99.

Brookes, K. J., Neale, B. M., Sugden, K., Khan, N., Asherson, P., & D'Souza, U. M. (2007). Relationship between VNTR polymorphisms of the human dopamine transporter gene and expression in post-mortem midbrain tissue. *American Journal of Medical Genetics.Part B, Neuropsychiatric Genetics, 144B*(8), 1070-1078.

Brown, G. L., Goodwin, F. K., Ballenger, J. C., Goyer, P. F., & Major, L. F. (1979). Aggression in humans correlates with cerebrospinal fluid amine metabolites. *Psychiatry Research, 1*(2), 131-139.

Brown, G. W., Craig, T. K. J., Harris, T. O., Handley, R. V., & Harvey, A. L. (2007). Validity of retrospective measures of early maltreatment and depressive episodes using the childhood experience of care and abuse (CECA) instrument—A life-course study of adult chronic depression—2. *Journal of Affective Disorders, 103*(1-3), 217-224.

Brown, H. (1976). *Brain and Behavior.* New York: Oxford University Press.

Browne, A., Miller, B., & Maguin, E. (1999). Prevalence and severity of lifetime physical and sexual victimization among incarcerated women. *International Journal of Law and Psychiatry, 22*(3-4), 301-322.

Brummett, B. H., Siegler, I. C., McQuoid, D. R., Svenson, I. K., Marchuk, D. A., & Steffens, D. C. (2003). Associations among the NEO personality inventory, revised and the serotonin transporter gene-linked polymorphic region in elders: Effects of depression and gender. *Psychiatric Genetics, 13*(1), 13-18.

Brunner, H. G., Nelen, M., Breakefield, X. O., Ropers, H. H., & van Oost, B. A. (1993). Abnormal behavior associated with a point mutation in the structural gene for monoamine oxidase A. *Science, 262*(5133), 578-580.

Buckholtz, J. W., & Meyer-Lindenberg, A. (2008). MAOA and the neurogenetic architecture of human aggression. *Trends in Neurosciences, 31*, 120-129.

Cadoret, R. J., Langbehn, D., Caspers, K., Troughton, E. P., Yucuis, R., Sandhu, H. K.,...Philibert, R. (2003). Associations of the serotonin transporter promoter polymorphism with aggressivity, attention deficit, and conduct disorder in an adoptee population. *Comprehensive Psychiatry, 44*(2), 88-101.

Cahill, L. (2006). Why sex matters for neuroscience. *Nature Reviews Neuroscience, 7*(6), 477-485.

Caldji, C., Francis, D., Sharma, S., Plotsky, P. M., & Meaney, M. J. (2000). The effects of early rearing environment on the development of the GABA$_A$ and central benzodiazepine receptor levels and novelty-induced fearfulness in the rat. *Neuropsychopharmacology, 22*, 219-229.

Canli, T., & Lesch, K. P. (2007). Long story short: The serotonin transporter in emotion regulation and social cognition. *Nature Neuroscience, 10*(9), 1103-1109.

Carlson, B.E., McNutt, L.A., Choi, D.Y., & Rose, I.M. (2002). Intimate partner violence and mental health: The role of social support and other protective factors. *Violence Against Women, 8*, 720-745.

Carrel, L., & Willard, H. F. (2005). X-inactivation profile reveals extensive variability in X-linked gene expression in females. *Nature, 434*, 400-404.

Cases, O., Seif, I., Grimsby, J., Gaspar, P., Chen, K., Pournin, S.,...De Maeyer, E. (1995). Aggressive behavior and altered amounts of brain serotonin and norepinephrine in mice lacking MAOA. *Science, 268*(5218), 1763-1766.

Caspi, A., & Herbener, E. S. (1990). Continuity and change: Assortative marriage and the consistency of personality in adulthood. *Journal of Personality and Social Psychology, 58*(2), 250-258.

Caspi, A., McClay, J., Moffitt, T. E., Mill, J., Martin, J., Craig, I. W.,…Poulton, R. (2002). Role of genotype in the cycle of violence in maltreated children. *Science, 297*(5582), 851-854.

Caspi, A., Sugden, K., Moffitt, T. E., Taylor, A., Craig, I. W., Harrington, H. L.,…Poulton, R. (2003). Influence of life stress on depression: Moderation by a polymorphism in the 5-HTT gene. *Science, 301*(5631), 386-389.

Caspi, A., Hariri, A. R., Holmes, A., Uher, R., & Moffitt, T. E. (2010). Genetic sensitivity to the environment: The case of the serotonin transporter gene and its implications for studying complex diseases and traits. *American Journal of Psychiatry, 167*, 509-527.

Castellanos, F. X., Elia, J., Kruesi, M. J., Gulotta, C. S., Mefford, I. N., Potter, W. Z.,…Rapoport, J. L. (1994). Cerebrospinal fluid monoamine metabolites in boys with attention-deficit hyperactivity disorder. *Psychiatry Research, 52*(3), 305-316.

Castellanos, F. X., Lau, E., Tayebi, N., Lee, P., Long, R. E., Giedd, J. N.,…Sidransky, E. (1998). Lack of an association between a dopamine-4 receptor polymorphism and attention-deficit/hyperactivity disorder: Genetic and brain morphometric analyses. *Molecular Psychiatry, 3*(5), 431-434.

Catena, M., Amedei, S.G., Faravelli, L., Rotella, F., Scarpato, A., Palla, A.,…Faravelli, C. (2007). Stress related disorders: Hypothalamic-pituitary-adrenal axis dysfunctions. *European Psychiatry, 22*, S269.

Cervilla, J. A., Molina, E., Rivera, M., Torres-Gonzalez, F., Bellon, J. A., Moreno, B.,…Gutiérrez, B. (2007). The risk for depression conferred by stressful life events is modified by variation at the serotonin transporter 5HTTLPR genotype: Evidence from the spanish PREDICT-gene cohort. *Molecular Psychiatry, 12*, 748-755.

Champagne, F. A., Weaver, I. C. G., Diorio, J., Dymov, S., Szyf, M., & Meaney, M. J. (2006). Maternal care associated with methylation of the estrogen receptor-α1b promoter and estrogen receptor-α expression in the medial preoptic area of female offspring. *Endocrinology, 147,* 2909-2915.

Champagne, F.A., & Curley, J.P. (2009). Epigenetic mechanisms mediating the long-term effects of maternal care on development. *Neuroscience and Biobehavioral Reviews, 33,* 593-600.

Chang, F. M., Kidd, J. R., Livak, K. J., Pakstis, A. J., & Kidd, K. K. (1996). The world-wide distribution of allele frequencies at the human dopamine D4 receptor locus. *Human Genetics, 98*(1), 91-101.

Chantala, K., & Tabor, J. (1999). Strategies to perform a design-based analysis using the Add Health data. University of North Carolina at Chapel Hill: Carolina Population Center.

Chantala, K., Kalsbeek, W. D., & Andraca, E. (2004). *Non-response in wave III of the add health study.* University of North Carolina at Chapel Hill: Carolina Population Center.

Chantala, K. (2006). *Guidelines for analyzing Add Health data.* Chapel Hill: Carolina Population Center, University of North Carolina.

Chen, T. J. H., Blum, K., Mathews, D., Fisher, L., Schnautz, N., Braverman, E. R.,…Comings, D. E. (2005). Are dopaminergic genes involved in a predisposition to pathological aggression? hypothesizing the importance of "super normal controls" in psychiatricgenetic research of complex behavioral disorders. *Medical Hypotheses, 65*(4), 703-707.

Chen, T. J. H., Blum, K., Mathews, D., Fisher, L., Schnautz, N., Braverman, E. R.,…Comings, D. E. (2007). Preliminary association of both the dopamine D2 receptor (DRD2)[Taq1 A1 allele] and the dopamine transporter (DAT1)[480 bp allele] genes with pathological aggressive behavior, a clinical subtype of reward deficiency syndrome (RDS) in adolescents. *Gene Ther Mol Biol, 11,* 93-112.

Cheon, K. A., Ryu, Y. H., Kim, J. W., & Cho, D. Y. (2005). The homozygosity for 10-repeat allele at dopamine transporter gene and dopamine transporter density in korean children with attention deficit hyperactivity disorder: Relating to treatment response to methylphenidate. *European Neuropsychopharmacology, 15*(1), 95-101.

Chesney-Lind, M. (1986). " Women and crime": The female offender. *Signs: Journal of Women in Culture and Society, 12*(1), 78-96.

Chesney-Lind, M., & Pasko, L. (2002). *The female offender: Girls, women, and crime.* Thousand Oaks: Sage Periodicals.

Chesney-Lind, M., & Shelden, R. G. (1998). *Girls, delinquency, and juvenile justice.* Belmont, CA: Wadsworth Publishing.

Cicchetti, D., Rogosch, F. A., & Sturge-Apple, M. L. (2007). Interactions of child maltreatment and serotonin transporter and monoamine oxidase A polymorphisms: Depressive symptomatology among adolescents from low socioeconomic status backgrounds. *Development and Psychopathology, 19*(04), 1161-1180.

Cicchetti, D., & Rogosch, F.A. (2001). Diverse patterns of neuroendocrine activity in maltreated children. *Development and Psychopathology, 13,* 677-693.

Cicchetti, D., Rogosch, F.A., Lynch, M., & Holt, K.D. (1993). Resilience in maltreated children: Processes leading to adaptive outcome. *Development and Psychopathology, 5,* 629-647.

Clarke, R. A., Murphy, D. L., & Constantino, J. N. (1999). Serotonin and externalizing behavior in young children. *Psychiatry Research, 86*(1), 29-40.

Clodfelter, K. H., Holloway, M. G., Hodor, P., Park, S. H., Ray, W. J., & Waxman, D. J. (2006). Sex-dependent liver gene expression is extensive and largely dependent upon signal transducer and activator of transcription 5b (STAT5b): STAT5b-dependent activation of male genes and repression of female genes revealed by microarray analysis. *Molecular Endocrinology, 20*(6), 1333-1351.

Clogg, C. C., Petkova, E., & Haritou, A. (1995). Statistical methods for comparing regression coefficients between models. *American Journal of Sociology, 100*(5), 1261-1293.

Coccaro, E. F., Berman, M. E., Kavoussi, R. J., & Hauger, R. L. (1996). Relationship of prolactin response to d-fenfluramine to behavioral and questionnaire assessments of aggression in personality-disordered men. *Biological Psychiatry, 40*(3), 157-164.

Coccaro, E. F., Kavoussi, R. J., Trestman, R. L., Gabriel, S. M., Cooper, T. B., & Siever, L. J. (1997). Serotonin function in human subjects: Intercorrelations among central 5-HT indices and aggressiveness. *Psychiatry Research, 73*(1-2), 1-14.

Coker, A. L., Davis, K. E., Arias, I., Desai, S., Sanderson, M., Brandt, H. M.,...Smith, P. H. (2002). Physical and mental health effects of intimate partner violence for men and women. *American Journal of Preventive Medicine, 23*(4), 260-268.

Comings, D. E., Gade-Andavolu, R., Gonzalez, N., Wu, S., Muhleman, D., Blake, H.,..., MacMurray, J. P. (2000a). Multivariate analysis of associations of 42 genes in ADHD, ODD and conduct disorder. *Clin Genet, 58*(1), 31-40.

Comings, D. E., Gade-Andavolu, R., Gonzalez, N., Wu, S., Muhleman, D., Blake, H., et al. (2000b). Comparison of the role of dopamine, serotonin, and noradrenaline genes in ADHD, ODD and conduct disorder: Multivariate regression analysis of 20 genes. *Clin Genet, 57*(3), 178-196.

Comings, D. E., Gade-Andavolu, R., Gonzalez, N., Wu, S., Muhleman, D., Chen, C.,...Rosenthal, R. J. (2001). The additive effect of neurotransmitter genes in pathological gambling. *Clin Genet, 60*(2), 107-116.

Conne, B., Stutz, A., & Vassalli, J. D. (2000). The 3'untranslated region of messenger RNA: A molecular 'hotspot' for pathology? *Nature Medicine, 6*, 637-641.

Connor, J. P., Young, R. M. D., Lawford, B. R., Ritchie, T. L., & Noble, E. P. (2002). D2 dopamine receptor (DRD2) polymorphism is associated with severity of alcohol dependence. *European Psychiatry, 17*(1), 17-23.

Contini, V., Marques, F. Z., Garcia, C. E., Hutz, M. H., & Bau, C. H. (2006). MAOA-uVNTR polymorphism in a Brazilian sample: Further support for the association with impulsive behaviors and alcohol dependence. *American Journal of Medical Genetics Part B, 141*(3), 305-308.

Cook, C. C., & Gurling, H. M. (1994). The D2 dopamine receptor gene and alcoholism: A genetic effect in the liability for alcoholism. *Journal of the Royal Society of Medicine, 87*(7), 400-402.

Couper, M. P., Singer, E., & Tourangeau, R. (2003). Understanding the effects of audio-CASI on self-reports of sensitive behavior. *Public Opinion Quarterly, 67*(3), 385-395.

Cowie, J., Cowie, V. A., & Slater, E. (1968). *Delinquency in girls.* Heinemann.

Cullerton-Sen, C., Cassidy, A.R., Murray-Close, D., Cicchetti, D., Crick, N.R., & Rogosch, F.A. (2008). Childhood maltreatment and the development of relational and physical aggression: The importance of a gender-informed approach. *Child Development, 79(6)*, 1736-1751.

Dagher, A., & Robbins, T. W. (2009). Personality, addiction, dopamine: Insights from Parkinson's disease. *Neuron, 61*, 502-510.

Daly, K. (1994). *Gender, Crime and Punishment.* New Haven: Yale University Press.

David, S. P., Murthy, N. V., Rabiner, E. A., Munafo, M. R., Johnstone, E. C., Jacob, R.,...Grasby, P. M. (2005). A functional genetic variation of the serotonin (5-HT) transporter affects 5-HT1A receptor binding in humans. *Journal of Neuroscience, 25*(10), 2586-2590.

de Almeida, R. M. M., Ferrari, P. F., Parmigiani, S., & Miczek, K. A. (2005). Escalated aggressive behavior: Dopamine, serotonin, and GABA. *European Journal of Pharmacology, 526*, 51-64.

DeBellis, M. D., & Keshavan, M. S. (2003). Sex differences in brain maturation in maltreatment-related pediatric posttraumatic stress disorder. *Neuroscience and Biobehavioral Reviews, 27*, 103-117.

Deckert, J. (1999). Excess of high activity monoamine oxidase A gene promoter alleles in female patients with panic disorder. *Human Molecular Genetics, 8*(4), 621-624.

DeHart, D. D. (2004). *Pathways to prison impact of victimization in the lives of incarcerated women.* The Center for Child & Family Studies, College of Social Work, University of South Carolina.

Delongchamp, R. R., Velasco, C., Dial, S., & Harris, A. J. (2005). Genome-wide estimation of gender differences in the gene expression of human livers: Statistical design and analysis. *BMC Bioinformatics, 6*, S13-S22.

Dembo, R., Williams, L., La Voie, L., Berry, E., Getreu, A., Wish, E. D.,...Washburn, M. (1989). Physical abuse, sexual victimization, and illicit drug use: Replication of a structural analysis among a new sample of high-risk youths. *Violence and Victims, 4*(2), 121-138.

Dembo, R., Williams, L., La Voie, L., Berry, E., Getreu, A., Kern, J.,...Mayo, J. (1990). Physical abuse, sexual victimization and marijuana/hashish and cocaine use over time: A structural analysis among a cohort of high risk youths. *Journal of Prison & Jail Health, 9*, 13-43.

Deroche, V., Marinelli, M., Maccari, S., Le Moal, M., Simon, H., & Piazza, P. V. (1995). Stress-induced sensitization and glucocorticoids. I. Sensitization of dopamine-dependent locomotor effects of amphetamine and morphine depends on stress-induced corticosterone secretion. *The Journal of Neuroscience, 15*, 7181-7188.

Desbonnet, L., Garrett, L., Daly, E., McDermott, K. W., & Dinan, T. G. (2008). Sexually dimorphic effects of maternal separation stress on corticotrophin-releasing factor and vasopressin systems in the adult rat brain. *International Journal of Developmental Neuroscience, 26*, 259-268.

Dewing, P., Shi, T., Horvath, S., & Vilain, E. (2003). Sexually dimorphic gene expression in mouse brain precedes gonadal differentiation. *Molecular Brain Research, 118*(1-2), 82-90.

Dmitrieva, J., Chen, C., Greenberger, E., Ogunseitan, O., & Ding, Y. (2010). Gender-specific expression of the DRD4 gene on adolescent delinquency, anger, and thrill seeking. *Social Cognitive & Affective Neuroscience* (forthcoming).

Dodge, K. A., Pettit, G. S., Bates, J. E., & Valente, E. (1995). Social information-processing patterns partially mediate the effect of early physical abuse on later conduct problems. *Journal of Abnormal Psychology, 104,* 632-643.

Dolan, M., Anderson, I. M., & Deakin, J. F. W. (2001). Relationship between 5-HT function and impulsivity and aggression in male offenders with personality disorders. *The British Journal of Psychiatry, 178*(4), 352-359.

Don, R. H., Cox, P. T., Wainwright, B. J., Baker, K., & Mattick, J. S. (1991). 'Touchdown'PCR to circumvent spurious priming during gene amplification. *Nucleic Acids Research, 19*(14), 4008-4008.

Du, L., Bakish, D., & Hrdina, P. D. (2000). Gender differences in association between serotonin transporter gene polymorphism and personality traits. *Psychiatric Genetics, 10*(4), 159-164.

Dube, S. R., Williamson, D. F., Thompson, T., Felitti, V. J., & Anda, R. F. (2004). Assessing the reliability of retrospective reports of adverse childhood experiences among adult HMO members attending a primary care clinic. *Child Abuse & Neglect, 28*(7), 729-737.

Ducci, F., Enoch, M. A., Hodgkinson, C., Xu, K., Catena, M., Robin, R. W.,...Goldman, D. (2008). Interaction between a functional MAOA locus and childhood sexual abuse predicts alcoholism and antisocial personality disorder in adult women. *Molecular Psychiatry, 13,* 334-347.

Durrett, C., Trull, T. J., & Silk, K. (2004). Retrospective measures of childhood abuse: Concurrent validity and reliability in a nonclinical sample with borderline features. *Journal of Personality Disorders, 18*(2), 178-192.

Eaton, D. K., Davis, K. S., Barrios, L., Brener, N. D., & Noonan, R. K. (2007). Associations of dating violence victimization with lifetime participation, co-occurrence, and early initiation of risk behaviors among US high school students. *Journal of Interpersonal Violence, 22*(5), 585-602.

Ehlert, U., Gaab, J., & Heinrichs, M. (2001). Psychoneuroendocrinological contributions to the etiology of depression, posttraumatic stress disorder, and stress related bodily disorders: The role of the hypothalamus-pituitary-adrenal axis. *Biological Psychology, 57,* 141-152.

Eisenberg, J., Zohar, A., Mei-Tal, G., Steinberg, A., Tartakovsky, E., Gritsenko, I.,...Ebstein, R. P. (2000). A haplotype relative risk study of the dopamine D4 receptor (DRD4) exon III repeat polymorphism and attention deficit hyperactivity disorder (ADHD). *Am J Med Genet (Neuropsychiatr Genet), 96,* 258-261.

Eley, T. C., Sugden, K., Corsico, A., Gregory, A. M., Sham, P., McGuffin, P.,...Craig, I. W. (2004). Gene-environment interaction analysis of serotonin system markers with adolescent depression. *Molecular Psychiatry, 9,* 908-915.

El-Faddagh, M., Laucht, M., Maras, A., Vöhringer, L., & Schmidt, M. H. (2004). Association of dopamine D4 receptor (DRD4) gene with attention-deficit/hyperactivity disorder (ADHD) in a high-risk community sample: A longitudinal study from birth to 11 years of age. *Journal of Neural Transmission, 111*(7), 883-889.

Ellis, L. (1991). Monoamine oxidase and criminality: Identifying an apparent biological marker for antisocial behavior. *Journal of Research in Crime and Delinquency, 28*(2), 227-251.

Elovainio, M., Jokela, M., Kivimaki, M., Pulkki-Raback, L., Lehtimaki, T., Airla, N.,...Keltikangas-Järvinen, L. (2007). Genetic variants in the DRD2 gene moderate the relationship between stressful life events and depressive symptoms in adults: Cardiovascular risk in young finns study. *Psychosomatic Medicine, 69*(5), 391-395.

English, D. J., Widom, C. S., & Brandford, C. (2002). *Childhood victimization and delinquency, adult criminality, and violent criminal behavior: A replication and extension: Final report.* Washington, DC: National Institute of Justice.

Fabre, V., Beaufour, C., Evrard, A., Rioux, A., Hanoun, N., Lesch, K. P.,...Martres, M. P. (2000). Altered expression and functions of serotonin 5-HT1A and 5-HT1B receptors in knock-out mice lacking the 5-HT transporter. *European Journal of Neuroscience, 12*(7), 2299-2310.

Fagan, J., Piper, E. S., & Cheng, Y. T. (1987). Contributions of victimization to delinquency in inner cities. *Journal of Criminal Law and Criminology, 78,* 586-613.

Falzone, T. L., Gelman, D. M., Young, J. I., Grandy, D. K., Low, M. J., & Rubinstein, M. (2002). Absence of dopamine D4 receptors results in enhanced reactivity to unconditioned, but not conditioned fear. *European Journal of Neuroscience, 15*, 158-164.

Faraone, S. V., Doyle, A. E., Mick, E., & Biederman, J. (2001). Meta-analysis of the association between the 7-repeat allele of the dopamine D4 receptor gene and attention deficit hyperactivity disorder. *American Journal of Psychiatry, 158*(7), 1052-1057.

Farrell, G., & Pease, K. (1993). *Once bitten, twice bitten: Repeat victimisation and its implications for crime prevention.* Home Office Police Research Group Unit Paper 46. London: Home Office.

Farrington, D. P. (1986). Age and crime. In M. Tonry (Ed.), *Crime and justice: A review of the research* (pp. 189-250). Chicago: University of Chicago Press.

Femina, D. D., Yeager, C. A., & Lewis, D. O. (1990). Child abuse: Adolescent records vs. adult recall. *Child Abuse & Neglect, 14*(2), 227-231.

Fergusson, D. M., Horwood, L. J., & Woodward, L. J. (2000). The stability of child abuse reports: A longitudinal study of the reporting behaviour of young adults. *Psychological Medicine, 30*(3), 529-544.

Ferrari, P. F., van Erp, A. M. M., Tornatzky, W., & Miczek, K. A. (2003). Accumbal dopamine and serotonin in anticipation of the next aggressive episode in rats. *European Journal of Neuroscience, 17*(2), 371-378.

Fink, G., Sumner, B., Rosie, R., Wilson, H., & McQueen, J. (1999). Androgen actions on central serotonin neurotransmission: Relevance for mood, mental state and memory. *Behavioural Brain Research, 105*(1), 53-68.

Fischette, C. T., Biegon, A., & McEwen, B. S. (1983). Sex differences in serotonin 1 receptor binding in rat brain. *Science, 222*(4621), 333-335.

Fishbein, D. H. (1990). Biological perspectives in criminology. *Criminology, 28*(1), 27-72.

Fishbein, D. H., Lozovsky, D., & Jaffe, J. H. (1989). Impulsivity, aggression, and neuroendocrine responses to serotonergic stimulation in substance abusers. *Biological Psychiatry, 25*(8), 1049-1066.

Fitzgerald, R. (2003). *An examination of sex differences in delinquency.* Statistics Canada, Canadian Centre for Justice Statistics.

Flory, J. D., Manuck, S. B., Ferrell, R. E., Dent, K. M., Peters, D. G., & Muldoon, M. F. (1999). Neuroticism is not associated with the serotonin transporter (5-HTTLPR) polymorphism. *Molecular Psychiatry, 4*(1), 93-96.

Foley, D. L., Eaves, L. J., Wormley, B., Silberg, J. L., Maes, H. H., Kuhn, J.,...Riley, B. (2004). Childhood adversity, monoamine oxidase A genotype, and risk for conduct disorder. *Archives of General Psychiatry, 61*(7), 738-744.

Franke, P., Schwab, S. G., Knapp, M., Gänsicke, M., Delmo, C., Zill, P.,...Maier, W. (1999). DAT1 gene polymorphism in alcoholism: A family-based association study. *Biological Psychiatry, 45*(5), 652-654.

Franke, P., Wang, T., Mothen, M. M., Knapp, M., Neith, H., Lichtermann, D.,...Maier, W. (2000). Susceptibility for alcoholism: DRD4 exon III polymorphism: A case-control and a family-based association approach. *Addiction Biology, 5*(3), 289-295.

Frisch, A., Postilnick, D., Rockah, R., Michaelovsky, E., Postilnick, S., Birman, E.,...Weizman, R. (1999). Association of unipolar major depressive disorder with genes of the serotonergic and dopaminergic pathways. *Molecular Psychiatry, 4*(4), 389-392.

Fuke, S., Suo, S., Takahashi, N., Koike, H., Sasagawa, N., & Ishiura, S. (2001). The VNTR polymorphism of the human dopamine transporter (DAT1) gene affects gene expression. *The Pharmacogenomics Journal, 1*, 152-156.

Fuster, J. M. (2001). The prefrontal cortex—An update: Time is of the essence. *Neuron, 30*, 319-333.

Gabel, S., Stadler, J., Bjorn, J., Shindledecker, R., & Bowden, C. L. (1993). Biodevelopmental aspects of conduct disorder in boys. *Child Psychiatry and Human Development, 24*(2), 125-141.

Garriock, H. A., Delgado, P., Kling, M. A., Carpenter, L. L., Burke, M., Burke, W. J.,...Moreno, F. A. (2006). Number of risk genotypes is a risk factor for major depressive disorder: A case control study. *Behavioral and Brain Functions, 2*, 24-32.

Gelernter, J., Kranzler, H., Coccaro, E. F., Siever, L. J., & New, A. S. (1998). Serotonin transporter protein gene polymorphism and personality measures in African American and European American subjects. *American Journal of Psychiatry, 155*(10), 1332-1338.

Gelernter, J., Kranzler, H., Cubells, J. F., Ichinose, H., & Nagatsu, T. (1998). DRD2 allele frequencies and linkage disequilibria, including the-141CIns/DelPromoter polymorphism, in European-American, African-American, and Japanese subjects. *Genomics, 51*(1), 21-26.

Gelernter, J., Cubells, J. F., Kidd, J. R., Pakstis, A. J., & Kidd, K. K. (1999). Population studies of polymorphisms of the serotonin transporter protein gene. *Am J Med Genet (Neuropsychiatr Genet), 88*, 61-66.

Genest, S., Gulemetova, R., Laforest, S., Drolet, G., & Kinkead, R. (2004). Neonatal maternal separation and sex-specific plasticity of the hypoxic ventilator response in awake rat. *Journal of Physiology, 554*, 543-557.

Gerra, G., Garofano, L., Pellegrini, C., Bosari, S., Zaimovic, A., Moi, G.,...Donnini, C. (2005). Allelic association of a dopamine transporter gene polymorphism with antisocial behaviour in heroin-dependent patients. *Addiction Biology, 10*(3), 275-281.

Ghanem, K. G., Hutton, H. E., Zenilman, J. M., Zimba, R., & Erbelding, E. J. (2005). Audio computer assisted self interview and face to face interview modes in assessing response bias among STD clinic patients. *Sexually Transmitted Infections, 81*(5), 421-425.

Gilfus, M. E. (1992). From victims to survivors to offenders: Women's routes of entry and immersion into street crime. *Women and Criminal Justice, 4*(1), 63-89.

Gill, M., Daly, G., Heron, S., Hawi, Z., & Fitzgerald, M. (1997). Confirmation of association between attention deficit hyperactivity disorder and a dopamine transporter polymorphism. *Molecular Psychiatry, 2*, 311-313.

Giordano, P., Deines, J. A., & Cernkovich, S. A. (2006). In and out of crime: A life course perspective on girls' delinquency. In K. Heimer and C. Kruttschnitt (Ed.), *In gender and crime: Patterns of victimization and offending* (pp. 17-40). New York: New York University Press.

Giros, B., Jaber, M., Jones, S. R., Wightman, R. M., & Caron, M. G. (1996). Hyperlocomotion and indifference to cocaine and amphetamine in mice lacking the dopamine transporter. *Nature, 379*(6566), 606-612.

Giros, B., & Caron, M. G. (1993). Molecular characterization of the dopamine transporter. *Trends in Pharmacological Sciences, 14*(2), 43-49.

Goldstein, A. L., Flett, G. L., & Wekerle, C. (2010). Child maltreatment, alcohol use and drinking consequences among male and female college students: An examination of drinking motives as mediators. *Addictive Behaviors, 35*, 636-639.

Gonda, X., Juhasz, G., Laszik, A., Rihmer, Z., & Bagdy, G. (2005). Subthreshold depression is linked to the functional polymorphism of the 5HT transporter gene. *Journal of Affective Disorders, 87*(2-3), 291-297.

Gorwood, P., Limosin, F., Batel, P., Hamon, M., Ades, J., & Boni, C. (2003). The A9 allele of the dopamine transporter gene is associated with delirium tremens and alcohol-withdrawal seizure. *Biological Psychiatry, 53*(1), 85-92.

Grabe, H. J., Lange, M., Wolff, B., Völzke, H., Lucht, M., Freyberger, H. J.,...Cascorbi, I. (2005). Mental and physical distress is modulated by a polymorphism in the 5-HT transporter gene interacting with social stressors and chronic disease burden. *Molecular Psychiatry, 10*, 220-224.

Grandy, D. K., Litt, M., Allen, L., Bunzow, J. R., Marchionni, M., Makam, H.,...Civelli, O. (1989). The human dopamine D2 receptor gene is located on chromosome 11 at q22-q23 and identifies a TaqI RFLP. *American Journal of Human Genetics, 45*(5), 778-785.

Grayson, C. E., & Nolen-Hoeksema, S. (2005). Motives to drink as mediators between childhood sexual assault and alcohol problems in adult women. *Journal of Traumatic Stress, 18*, 137-145.

Grove, W. M., Eckert, E. D., Heston, L., Bouchard, T. J., Segal, N., & Lykken, D. T. (1990). Heritability of substance abuse and antisocial behavior: A study of monozygotic twins reared apart. *Biol Psychiatry, 27*(12), 1293-1304.

Gundlah, C., Lu, N. Z., & Bethea, C. L. (2002). Ovarian steroid regulation of monoamine oxidase-A and B mRNAs in the macaque dorsal raphe and hypothalamic nuclei. *Psychopharmacology, 160*(3), 271-282.

Guo, G., Roettger, M. E., & Shih, J. C. (2007a). Contributions of the DAT1 and DRD2 genes to serious and violent delinquency among adolescents and young adults. *Human Genetics, 121*(1), 125-136.

Guo, G., Wilhelmsen, K., & Hamilton, N. (2007b). Gene-lifecourse interaction for alcohol consumption in adolescence and young adulthood: Five monoamine genes. *American Journal of Medical Genetics.Part B, Neuropsychiatric Genetics, 144*(4), 417-423.

Gur, R., Gunning-Dixon, F., Bilker, W.B., & Gur, R.E. (2002). Sex differences in temporo-limbic and frontal brain volumes on healthy adults. *Cerebral Cortex, 12*, 998-1047.

Haberstick, B. C., & Smolen, A. (2004). Genotyping of three single nucleotide polymorphisms following whole genome preamplification of DNA collected from buccal cells. *Behavior Genetics, 34*(5), 541-547.

Haberstick, B. C., Lessem, J. M., Hopfer, C. J., Smolen, A., Ehringer, M. A., Timberlake, D.,...Hewitt, J. K. (2005). Monoamine oxidase A(MAOA) and antisocial behaviors in the presence of childhood and adolescent maltreatment. *American Journal of Medical Genetics Part B Neuropsychiatric Genetics, 135*(1), 59-64.

Haberstick, B. C., Smolen, A., & Hewitt, J. K. (2006). Family-based association test of the 5HTTLPR and aggressive behavior in a general population sample of children. *Biological Psychiatry, 59*(9), 836-843.

Haddley, K., Vasiliou, A. S., Ali, F. R., Paredes, U. M., Bubb, V. J., & Quinn, J. P. (2008). Molecular genetics of monoamine transporters: Relevance to brain disorders. *Neurochemical Research, 33*(4), 652-667.

Hallikainen, T., Hietala, J., Kauhanen, J., Pohjalainen, T., Syvalahti, E., Salonen, J. T.,…Tihonen, J. (2003). Ethanol consumption and DRD2 gene TaqI a polymorphism among socially drinking males. *American Journal of Medical Genetics Part A, 119*(2), 152-155.

Halperin, J. M., Sharma, V., Siever, L. J., Schwartz, S. T., Matier, K., Wornell, G.,…Newcorn, J. H. (1994). Serotonergic function in aggressive and nonaggressive boys with attention deficit hyperactivity disorder. *American Journal of Psychiatry, 151*(2), 243-248.

Ham, B. J., Lee, Y. M., Kim, M. K., Lee, J., Ahn, D. S., Choi, M. J.,…Lee, M. S. (2006). Personality, dopamine receptor D4 exon III polymorphisms, and academic achievement in medical students. *Neuropsychobiology, 53*(4), 203-209.

Hammen, C., Ellicott, A., Gitlin, M., & Jamison, K. R. (1989). Sociotropy/autonomy and vulnerability to specific life events in patients with unipolar depression and bipolar disorders. *Journal of Abnormal Psychology, 98*(2), 154-160.

Haney, M., Noda, K., Kream, R., & Miczek, K. A. (1990). Regional serotonin and dopamine activity: Sensitivity to amphetamine and aggressive behavior in mice. *Aggress Behav, 16*, 259-270.

Hanna, G. L., Yuwiler, A., & Coates, J. K. (1995). Whole blood serotonin and disruptive behaviors in juvenile obsessive-compulsive disorder. *Journal of the American Academy of Child & Adolescent Psychiatry, 34*(1), 28-35.

Hardt, J., & Rutter, M. (2004). Validity of adult retrospective reports of adverse childhood experiences: Review of the evidence. *Journal of Child Psychology and Psychiatry, 45*(2), 260-273.

Hardt, J., Sidor, A., Bracko, M., & Egle, U. T. (2006). Reliability of retrospective assessments of childhood experiences in Germany. *The Journal of Nervous and Mental Disease, 194*(9), 676-683.

Harris, K. M., Florey, F., Tabor, J., Bearman, P. S., Jones, J., & Udry, J. R. (2003). The National Longitudinal Study of Adolescent Health: Research design [www document] *URL: Http://www.Cpc.Unc.edu/projects/addhealth/design.,*

Heils, A., Teufel, A., Petri, S., Stober, G., Riederer, P., Bengel, D.,...Lesch, K. P. (1996). Allelic variation of human serotonin transporter gene expression. *Journal of Neurochemistry, 66*(6), 2621-2624.

Heinz, A., Goldman, D., Jones, D. W., Palmour, R., Hommer, D., Gorey, J. G.,...Weinberger, D. R. (2000). Genotype influences in vivo dopamine transporter availability in human striatum. *Neuropsychopharmacology, 22*(2), 133-139.

Herman, A. I., Philbeck, J. W., Vasilopoulos, N. L., & Depetrillo, P. B. (2003). Serotonin transporter promoter polymorphism and differences in alcohol consumption behavior in a college student population. *Alcohol and Alcoholism, 38*(5), 446-449.

Hill, S. Y., Zezza, N., Wipprecht, G., Locke, J., & Neiswanger, K. (1999). Personality traits and dopamine receptors (D2 and D4): Linkage studies in families of alcoholics. *Am J Med Genet Neuropsychiatr Genet, 88,* 634-641.

Hindelang, M. J., Gottfredson, M. R., & Garofalo, J. (1978). *Victims of personal crime: An empirical foundation for a theory of personal victimization.* Thousand Oaks: Sage.

Hines, D. A., & Saudino, K. J. (2004). Genetic and environmental influences on intimate partner aggression: A preliminary study. *Violence and Victims, 19*(6), 701-718.

Hirschi, T. (1969). *Causes of delinquency.* Berkeley: University of California Press.

Hirschi, T., & Gottfredson, M. (1983). Age and the explanation of crime. *American Journal of Sociology, 89*(3), 552-584.

Hitzemann, R. J. (1998). The regulation of D2 dopamine receptor expression. *Molecular Psychiatry, 3,* 198-203.

Hokanson, J. E., & Butler, A. C. (1992). Cluster analysis of depressed college students' social behaviors. *Journal of Personality and Social Psychology, 62*(2), 273-280.

Holmes, A., le Guisquet, A.M., Vogel, E., Millstein, R.A., Leman, S., & Belzung, C. (2005). Early life genetic, epigenetic, and environmental factors shaping emotionality in rodents. *Neuroscience and Biobehavioral Reviews, 29*, 1335-1346.

Holmes, J., Payton, A., Barrett, J. H., Hever, T., Fitzpatrick, H., Trumper, A. L.,…Thapar, A. (2000). A family-based and case-control association study of the dopamine D4 receptor gene and dopamine transporter gene in attention deficit hyperactivity disorder. *Molecular Psychiatry, 5*, 523-530.

Hong, H.J., Shin, D.W., Lee, E.H., Oh, Y.H., & Noh, K.S. (2003). Hypothalamic-pituitary-adrenal reactivity in boys with attention deficit hyperactivity disorder. *Yonsei Medical Journal, 44*, 608-614.

Hopfer, C. J., Timberlake, D., Haberstick, B., Lessem, J. M., Ehringer, M. A., Smolen, A.,…Hewitt, J. K. (2005). Genetic influences on quantity of alcohol consumed by adolescents and young adults. *Drug and Alcohol Dependence, 78*(2), 187-193.

Hrdina, P. D. (1994). Platelet serotonergic markers in psychiatric disorders: Use, abuse and limitations. *Journal of Psychiatry and Neuroscience, 19*(2), 87-90.

Hu, X., Lipsky, R. H., Zhu, G., Akhtar, L. A., Taubman, J., Greenberg, B. D.,…Goldman, D. (2006). Serotonin transporter promoter gain-of-function genotypes are linked to obsessive-compulsive disorder. *American Journal of Human Genetics, 78*, 815-826.

Hubbard, D. J., & Pratt, T. C. (2002). A meta-analysis of the predictors of delinquency among girls. *Journal of Offender Rehabilitation, 34*(3), 1-14.

Hughes, C. W., Petty, F., Sheikha, S., & Kramer, G. L. (1996). Whole-blood serotonin in children and adolescents with mood and behavior disorders. *Psychiatry Research, 65*(2), 79-95.

Huizinga, D., Haberstick, B. C., Smolen, A., Menard, S., Young, S. E., Corley, R. P.,…Hewitt, J. K. (2006). Childhood maltreatment, subsequent antisocial behavior, and the role of monoamine oxidase A genotype. *Biological Psychiatry, 60*(7), 677-683.

Hussey, J. M., Chang, J. J., & Kotch, J. B. (2006). Child maltreatment in the United States: Prevalence, risk factors, and adolescent health consequences. *Pediatrics, 118*(3), 933-942.

Hutchinson, K. E., McGeary, J., Smolen, A., Bryan, A., & Swift, R. M. (2002). The DRD4 VNTR polymorphism moderates craving after alcohol consumption. *Health Psychology, 21*(2), 139-146.

Ichise, M., Vines, D.C., Gura, T., Anderson, G.M., Suomi, S.J., Higley, J.D.,…Innis, R.B. (2006). Effects of early life stress on [^{11}C]DASB positron emission tomography imaging of serotonin transporters in adolescent peer- and mother-reared rhesus monkeys. *The Journal of Neuroscience, 26(17)*, 4638-4643.

Ilia, M., Sugiyama, Y., & Price, J. (2003). Gender and age related expression of oct-6–a POU III domain transcription factor, in the adult mouse brain. *Neuroscience Letters, 344*(2), 138-140.

Ireland, T. O., Smith, C. A., & Thornberry, T. P. (2002). Developmental issues in the impact of child maltreatment on later delinquency and drug use. *Criminology, 40*(2), 359-400.

Irvine, R. A., Yu, M. C., Ross, R. K., & Coetzee, G. A. (1995). The CAG and GGC microsatellites of the androgen receptor gene are in linkage disequilibrium in men with prostate cancer. *Cancer Research, 55*(9), 1937-1940.

Ishiguro, H., Arinami, T., Saito, T., Akazawa, S., Enomoto, M., Mitushio, H.,…Shibuya, H. (1998). Association study between the 441C Ins/Del and TaqI A polymorphisms of the dopamine D2 receptor gene and alcoholism. *Alcoholism: Clinical and Experimental Research, 22*(4), 845-848.

Iwasa, Y., & Pomiankowski, A. (2001). The evolution of X-linked genomic imprinting. *Genetics, 158*(4), 1801-1809.

Jaccard, J., & Turrisi, R. (2003). *Interaction Effects in Multiple Regression.* Thousand Oaks: Sage.

Jacobs, B. L., & Azmitia, E. C. (1992). Structure and function of the brain serotonin system. *Physiological Reviews, 72*(1), 165-229.

Jaffee, S. R., Caspi, A., Moffitt, T. E., Dodge, K. A., Rutter, M., Taylor, A.,…Tully, L. A. (2005). Nature× nurture: Genetic vulnerabilities interact with physical maltreatment to promote conduct problems. *Development and Psychopathology, 17*(01), 67-84.

Jarry, J. L., & Vaccarino, F. J. (1996). Eating disorder and obsessive-compulsive disorder: Neurochemical and phenomenological commonalities. *Journal of Psychiatry and Neuroscience, 21*(1), 36-48.

Jockin, V., McGue, M., & Lykken, D. T. (1996). Personality and divorce: A genetic analysis. *Journal of Personality and Social Psychology, 71,* 288-299.

Joffe, H., & Cohen, L. S. (1998). Estrogen, serotonin, and mood disturbance: Where is the therapeutic bridge? *Biological Psychiatry, 44*(9), 798-811.

Joiner, T. E., Jr, & Metalsky, G. I. (1995). A prospective test of an integrative interpersonal theory of depression: A naturalistic study of college roommates. *Journal of Personality and Social Psychology, 69*(4), 778-788.

Jones, G. H., Hernandez, T. D., Kendall, D. A., Marsden, C. A., & Robbins, T. W. (1992). Dopaminergic and serotonergic function following isolation rearing in rats: Study of behavioral responses and postmortem and in vivo neurochemistry. *Pharmacology Biochemistry and Behavior, 43,* 17-35.

Jönsson, E. G., Noethen, M. M., Gruenhage, F., Farde, L., Nakashima, Y., Propping, P.,...Sedvall, G. C. (1999). Polymorphisms in the dopamine D2 receptor gene and their relationships to striatal dopamine receptor density of healthy volunteers. *Molecular Psychiatry, 4*(3), 290-296.

Kang, A. M., Palmatier, M. A., & Kidd, K. K. (1999). Global variation of a 40-bp VNTR in the 3'-untranslated region of the dopamine transporter gene (SLC6A3). *Biological Psychiatry, 46*(2), 151-160.

Kapur, S., & Mann, J. J. (1992). Role of the dopaminergic system in depression. *Biological Psychiatry(1969), 32*(1), 1-17.

Katzenellenbogen, J. A., O'Malley, B. W., & Katzenellenbogen, B. S. (1996). Tripartite steroid hormone receptor pharmacology: Interaction with multiple effector sites as a basis for the cell- and promoter-specific action of these hormones. *Molecular Endocrinology, 10,* 119-131.

Kaufman, J. G., & Widom, C. S. (1999). Childhood victimization, running away, and delinquency. *Journal of Research in Crime and Delinquency, 36*(4), 347-370.

Kaufman, J., Yang, B. Z., Douglas-Palumberi, H., Houshyar, S., Lipschitz, D., Krystal, J. H.,...McEwen, B. S. (2004). Social supports and serotonin transporter gene moderate depression in maltreated children. *Proceedings of the National Academy of Sciences, 101*(49), 17316-17321.

Kaufman, J., Yang, B., Douglas-Palumberi, H., Crouse-Artus, M., Lipschitz, D., Krystal, J. H.,...Gelernter, J. (2007). Genetic and environmental predictors of early alcohol use. *Biological Psychiatry, 61,* 1228-1234.

Kendler, K. S., Kessler, R. C., & Neale, M. C. (1993). The prediction of major
     depression in women: Toward an integrated etiologic model. *American
     Journal of Psychiatry, 1*(50), 1139-1148.

Kendler, K. S., Bulik, C. M., Silberg, J., Hettema, J. M., Myers, J., & Prescott,
     C. A. (2000). Childhood sexual abuse and adult psychiatric and
     substance use disorders in women. *Archives of General Psychiatry, 57,*
     953-959.

Kendler, K. S. (2001). Twin studies of psychiatric illness an update. *Archives of
     General Psychiatry, 58*(11), 1005-1014.

Kendler, K. S., Thornton, L. M., & Prescott, C. A. (2001). Gender differences
     in the rates of exposure to stressful life events and sensitivity to their
     depressogenic effects. *American Journal of Psychiatry, 158,* 587-593.

Kendler, K. S., Kuhn, J. W., Vittum, J., Prescott, C. A., & Riley, B. (2005). The
     interaction of stressful life events and a serotonin transporter
     polymorphism in the prediction of episodes of major depression A
     replication. *Archives of General Psychiatry, 62*(5), 529-535.

Kent, L., Doerry, U., Hardy, E., Parmar, R., Gingell, K., Hawi, Z.,...Craddock,
     N. (2002). Evidence that variation at the serotonin transporter gene
     influences susceptibility to attention deficit hyperactivity disorder
     (ADHD): Analysis and pooled analysis. *Molecular Psychiatry, 7,* 908-
     912.

Kim, D. K., Tolliver, T. J., Huang, S. J., Martin, B. J., Andrews, A. M.,
     Wichems, C.,...Murphy, D. L. (2005). Altered serotonin synthesis,
     turnover and dynamic regulation in multiple brain regions of mice
     lacking the serotonin transporter. *Neuropharmacology, 49*(6), 798-810.

Kim-Cohen, J., Caspi, A., Taylor, A., Williams, B., Newcombe, R., Craig, I.
     W.,...Moffitt, T. E. (2006). MAOA, maltreatment, and gene–
     environment interaction predicting children's mental health: New
     evidence and a meta-analysis. *Molecular Psychiatry, 11,* 903-913.

Kingree, J. B., Phan, D., & Thompson, M. (2003). Child maltreatment and
     recidivism among adolescent detainees. *Criminal Justice and Behavior,
     30*(6), 623-643.

Kirley, A., Lowe, N., Mullins, C., McCarron, M., Daly, G., Waldman, I., Hawi,
     Z. (2004). Phenotype studies of the DRD4 gene polymorphisms in
     ADHD: Association with oppositional defiant disorder and positive
     family history. *AMERICAN JOURNAL OF MEDICAL GENETICS PART
     B, 131,* 38-42.

Klein, T.A., Neumann, J., Reuter, M., Hennig, J., vonCramon, D.Y., & Ullsperger, M. (2007). Genetically determined differences in learning from errors. *Science, 318*, 1642-1645.

Koller, G., Bondy, B., Preuss, U. W., Bottlender, M., & Soyka, M. (2003). No association between a polymorphism in the promoter region of the MAOA gene with antisocial personality traits in alcoholics. *Alcohol and Alcoholism, 38*(1), 31-34.

Konishi, T., Calvillo, M., Leng, A. S., Lin, K. M., & Wan, Y. J. Y. (2004). Polymorphisms of the dopamine D2 receptor, serotonin transporter, and GABAA receptor β3 subunit genes and alcoholism in Mexican-Americans. *Alcohol, 32*(1), 45-52.

Kono, Y., Yoneda, H., Sakai, T., Nonomura, Y., Inayama, Y., Koh, J.,...Asaba, H. (1997). Association between early-onset alcoholism and the dopamine D2 receptor gene. *American Journal of Medical Genetics (Neuropsychiatric Genetics), 74*, 179-182.

Kreek, M. J., Nielsen, D. A., Butelman, E. R., & LaForge, K. S. (2005). Genetic influence on impulsivity, risk-taking, stress responsivity, and vulnerability to drug abuse and addiction. *Nature Neuroscience, 8*, 1450-1457.

Kruttschnitt, C., & Mac Millan, R. (2006). The violent victimization of women. A life course perspective. In K. Heimer, & C. Kruttschnitt (Eds.), *Gender and crime. patterns of victimization and offending* (pp. 139-170). New York: New York University Press.

Kunitz, S. J., Levy, J. E., McCloskey, J., & Gabriel, K. R. (1998). Alcohol dependence and domestic violence as sequelae of abuse and conduct disorder in childhood. *Child Abuse & Neglect, 22*, 1079-1091.

Kurtz, P. D., Kurtz, G. L., & Jarvis, S. V. (1991). Problems of maltreated runaway youth. *Adolescence, 26*(103), 543-555.

Kwok, P., & Gu, Z. (1999). Single nucleotide polymorphism libraries: Why and how we are building them? *Molecular Medicine Today, 5*, 538-543.

Laakso, A., Pohjalainen, T., Bergman, J., Kajander, J., Haaparanta, M., Solin, O.,...Hietala, J. (2005). The A1 allele of the human D2 dopamine receptor gene is associated with increased activity of striatal L-amino acid decarboxylase in healthy subjects. *Pharmacogenetics and Genomics, 15*(6), 387.

Landegren, U., Nilsson, M., & Kwok, P. Y. (1998). Reading bits of genetic information: Methods for single-nucleotide polymorphism analysis. *Genome Research, 8*(8), 769-776.

Lang, A. J., Stein, M. B., Kennedy, C. M., & Foy, D. W. (2004). Adult psychopathology and intimate partner violence among survivors of childhood maltreatment. *Journal of Interpersonal Violence, 19*(10), 1102-1118.

Lansford, J. E., Malone, P. S., Stevens, K. I., Dodge, K. A., Bates, J. E., & Pettit, G. S. (2006). Developmental trajectories of externalizing and internalizing behaviors: Factors underlying resilience in physically abused children. *Development and Psychopathology, 18*(01), 35-55.

Lansford, J. E., Miller-Johnson, S., Berlin, L. J., Dodge, K. A., Bates, J. E., Pettit, G. S. (2007). Early physical abuse and later violent delinquency: A prospective longitudinal study. *Childhood Maltreatment, 12*, 233-245.

Laruelle, M., Gelernter, J., & Innis, R. B. (1998). D2 receptors binding potential is not affected by Taq1 polymorphism at the D2 receptor gene. *Molecular Psychiatry, 3*, 261-265.

Lasiuk, G. C., & Hegadoren, K. M. (2007). The effects of estradiol on central serotonergic systems and its relationship to mood in women. *Biological Research for Nursing, 9*(2), 147-160.

Lauritsen, J. L., Sampson, R. J., & Laub, J. H. (1991). The link between offending and victimization among adolescents. *Criminology, 29*(2), 265-292.

Lawford, B. R., Young, R. M. D., Rowell, J. A., Gibson, J. N., Feeney, G. F. X., Ritchie, T. L.,... Noble, E. P. (1997). Association of the D2 dopamine receptor A1 allele with alcoholism: Medical severity of alcoholism and type of controls. *Biological Psychiatry, 41*(4), 386-393.

Lawson, D. C., Turic, D., Langley, K., Pay, H. M., Govan, C. F., Norton, N.,...Thapar, A. (2003). Association analysis of monoamine oxidase A and attention deficit hyperactivity disorder. *American Journal of Medical Genetics, 116*(1), 84-89.

Le Saux, M., & Di Paolo, T. (2006). Influence of oestrogenic compounds on monoamine transporters in rat striatum. *Journal of Neuroendocrinology, 18*(1), 25-32.

Lee, H. J., Lee, H. S., Kim, Y. K., Kim, S. H., Kim, L., Lee, M. S.,...Kim, S. (2003). Allelic variants interaction of dopamine receptor D4 polymorphism correlate with personality traits in young korean female population. *American Journal of Medical Genetics, 118*(1), 76-80.

Lemmon, J. H. (1999). How child maltreatment affects dimensions of juvenile delinquency in a cohort of low-income urban youths. *Justice Quarterly, 16*, 357-376.

Lenze, E. J., Munin, M. C., Ferrell, R. E., Pollock, B. G., Skidmore, E., Lotrich, F.,...Reynolds, C. F. (2005). Association of the serotonin transporter gene-linked polymorphic region (5-HTTLPR) genotype with depression in elderly persons after hip fracture. *Archives of General Psychiatry, 13*(5), 428-432.

Lesch, K. P., Bengel, D., Heils, A., Sabol, S. Z., Greenberg, B. D., Petri, S.,...Murphy, D. L. (1996). Association of anxiety-related traits with a polymorphism in the serotonin transporter gene regulatory region. *Science, 274*(5292), 1527-1531.

Leussis, M. P., & Andersen, S. L. (2008). Neuroanatomical findings from a social stress model. *Synapse, 62*, 22-30.

Lewis, R. (2001). *Human genetics: Concepts and applications* (6th ed.) New York: McGraw-Hill.

Li, D., Sham, P. C., Owen, M. J., & He, L. (2006). Meta-analysis shows significant association between dopamine system genes and attention deficit hyperactivity disorder (ADHD). *Human Molecular Genetics, 15*(14), 2276-2284.

Liao, D. L., Hong, C. J., Shih, H. L., & Tsai, S. J. (2004). Possible association between serotonin transporter promoter region polymorphism and extremely violent crime in chinese males. *Neuropsychobiology, 50*(4), 284-287.

Lichter, J. B., Barr, C. L., Kennedy, J. L., Van Tol, H. H. M., Kidd, K. K., & Livak, K. J. (1993). A hypervariable segment in the human dopamine receptor D4 (DRD4) gene. *Human Molecular Genetics, 2*(6), 767-773.

Linnoila, M., Virkkunen, M., Scheinin, M., Nuutila, A., Rimon, R., & Goodwin, F. K. (1983). Low cerebrospinal fluid 5-hydroxyindoleacetic acid concentration differentiates impulsive from nonimpulsive violent behavior. *Life Sciences, 33*(26), 2609-2614.

Liu, D., Diorio, J., Tannenbaum, B., Caldji, C., Francis, D., Freedman, A.,...Meaney, M. J. (1997). Maternal care, hippocampal glucocorticoid receptors, and hypothalamic-pituitary-adrenal responses to stress. *Science, 5332*, 1659-1662.

Llorente, R., Llorente-Berzal, A., Petrosino, S., Marco, E., Guaza, C., Prada, C.,...Viveros, M. (2008). Gender-dependent cellular and biochemical effects of maternal deprivation on the hippocampus of neonatal rats: A possible role for the endocannabinoid system. *Developmental Neurobiology, 68*, 1334-1347.

Lombroso, C., & Ferrero, G. (2004). *Criminal woman, the prostitute, and the normal woman* (N. H. Rafter, M. Gibson Trans.). Durham, NC: Duke University Press.

López León, S., Croes, E. A., Sayed-Tabatabaei, F. A., Claes, S., Broeckhoven, C. V., & van Duijn, C. M. (2005). The dopamine D4 receptor gene 48-base-pair-repeat polymorphism and mood disorders: A meta-analysis. *Biological Psychiatry, 57*(9), 999-1003.

López-León, S., Janssens, A. C., González-Zuloeta Ladd, A. M., Del-Favero, J., Claes, S. J., Oostra, B. A.,...van Duijn, C. M. (2007). Meta-analyses of genetic studies on major depressive disorder. *Molecular Psychiatry, 13*(8), 772-785.

Louilot, A., Le Moal, M., & Simon, H. (1986). Differential reactivity of dopaminergic neurons in the nucleus accumbens in response to different behavioral situations. an in vivo voltammetric study in free moving rats. *Brain Research., 397*(2), 395-400.

Lu, R. B., Ko, H. C., Chang, F. M., Castiglione, C. M., Schoolfield, G., Pakstis, A. J.,...Kidd, K. K. (1996). No association between alcoholism and multiple polymorphisms at the dopamine D2 receptor gene (DRD2) in three distinct Taiwanese populations. *Biological Psychiatry, 39*(6), 419-429.

Lu, R. B., Lee, J. F., Ko, H. C., Lin, W. W., Chen, K., & Shih, J. C. (2002). No association of the MAOA gene with alcoholism among Han Chinese males in Taiwan. *Progress in Neuro-Psychopharmacology & Biological Psychiatry, 26*(3), 457-461.

Lu, R. B., Lin, W. W., Lee, J. F., Ko, H. C., & Shih, J. C. (2003). Neither antisocial personality disorder nor antisocial alcoholism is associated with the MAO-A gene in Han Chinese males. *Alcoholism: Clinical and Experimental Research, 27*(6), 889-893.

Lucki, I. (1998). The spectrum of behaviors influenced by serotonin. *Biological Psychiatry, 44*(3), 151-162.

Lynn, P. M. Y., & Davies, W. (2007). The 39, XO mouse as a model for the neurobiology of Turner syndrome and sex-biased neuropsychiatric disorders. *Behavioural Brain Research, 179*(2), 173-182.

Lyon, M. F. (1961). Gene action in the X-chromosome of the mouse (mus musculus L.). *Nature, 190*(4773), 372-373.

Ma, Z. Q., Bondiolotti, G. P., Olasmaa, M., Violani, E., Patrone, C., Picotti, G. B.,…Maggi, A. (1993). Estrogen modulation of catecholamine synthesis and monoamine oxidase A activity in the human neuroblastoma cell line SK-ER3. *Journal of Steroid Biochemistry and Molecular Biology, 47*(1-6), 207-211.

Macmillan, R. (2001). Violence and the life course: The consequences of victimization for personal and social development. *Annual Reviews in Sociology, 27*(1), 1-22.

Maestripieri, D., McCormack, K., Lindell, S. G., Higley, J. D., & Sanchez, M. M. (2006). Influence of parenting style on the offspring's behaviour and CSF monoamine metabolite levels in crossfostered and noncrossfostered female rhesus macaques. *Behavioural Brain Research, 175*, 90-95.

Maestripieri, D. (2005). Neuroendocrine mechanisms underlying the intergenerational transmission of maternal behavior and infant abuse in rhesus macaques. In D. Pfaff, C. Kordon, P. Chanson, & Y. Christen (Eds.), *Research and Perspectives in Endocrine Interactions: Hormones and Social Behavior* (pp. 121-131). New York: Springer.

Mandelli, L., Serretti, A., Marino, E., Pirovano, A., Calati, R., & Colombo, C. (2007). Interaction between serotonin transporter gene, catechol-O-methyltransferase gene and stressful life events in mood disorders. *The International Journal of Neuropsychopharmacology, 10*(04), 437-447.

Manki, H., Kanba, S., Muramatsu, T., Higuchi, S., Suzuki, E., Matsushita, S.,…Asai, M. (1996). Dopamine D2, D3 and D4 receptor and transporter gene polymorphisms and mood disorders. *Journal of Affective Disorders, 40*(1-2), 7-13.

Manor, I., Eisenberg, J., Tyano, S., Sever, Y., Cohen, H., Ebstein, R. P.,…Kotler, M. (2001). Family-based association study of the serotonin transporter promoter region polymorphism (5-HTTLPR) in attention deficit hyperactivity disorder. *Am J Med Genet, 105B*, 91-95.

Manuck, S. B., Flory, J. D., Ferrell, R. E., Mann, J. J., & Muldoon, M. F. (2000). A regulatory polymorphism of the monoamine oxidase-A gene may be associated with variability in aggression, impulsivity, and central nervous system serotonergic responsivity. *Psychiatry Research, 95*(1), 9-23.

Marco, E. M., Adriani, W., Llorente, R., Laviola, G., & Viveros, M. P. (2009). Detrimental psychophysiological effects of early maternal deprivation in adolescent and adult rodents: Altered responses to cannabinoid exposure. *Neuroscience and Biobehavioral Reviews, 33*, 498-507.

Martinez, D., Gelernter, J., Abi-Dargham, A., van Dyck, C. H., Kegeles, L., Innis, R. B.,...Laruelle, M. (2001). The variable number of tandem repeats polymorphism of the dopamine transporter gene is not associated with significant change in dopamine transporter phenotype in humans. *Neuropsychopharmacology, 24*(5), 553-560.

Masi, G. (2004). Pharmacotherapy of pervasive developmental disorders in children and adolescents. *CNS Drugs, 18*(14), 1031-1052.

Mason, D. A., & Frick, P. J. (1994). The heritability of antisocial behavior: A meta-analysis of twin and adoption studies. *Journal of Psychopathology and Behavioral Assessment, 16*(4), 301-323.

Matsushita, S., Yoshino, A., Murayama, M., Kimura, M., Muramatsu, T., & Higuchi, S. (2001). Association study of serotonin transporter gene regulatory region polymorphism and alcoholism. *Am J Med Genet, 105B*, 446-450.

Matthews, K., Dalley, J. W., Matthews, C., Tsai, T. H., & Robbins, T. W. (2001). Periodic maternal separation of neonatal rats produces region and gender specific effects on biogenic amine content in postmortem adult brain. *Synapse, 40*, 1-10.

Maxfield, M. G., & Widom, C. S. (1996). The cycle of violence. revisited 6 years later. *Archives of Pediatrics and Adolescent Medicine, 150*(4), 390-395.

McCormick, C. M. (2010). An animal model of social instability stress in adolescence and risk for drugs of abuse. *Physiology & Behavior, 99*, 194-203.

McEwen, B. S. (1999). The molecular and neuroanatomical basis for estrogen effects in the central nervous system. *Journal of Clinical Endocrinology & Metabolism, 84*(6), 1790-1797.

McGeary, J. E., Esposito-Smythers, C., Spirito, A., & Monti, P. M. (2007). Associations of the dopamine D4 receptor gene VNTR polymorphism with drug use in adolescent psychiatric inpatients. *Pharmacology, Biochemistry and Behavior, 86*(2), 401-406.

McGloin, J. M., & Widom, C. S. (2001). Resilience among abused and neglected children grown up. *Development and Psychopathology, 13*(04), 1021-1038.

McGowan, P. O., Sasaki, A., D'Alessio, A. C., Dymov, S., Labonté, B., Szyf, M.,...Meaney, M. J. (2009). Epigenetic regulation of the glucocorticoid receptor in human brain associates with childhood abuse. *Nature Neuroscience, 12*, 342-348.

McGue, M., & Lykken, D. T. (1992). Genetic influence on the risk of divorce. *Psychological Science, 3*(6), 368-373.

McGuffin, P., Katz, R., & Bebbington, P. (1988). The Camberwell Collaborative Depression Study. III. Depression and adversity in the relatives of depressed probands. *The British Journal of Psychiatry, 152*(6), 775-782.

Meaney, M.J., Brake, W., & Gratton, A. (2002). Environmental regulation of the development of mesolimbic dopamine systems: A neurobiological mechanism for vulnerability to drug abuse? *Psychoneuroendocrinology, 27*, 127-138.

Meaney, M. J. (2001). Maternal care, gene expression, and the transmission of individual differences in stress reactivity across generations. *Annual Review of Neuroscience, 24*, 1161-1192.

Meaney, M. J., Diorio, J., Francis, D., Weaver, S., Yau, J., Chapman, K.,...Seckl, J. R. (2000). Postnatal handling increases the expression of cAMP-inducible transcription factors in the rat hippocampus: The effects of thyroid hormones and serotonin. *The Journal of Neuroscience, 20*, 3926-3935.

Messina, N., & Grella, C. (2006). Childhood trauma and women's health outcomes in a California prison population. *American Journal of Public Health, 96*, 1842-1848.

Meyer-Lindenberg, A., Buckholtz, J. W., Kolachana, B., R. Hariri, A., Pezawas, L., Blasi, G., Weinberger, D. R. (2006). Neural mechanisms of genetic risk for impulsivity and violence in humans. *Proceedings of the National Academy of Sciences, 103*(16), 6269-6274.

Miethe, T. D., Stafford, M. C., & Long, J. S. (1987). Social differentiation in criminal victimization: A test of routine activities/lifestyle theories. *American Sociological Review, 52*(2), 184-194.

Mill, J., Asherson, P., Browes, C., D'Souza, U., & Craig, I. (2002). Expression of the dopamine transporter gene is regulated by the 3' UTR VNTR:

Evidence from brain and lymphocytes using quantitative RT-PCR. *American Journal of Medical Genetics (Neuropsychiatric Genetics), 114,* 975-979.

Mill, J., Xu, X., Ronald, A., Curran, S., Price, T., Knight, J.,...Asherson, P. (2005a). Quantitative trait locus analysis of candidate gene alleles associated with attention deficit hyperactivity disorder(ADHD) in five genes: DRD 4, DAT 1, DRD 5, SNAP-25, and 5 HT 1 B. *American Journal of Medical Genetics Part B Neuropsychiatric Genetics, 133*(1), 68-73.

Mill, J., Asherson, P., Craig, I., & D'Souza, U. M. (2005b). Transient expression analysis of allelic variants of a VNTR in the dopamine transporter gene (DAT1). *BMC Genetics, 6,* 3-10.

Miller, E. M. (1986). *Street woman.* Temple University Press.

Moffitt, T. E., Brammer, G. L., Caspi, A., Fawcett, J. P., Raleigh, M., Yuwiler, A.,...Silva, P. (1998). Whole blood serotonin relates to violence in an epidemiological study. *Biological Psychiatry, 43*(6), 446-457.

Monroe, S. M., & Simons, A. D. (1991). Diathesis-stress theories in the context of life stress research: Implications for the depressive disorders. *Psychological Bulletin, 110*(3), 406-425.

Moore, T. M., Scarpa, A., & Raine, A. (2002). A meta-analysis of serotonin metabolite 5-HIAA and antisocial behavior. *Aggressive Behavior, 28*(4), 299-316.

Moss, H. B., Yao, J. K., & Panzak, G. L. (1990). Serotonergic responsivity and behavioral dimensions in antisocial personality disorder with substance abuse. *Biological Psychiatry, 28*(4), 325-338.

Munafò, M. R., Johnstone, E. C., Welsh, K. I., & Walton, R. T. (2005). Association between the DRD2 gene Taq1A (C32806T) polymorphism and alcohol consumption in social drinkers. *The Pharmacogenomics Journal, 5,* 96-101.

Munafò, M. R., Yalcin, B., Willis-Owen, S. A., & Flint, J. (2008). Association of the dopamine D4 receptor (DRD4) gene and approach-related personality traits: Meta-analysis and new data. *Biological Psychiatry, 63*(2), 197-206.

Murgatroyd, C., Patchev, A. V., Wu, Y., Micale, V., Bockmühl, Y., Fischer, D.,...Spengler, D. (2009). Dynamic DNA methylation programs persistent adverse effects of early-life stress. *Nature Neuroscience, 12,* 1559-1566.

Murphy, D. L., Uhl, G. R., Holmes, A., Ren-Patterson, R., Hall, F. S., Sora, I.,...Lesch, K. P. (2003). Experimental gene interaction studies with SERT mutant mice as models for human polygenic and epistatic traits and disorders. *Genes, Brain & Behavior, 2*(6), 350-364.

Nakamura, M., Ueno, S., Sano, A., & Tanabe, H. (2000). The human serotonin transporter gene linked polymorphism (5-HTTLPR) shows ten novel allelic variants. *Molecular Psychiatry, 5*, 32-38.

Nguyen, D. K., & Disteche, C. M. (2006). Dosage compensation of the active X chromosome in mammals. *Nature Genetics, 38*(1), 47-53.

Nishizawa, S., Benkelfat, C., Young, S. N., Leyton, M., Mzengeza, S., de Montigny, C.,...Diksic, M. (1997). Differences between males and females in rates of serotonin synthesis in human brain. *Proceedings of the National Academy of Sciences, 94*(10), 5308-5313.

Noble, E. P. (1991). Genetic studies in alcoholism--CNS functioning and molecular biology. *Psychiatric Annals, 21*, 215-229.

Noble, E. P., Blum, K., Ritchie, T., Montgomery, A., & Sheridan, P. J. (1991). Allelic association of the D2 dopamine receptor gene with receptor binding characteristics in alcoholism. *Archives of General Psychiatry, 48*, 648-654.

Noble, E. P. (1993). The D 2 dopamine receptor gene: A review of association studies in alcoholism. *Behavior Genetics, 23*(2), 119-129.

Noble, E. P., Gottschalk, L. A., Fallon, J. H., Ritchie, T. L., & Wu, J. C. (1997). D2 dopamine receptor polymorphism and brain regional glucose metabolism. *American Journal of Medical Genetics, 74*(2), 162-166.

Noble, E. P. (1998). The D2 dopamine receptor gene A review of association studies in alcoholism and phenotypes. *Alcohol, 16*(1), 33-45.

Noble, E. P. (2003). D 2 dopamine receptor gene in psychiatric and neurologic disorders and its phenotypes. *American Journal of Medical Genetics, 116*(1), 103-125.

Oades, R. D., Röpcke, B., & Eggers, C. (1994). Monoamine activity reflected in urine of young patients with obsessive compulsive disorder, psychosis with and without reality distortion and healthy subjects: An explorative analysis. *Journal of Neural Transmission, 96*(2), 143-159.

Oomen, C. A., Girardi, C. E. N., Cahyadi, R., Verbeek, E. C., Krugers, H., Joël, M.,...Lucassen, P. J. (2009). Opposite effects of early maternal deprivation on neurogenesis in male versus female rats. *PLoS, 4*, e3675.

Ostrer, H. (2001). Invited review: Sex-based differences in gene expression. *Journal of Applied Physiology, 91*(5), 2384-2388.

Ou, X. M., Chen, K., & Shih, J. C. (2006). Glucocorticoid and androgen activation of monoamine oxidase A is regulated differently by R1 and Sp1. *Journal of Biological Chemistry, 281*(30), 21512-21525.

Parsian, A., Chakraverty, S., Fisher, L., & Cloninger, C. R. (1997). No association between polymorphisms in the human dopamine D3 and D4 receptor genes and alcoholism. *American Journal of Medical Genetics, 74*, 281-285.

Parsian, A., & Zhang, Z. H. (1997). Human dopamine transporter gene polymorphism (VNTR) and alcoholism. *Am J Med Genet (Neuropsychiatr Genet), 74*, 480-482.

Parsian, A., Cloninger, C. R., Sinha, R., & Zhang, Z. H. (2003). Functional variation in promoter region of monoamine oxidase A and subtypes of alcoholism: Haplotype analysis. *American Journal of Medical Genetics, 117*(1), 46-50.

Passamonti, L., Cerasa, A., Gioia, M. C., Magariello, A., Muglia, M., Quattrone, A.,…Fera, F. (2008). Genetically dependent modulation of serotonergic inactivation in the human prefrontal cortex. *NeuroImage, 40*(3), 1264-1273.

Patkar, A. A., Gottheil, E., Berrettini, W. H., Hill, K. P., Thornton, C. C., & Weinstein, S. P. (2003). Relationship between platelet serotonin uptake sites and measures of impulsivity, aggression, and craving among African-American cocaine abusers. *American Journal on Addictions, 12*(5), 432-447.

Pato, C. N., Macciardi, F., Pato, M. T., Verga, M., & Kennedy, J. L. (1993). Review of the putative association of dopamine D2 receptor and alcoholism: A meta-analysis. *American Journal of Medical Genetics, 48*(2), 78-82.

Patterson, G. R. (1982). *Coercive family process* Castalia Publishing Company.

Pecins-Thompson, M., A. Brown, N., & Bethea, C. L. (1998). Regulation of serotonin re-uptake transporter mRNA expression by ovarian steroids in rhesus macaques. *Molecular Brain Research, 53*(1-2), 120-129.

Petronis, A., Gottesman, I.I., Kan, P., Kennedy, J.L., Basile, V.S., Paterson, A.D.,… Popendikyte, V. (2003). Monozygotic twins exhibit numerous epigenetic differences: Clues to twin discordance? *Schizophrenia Bulletin, 29*, 169-178.

Plomin, R. (1990). *Nature and nurture: An introduction to human behavioral genetics.* Pacific Grove, CA: Brooks/Cole Pub. Co.

Plomin, R., Lichtenstein, P., Pedersen, N. L., McClearn, G. E., & Nesselroade, J. R. (1990). Genetic influence on life events during the last half of the life span. *Psychology and Aging, 5*(1), 25-30.

Pohjalainen, T., Rinne, J. O., Nagren, K., Lehikoinen, P., Anttila, K., Syvalahti, E. K. G.,...Hietala, J. (1998). The A1 allele of the human D2 dopamine receptor gene predicts low D2 receptor availability in healthy volunteers. *Molecular Psychiatry, 3,* 256-260.

Ponce, G., Jimenez-Arriero, M. A., Rubio, G., Hoenicka, J., Ampuero, I., Ramos, J. A.,...Palomo, T. (2003). The A1 allele of the DRD2 gene (TaqIA polymorphisms) is associated with antisocial personality in a sample of alcohol-dependent patients. *European Psychiatry, 18,* 356-360.

Primus, R. J., Thurkauf, A., Xu, J., Yevich, E., Mcinerney, S., Shaw, K.,...Gallager, D. W. (1997). II. localization and characterization of dopamine D4 binding sites in rat and human brain by use of the novel, D4 receptor-selective ligand [3H] NGD 94-1. *Journal of Pharmacology and Experimental Therapeutics, 282*(2), 1020-1027.

Pruessner, J. C., Champagne, F., Meaney, M. J., & Dagher, A. (2004). Dopamine release in response to a psychological stress in humans and its relationship to early life maternal care: A positron emission tomography study using [^{11}C]Raclopride. *The Journal of Neuroscience, 24(11),* 2825-2831.

Pyeritz, R. E. (1989). Pleiotropy revisited: Molecular explanations of a classic concept. *American Journal of Medical Genetics, 34,* 124-134.

Reif, A., & Lesch, K. P. (2003). Toward a molecular architecture of personality. *Behavioural Brain Research, 139*(1-2), 1-20.

Reisig, M. D., Holtfreter, K., & Morash, M. (2006). Assessing recidivism risk across female pathways to crime. *Justice Quarterly, 23,* 384-405.

Renard, G. M., Rivarola, M., & Suárez, M. M. (2007). Sexual dimorphism in rats: Effects of early maternal deprivation and variable chronic stress on pituitary-adrenal axis and behavior. *International Journal of Developmental Neuroscience, 25,* 373-379.

Retz, W., Retz-Junginger, P., Supprian, T., Thome, J., & Rösler, M. (2004). Association of serotonin transporter promoter gene polymorphism with violence: Relation with personality disorders, impulsivity, and childhood ADHD psychopathology. *Behav Sci Law, 22*(3), 415-425.

Rinn, J. L., & Snyder, M. (2005). Sexual dimorphism in mammalian gene expression. *Trends in Genetics, 21*(5), 298-305.

Ritchie, T., & Noble, E. P. (2003). Association of seven polymorphisms of the D2 dopamine receptor gene with brain receptor-binding characteristics. *Neurochemical Research, 28*(1), 73-82.

Rivera, B., & Widom, C. S. (1990). Childhood victimization and violent offending. *Violence and Victims, 5*(1), 19-35.

Roberts, T. A., & Klein, J. D. (2003). Intimate partner abuse and high risk behavior in adolescents. *Archives of Pediatrics and Adolescent Medicine, 157*, 375-380.

Roberts, T. A., Klein, J. D., & Fisher, S. (2003). Longitudinal effect of intimate partner abuse on high-risk behavior among adolescents. *Archives of Pediatrics and Adolescent Medicine, 157*, 875-881.

Rodríguez, E., Ribot, J., Rodríguez, A. M., & Palou, A. (2004). PPAR-big gamma 2 expression in response to cafeteria diet: Gender-and depot-specific effects. *Obesity Research, 12*, 1455-1463.

Rogers, W. (1993). Calculation of quantile regression standard errors. *Stata Technical Bulletin, 13*, 18-19.

Roth, J. A., Breakefield, X. O., & Castiglione, C. M. (1976). Monoamine oxidase and catechol-O-methyltransferase activities in cultured human skin fibroblasts. *Life Sciences, 19*(11), 1705-1710.

Rowe, D. C., & Farrington, D. P. (1997). The familial transmission of criminal convictions. *Criminology, 35*(1), 177-202.

Rowe, D. C., Stever, C., Gard, J. M. C., Cleveland, H. H., Sanders, M. L., Abramowitz, A.,...Waldman, I. D. (1998). The relation of the dopamine transporter gene (DAT1) to symptoms of internalizing disorders in children. *Behavior Genetics, 28*(3), 215-225.

Rowe, D. C., Stever, C., Chase, D., Sherman, S., Abramowitz, A., & Waldman, I. D. (2001). Two dopamine genes related to reports of childhood retrospective inattention and conduct disorder symptoms. *Molecular Psychiatry, 6*, 429-433.

Rubinow, D. R., Schmidt, P. J., & Roca, C. A. (1998). Estrogen–serotonin interactions: Implications for affective regulation. *Biological Psychiatry, 44*(9), 839-850.

Rutter, M. (2006). *Genes and behavior: Nature-nurture interplay explained.* Malden, MA: Blackwell.

Rutter, M., & Pickles, A. (1991). Person-environment interactions: Concepts, mechanisms, and implications for data analysis. In T. D. Wachs and R. Plomin (ed.), *Conceptualization and Measurement of Organism-Environment Interaction* (p. 105-141). Washington, DC: American Psychological Association.

Sabol, S. Z., Hu, S., & Hamer, D. (1998). A functional polymorphism in the monoamine oxidase A gene promoter. *Human Genetics, 103*(3), 273-279.

Salisbury, E. J., & Van Voorhis, P. (2009). Gendered pathways: A quantitative investigation of women probationers' paths to incarceration. *Criminal Justice and Behavior, 36*, 541-566.

Salzinger, S., Rosario, M., & Felson, R. S. (2007). Physical child abuse and adolescent violent delinquency: The mediating and moderating roles of personal relationships. *Child Maltreatment, 12*, 208-219.

Samochowiec, J., Lesch, K. P., Rottmann, M., Smolka, M., Syagailo, Y. V., Okladnova, O.,...Sander, T. (1999). Association of a regulatory polymorphism in the promoter region of the monoamine oxidase A gene with antisocial alcoholism. *Psychiatry Research, 86*(1), 67-72.

Samochowiec, J., Kucharska-Mazur, J., Grzywacz, A., Jabłoński, M., Rommelspacher, H., Samochowiec, A.,...Pelka-Wysiecka, J. (2006). Family-based and case-control study of DRD2, DAT, 5HTT, COMT genes polymorphisms in alcohol dependence. *Neuroscience Letters, 410*(1), 1-5.

Samochowiec, J., Kucharska-Mazur, J., Grzywacz, A., Pelka-Wysiecka, J., Mak, M., Samochowiec, A.,...Bienkowski, P. (2008). Genetics of Lesch's typology of alcoholism. *Progress in Neuropsychopharmacology & Biological Psychiatry, 32*(2), 423-427.

Sampson, R. J., & Lauritsen, J. L. (1990). Deviant lifestyles, proximity to crime, and the offender-victim link in personal violence. *Journal of Research in Crime and Delinquency, 27*(2), 110.

Sampson, R. J., & Lauritsen, J. L. (1993). Violent victimization and offending: Individual-, situational-, and community-level risk factors. In A. J. Reiss, J. A. Roth & K. A. Miczek (Eds.), *Understanding and preventing violence* (pp. 1-114) National Academy Press.

Sander, T., Harms, H., Podschus, J., Finckh, U., Nickel, B., Rolfs, A., Schmidt, L. G. (1997). Allelic association of a dopamine transporter gene polymorphism in alcohol dependence with withdrawal seizures or delirium. *Biological Psychiatry, 41*(3), 299-304.

Schaeffer, C. M., Petras, H., Ialongo, N., Poduska, J., & Kellam, S. (2003).
Modeling growth in boys' aggressive behavior across elementary school:
Links to later criminal involvement, conduct disorder, and antisocial
personality disorder. *Developmental Psychology, 39*(6), 1020-1035.

Scheid, J. M., Holzman, C. B., Jones, N., Friderici, K. H., Nummy, K. A.,
Symonds, L. L.,...Fisher, R. (2007). Depressive symptoms in mid-
pregnancy, lifetime stressors and the 5-HTTLPR genotype. *Genes, Brain
and Behavior, 6*(5), 453-464.

Schepis, T. S., Adinoff, B., & Rao, U. (2008). Neurobiological processes in
adolescent addictive disorders. *American Journal of Addictions, 17*, 6-
23.

Schmidt, L. G., Harms, H., Kuhn, S., Rommelspacher, H., & Sander, T. (1998).
Modification of alcohol withdrawal by the A9 allele of the dopamine
transporter gene. *American Journal of Psychiatry, 155*(4), 474-478.

Schmidt, L. G., Sander, T., Kuhn, S., Smolka, M., Rommelspacher, H.,
Samochowiec, J.,...Lesch, K. P. (2000). Different allele distribution of a
regulatory MAOA gene promoter polymorphism in antisocial and
anxious-depressive alcoholics. *Journal of Neural Transmission, 107*(6),
681-689.

Schoots, O., & Van Tol, H. H. M. (2003). The human dopamine D4 receptor
repeat sequences modulate expression. *The Pharmacogenomics Journal,
3*, 343-348.

Schreck, C. J. (1999). Criminal victimization and low self-control: An
extension and test of a general theory of crime. *Justice Quarterly, 16*,
633-654.

Schreck, C. J., Wright, R. A., & Miller, J. M. (2002). Study of individual and
situational antecedents of violent victimization, A. *Justice Quarterly, 19*,
159-180.

Schuck, A. M., & Widom, C. S. (2001). Childhood victimization and alcohol
symptoms in females: Causal inferences and hypothesized mediators.
Child Abuse & Neglect, 25, 1069-1092.

Schulz-Heik, R.J., Rhee, S.H., Silvern, L., Lessem, J.M., Haberstick, B.C.,
Hopfer, C., & Hewitt, J.K. (2009). Investigation of genetically mediated
child effects on maltreatment. *Behavioral Genetics, 39*, 265-276.

Seccombe, K. (2002). "Beating the odds" versus "changing the odds": Poverty,
resilience, and family policy. *Journal of Marriage and Family, 64*(2),
384-394.

Sen, S., Burmeister, M., & Ghosh, D. (2004). Meta-analysis of the association between a serotonin transporter promoter polymorphism (5-HTTLPR) and anxiety-related personality traits. *AMERICAN JOURNAL OF MEDICAL GENETICS PART B, 127,* 85-89.

Shaffer, J. N., & Ruback, R. B. (2002). *Violent victimization as a risk factor for violent offending among juveniles.* US Dept. of Justice, Office of Justice Programs, Office of Juvenile Justice and Delinquency Prevention.

Shaikh, K. J., Naveen, D., Sherrin, T., Murthy, A., Thennarasu, K., Anand, A.,...Jain, S. (2001). Polymorphisms at the DRD2 locus in early-onset alcohol dependence in the Indian population. *Addiction Biology, 6*(4), 331-335.

Shannon, C., Schwandt, M. L., Champoux, M., Shoaf, S. E., Suomi, S. J., Linnoila, M.,... Higley, J. D. (2005). Maternal absence and stability of individual differences in CSF 5HIAA concentrations in rhesus monkey infants. *The American Journal of Psychiatry, 162,* 1658-1664.

Shih, J. C., Chen, K., & Ridd, M. J. (1999). Monoamine oxidase: From genes to behavior. *Annual Reviews in Neuroscience, 22*(1), 197-217.

Shih, J. C., & Thompson, R. F. (1999). Monoamine oxidase in neuropsychiatry and behavior. *The American Journal of Human Genetics, 65*(3), 593-598.

Shih, J. C. (2004). Cloning, after cloning, knock-out mice, and physiological functions of MAO A and B. *Neurotoxicology, 25*(1-2), 21-30.

Siegel, J. A., & Williams, L. M. (2003). The relationship between child sexual abuse and female delinquency and crime: A prospective study. *Journal of Research in Crime and Delinquency, 40*(1), 71.

Silberg, J., Pickles, A., Rutter, M., Hewitt, J., Simonoff, E., Maes, H.,...Eaves, L. (1999). The influence of genetic factors and life stress on depression among adolescent girls. *Archives of General Psychiatry, 56*(3), 225-232.

Silverman, J. G., Raj, A., Mucci, L. A., & Hathaway, J. E. (2001). Dating violence against adolescent girls and associated substance use, unhealthy weight control, sexual risk behavior, pregnancy, and suicidality. *JAMA, 286*(5), 572-579.

Simpson, T. L., & Miller, W. R. (2002). Concomitance between childhood sexual and physical abuse and substance use problems: A review. *Clinical Psychology Review, 22,* 27-77.

Singer, S. I. (1986). Victims of serious violence and their criminal behavior: Subcultural theory and beyond. *Violence and Victims, 1*(1), 61-70.

Sjöberg, R. L., Nilsson, K. W., Nordquist, N., Öhrvik, J., Leppert, J., Lindström, L.,...Oreland, L. (2006). Development of depression: Sex and the interaction between environment and a promoter polymorphism of the serotonin transporter gene. *The International Journal of Neuropsychopharmacology, 9*(04), 443-449.

Sjöberg, R., Ducci, F., Barr, C. S., Newman, T. K., Dell'Osso, L., Virkkunen, M.,...Goldman, D. (2008). A non-additive interaction of a functional MAO-A VNTR and testosterone predicts antisocial behavior. *Neuropsychopharmacology, 33*, 425-430.

Skuse, D. H., James, R. S., Bishop, D. V. M., Coppin, B., Dalton, P., Aamodt-Leeper, G.,...Jacobs, P. A. (1997). Evidence from Turner's syndrome of an imprinted X-linked locus affecting cognitive function. *Nature, 387*, 705-708.

Skuse, D. H. (2006). Sexual dimorphism in cognition and behaviour: The role of X-linked genes. *European Journal of Endocrinology, 155*(Suppl 1), 99-106.

Smith, C., & Thornberry, T. P. (1995). The relationship between childhood maltreatment and adolescent involvement in delinquency. *Criminology, 33*(4), 451-481.

Smith, L. J., Henderson, J. A., Abell, C. W., & Bethea, C. L. (2004). Effects of ovarian steroids and raloxifene on proteins that synthesize, transport, and degrade serotonin in the raphe region of macaques. *Neuropsychopharmacology, 29*, 2035-2045.

Smith, L., Watson, M., Gates, S., Ball, D., & Foxcroft, D. (2008). Meta-analysis of the association of the Taq1A polymorphism with the risk of alcohol dependency: A HuGE gene-disease association review. *American Journal of Epidemiology, 167*(2), 125-138.

Snell, T. L., & Morton, D. C. (1994). *Women in prison.* Washington, DC: Bureau of Justice Statistics, Special Report.

Steffensmeier, D. (1993). National trends in female arrests, 1960–1990: Assessment and recommendations for research. *Journal of Quantitative Criminology, 9*(4), 411-441.

Steffensmeier, D., & Allan, E. (1996). Gender and crime: Toward a gendered theory of female offending. *Annual Reviews in Sociology, 22*(1), 459-487.

Stein, M. B., Jang, K. L., Taylor, S., Vernon, P. A., & Livesley, W. J. (2002). Genetic and environmental influences on trauma exposure and posttraumatic stress disorder symptoms: A twin study. *American Journal of Psychiatry, 159*(10), 1675-1681.

Stoff, D. M., Pasatiempo, A. P., Yeung, J., Cooper, T. B., Bridger, W. H., & Rabinovich, H. (1992). Neuroendocrine responses to challenge with dl-fenfluramine and aggression in disruptive behavior disorders of children and adolescents. *Psychiatry Research, 43*(3), 263-276.

Stoff, D. M. Pollock, L., Vitiello, B., Behar, D., & Bridger, W. H. (1987). Reduction of (3H)-imipramine binding sites on platelets of conduct-disordered children. *Neuropsychopharmacology, 1*, 55-62.

Stouthamer–Loeber, M., Loeber, R., Homish, D. L., & Wei, E. (2001). Maltreatment of boys and the development of disruptive and delinquent behavior. *Development and Psychopathology, 13*(04), 941-955.

Straus, M.A. (2004). Cross-cultural reliability and validity of the Revised Conflict Tactics Scales: A study of university student dating couples in 17 nations. *Cross-Cultural Research, 37*, 1-26.

Straus, M. A., Hamby, S. L., Boney-McCoy, S., & Sugarman, D. B. (1996). The Revised Conflict Tactics Scales (CTS2): Development and preliminary psychometric data. *Journal of Family Issues, 17*(3), 283-316.

Stuewig, J., & McCloskey, L. A. (2005). The relation of child maltreatment to shame and guilt among adolescents: Psychological routes to depression and delinquency. *Child Maltreatment, 10*, 324-336.

Suarez, B. K., Parsian, A., Hampe, C. L., Todd, R. D., Reich, T., & Cloninger, C. R. (1994). Linkage disequilibria at the D2 dopamine receptor locus (DRD2) in alcoholics and controls. *Genomics, 19*, 12-20.

Surtees, P. G., Wainwright, N. W. J., Willis-Owen, S. A. G., Luben, R., Day, N. E., & Flint, J. (2006). Social adversity, the serotonin transporter (5-HTTLPR) polymorphism and major depressive disorder. *Biological Psychiatry, 59*(3), 224-229.

Swanson, J. M., Sunohara, G. A., Kennedy, J. L., Regino, R., Fineberg, E., Wigal, T.,...Wigal, S. (1998). Association of the dopamine receptor D4 (DRD4) gene with a refined phenotype of attention deficit hyperactivity disorder (ADHD): A family-based approach. *Molecular Psychiatry, 3*(1), 38-41.

Sweidan, S., Edinger, H., & Siegel, A. (1991). D2 dopamine receptor-mediated mechanisms in the medial preoptic-anterior hypothalamus regulate effective defense behavior in the cat. *Brain Research, 549*(1), 127-137.

Szyf, M., Weaver, I. C. G., Champagne, F. A., Diorio, J., & Meaney, M. J. (2005). Maternal programming of steroid receptor expression and phenotype through DNA methylation in the rat. *Frontiers in Neuroendocrinology, 26*, 139-162.

Tarullo, A.R., & Gunnar, M.R. (2006). Childhood maltreatment and the developing HPA axis. *Hormones and Behavior, 50*, 632-639.

Taylor, S. E., Way, B. M., Welch, W. T., Hilmert, C. J., Lehman, B. J., & Eisenberger, N. I. (2006). Early family environment, current adversity, the serotonin transporter promoter polymorphism, and depressive symptomatology. *Biological Psychiatry, 60*(7), 671-676.

Teague, R., Mazerolle, P., Legosz, M., & Sanderson, J. (2008). Linking childhood exposure to physical abuse and adult offending: Examining mediating factors and gendered relationships. *Justice Quarterly, 25*, 313-348.

Teicher, M.H., Andersen, S.L., Polcari, A., Anderson, C.M., Navalta, C.P., & Kim, D.M. (2003). The neurobiological consequences of early stress and childhood maltreatment. *Neuroscience and Biobehavioral Reviews, 27*, 33-44.

Teicher, M. H., Tomoda, A., & Andersen, S. L. (2006). Neurobiological consequences of early stress and childhood maltreatment: Are results from human and animal studies comparable? *Annals New York Academic of Sciences, 1071*, 313-323.

Thapar, A., & McGuffin, P. (1996). Genetic influences on life events in childhood. *Psychological Medicine, 26*(4), 813-820.

Thompson, J., Thomas, N., Singleton, A., Piggott, M., Lloyd, S., Perry, E. K.,...Court J. A. (1997). D2 dopamine receptor gene (DRD2) Taq1 A polymorphism: Reduced dopamine D2 receptor binding in the human striatum associated with the A1 allele. *Pharmacogenetics, 7*(6), 479-484.

Tourangeau, R., & Shin, H. (1999). *The longitudinal study of adolescent health: Grand sample weight.* Chapel Hill, NC: Carolina Population Center, University of North Carolina at Chapel Hill.

Todd, R. D., Huang, H., Smalley, S. L., Nelson, S. F., Willcutt, E. G., Pennington, B. F....Neuman, J. (2005). Collaborative analysis of DRD4 and DAT genotypes in population-defined ADHD subtypes. *Journal of Child Psychology and Psychiatry, 46*, 1067-1073.

Treister, N. S., Richards, S. M., Lombardi, M. J., Rowley, P., Jensen, R. V., & Sullivan, D. A. (2005). Sex-related differences in gene expression in salivary glands of BALB/c mice. *Journal of Dental Research, 84*(2), 160-165.

Türker, T., Sodmann, R., Goebel, U., Jatzke, S., Knapp, M., Lesch, K. P.,... Stöber, G. (1998). High ethanol tolerance in young adults is associated with the low-activity variant of the promoter of the human serotonin transporter gene. *Neuroscience Letters, 248*(3), 147-150.

Turner, E., Ewing, J., Shilling, P., Smith, T. L., Irwin, M., Schuckit, M.,...Kelsoe, J. R. (1992). Lack of association between an RFLP near the D2 dopamine receptor gene and severe alcoholism. *Biological Psychiatry, 31*, 285-290.

Tuvblad, C., Grann, M. & Lichtenstein, P. (2006). Heritability for adolescent antisocial behavior differs with socioeconomic status: Gene-environment interaction. *Journal of Child Psychology and Psychiatry, 47*, 734-743.

Uhl, G. R. Drgon, T., Johnson, C., Fatusin, O. O., Liu, Q. R., Contoreggi, C.,...Crabbe, J. (2008). "Higher order" addiction molecular genetics: Convergent data from genome-wide association in humans and mice. *Biochemical Pharmacology, 75*, 98-111.

Unis, A. S., Cook, E. H., Vincent, J. G., Gjerde, D. K., Perry, B. D., Mason, C.,...Mitchell, J. (1997). Platelet serotonin measures in adolescents with conduct disorder. *Biological Psychiatry, 42*(7), 553-559.

Unnever, J. D., Cullen, F. T., & Agnew, R. (2006). Why is" bad" parenting criminogenic? implications from rival theories. *Youth Violence and Juvenile Justice, 4*(1), 3.

Van Craenenbroeck, K., Clark, S. D., Cox, M. J., Oak, J. N., Liu, F., & Van Tol, H. H. M. (2005). Folding efficiency is rate-limiting in dopamine D4 receptor biogenesis. *Journal of Biological Chemistry, 280*(19), 19350-19357.

van Erp, A. M. M., & Miczek, K. A. (2000). Aggressive behavior, increased accumbal dopamine, and decreased cortical serotonin in rats. *Journal of Neuroscience, 20*(24), 9320.

van Goozen, S. H. M., Matthys, W., Cohen-Kettenis, P. T., Westenberg, H., & van Engeland, H. (1999). Plasma monoamine metabolites and aggression: Two studies of normal and oppositional defiant disorder children. *European Neuropsychopharmacology, 9*(1-2), 141-147.

Van Tol, H. H., Wu, C. M., Guan, H. C., Ohara, K., Bunzow, J. R., Civelli, O.,...Jovanovic, V. (1992). Multiple dopamine D4 receptor variants in the human population. *Nature, 358*(6382), 149-152.

Vandenbergh, D. J., Persico, A. M., Hawkins, A. L., Griffin, C. A., Li, X., Jabs, E. W., et al. (1992). Human dopamine transporter gene (DAT1) maps to chromosome 5p15.3 and displays a VNTR. *Genomics, 14*, 1104-1106.

Vandenbergh, D. J., Rodriguez, L. A., Hivert, E., Schiller, J. H., Villareal, G., Pugh, E. W.,...Uhl, G. R. (2000). Long forms of the dopamine receptor (DRD4) gene VNTR are more prevalent in substance abusers: No interaction with functional alleles of the catechol-o-methyltransferase (COMT) gene. *American Journal of Medical Genetics, 96*(5), 678-683.

VanNess, S. H., Owens, M. J., & Kilts, C. D. (2005). The variable number of tandem repeats element in DAT1 regulates in vitro dopamine transporter density. *BMC Genetics, 6*, 55-66.

Vaske, J., Makarios, M., Boisvert, D., Beaver, K. M., & Wright, J. P. (2008). The interaction of DRD2 and violent victimization on depression: An analysis by gender and race. *Journal of Affective Disorders*, (forthcoming)

Vaske, J., Wright, J. P., & Beaver, K. M. (2008). A dopamine gene (DRD2) predicts serious victimization and distinguishes between offenders who have and have not been violently victimized. *International Journal of Offender Therapy and Comparative Criminology*, (forthcoming)

Vaske, J., Wright, J. P., Boisvert, D., & Beaver, K. M. (2010). Gender, genetic risk, and criminal behavior. *Psychiatry Research* (forthcoming).

Vaske, J., Boisvert, D. B., & Wright, J. P. (forthcoming). Genetic and environmental contributions to the relationship between violent victimization and criminal behavior.

Vawter, M. P., Evans, S., Choudary, P., Tomita, H., Meador-Woodruff, J., Molnar, M.,...Bunney, W. E. (2004). Gender-specific gene expression in post-mortem human brain: Localization to sex chromosomes. *Neuropsychopharmacology, 29*(2), 373-384.

Vermeersch, H., T'Sjoen, G., Kaufman, J. M., Vincke, J., & Van Houtte, M. (2010). Testosterone, androgen receptor gene CAG repeat length, mood and behavior in adolescent males. *European Journal of Endocrinology, 163*, 319-328.

Virkkunen, M., De Jong, J., Bartko, J., Goodwin, F. K., & Linnoila, M. (1989). Relationship of psychobiological variables to recidivism in violent offenders and impulsive fire setters. A follow-up study. *Archives of General Psychiatry, 46*(7), 600-603.

Virkkunen, M., Goldman, D., Nielsen, D. A., & Linnoila, M. (1995). Low brain serotonin turnover rate (low CSF 5-HIAA) and impulsive violence. *Journal of Psychiatry and Neuroscience, 20*(4), 271-275.

Walsh, A. (1995). *Biosociology: An emerging paradigm.* Westport, CT: Praeger/Greenwood.

Walters, G. D. (1992). A meta-analysis of the gene-crime relationship. *Criminology, 30*(4), 595-614.

Wang, X., Trivedi, R., Treiber, F., & Snieder, H. (2005). Genetic and environmental influences on anger expression, John Henryism, and stressful life events: The georgia cardiovascular twin study. *Psychosomatic Medicine, 67*(1), 16-23.

Warren, D. E., Tedford, W. H., Jr, & Flynn, W. E. (1979). Behavioral effects of cyclic changes in serotonin during the human menstrual cycle. *Medical Hypotheses, 5*(3), 359-364.

Weaver, I. C. G., Cervoni, N., Champagne, F. A., D'Alessio, A. C., Sharma, S., Seckl, J. R.,…Meaney, M. J. (2004). Epigenetic programming by maternal behavior. *Nature Neuroscience, 7*, 847-854.

Weaver, I. C. G., Meaney, M. J., & Szyf, M. (2006). Maternal care effects on the hippocampal transcriptome and anxiety mediated behaviors in the offspring that are reversible in adulthood. *Proceedings of the National Academy of Sciences, 103*, 3480-3485.

Weaver, I. C. G., D'Alessio, A. C., Brown, S. E., Hellstrom, I. C., Dymov, S., Sharma, S.,…Meaney, M. J. (2007). The transcription factor nerve growth factor-inducible protein A mediates epigenetic programming: Altering epigenetic marks by immediate-early genes. *The Journal of Neuroscience, 27*, 1756-1768.

Welle, S., Tawil, R., & Thornton, C. A. (2008). Sex-related differences in gene expression in human skeletal muscle. *PLoS ONE, 3*(1)

Weickert, C. S., Elashoff, M., Richards, A. B., Sinclair, D., Bahn, S., Paabo, S.…Webster, M. J. (2009). Transcriptome analysis of male-female differences in prefrontal cortical development. *Molecular Psychiatry, 14*, 558-561.

Weiler, B. L., & Widom, C. S. (1996). Psychopathy and violent behavior in abused and neglected young adults. *Criminal Behaviour and Mental Health, 6*, 253-271.

Werner, E. E., & Smith, R. S. (1989). *Vulnerable but invincible: A longitudinal study of resilient children and youth.* New York: Adams-Bannister-Cox.

Westlund, K. N., Denney, R. M., Kochersperger, L. M., Rose, R. M., & Abell, C. W. (1985). Distinct monoamine oxidase A and B populations in primate brain. *Science, 230*(4722), 181-183.

White, H. R., & Widom, C. S. (2008). Three potential mediators of the effects of child abuse and neglect on adulthood substance use among women. *Journal of Studies on Alcohol and Drugs, 69*, 337-347.

Widom, C. S. (1989a). Child abuse, neglect, and violent criminal behavior. *Criminology, 27*, 251-271.

Widom, C. S. (1989b). The cycle of violence. *Science, 244*(4901), 160-166.

Widom, C. P., & Ames, M. A. (1994). Criminal consequences of childhood sexual victimization. *Child Abuse & Neglect, 18*(4), 303-318.

Widom, C. S., & Shepard, R. L. (1996). Accuracy of adult recollections of childhood victimization: Part 1. childhood physical abuse. *Psychological Assessment, 8*(4), 412-421.

Widom, C. S., & Morris, S. (1997). Accuracy of adult recollections of childhood victimization: Part 2. childhood sexual abuse. *Psychological Assessment, 9*(1), 34-46.

Widom, C. S., & White, H. R. (1997). Problem behaviours in abused and neglected children grown up: Prevalence and co-occurrence of substance abuse, crime and violence. *Criminal Behaviour and Mental Health, 7*, 287-310.

Widom, C. S., Weiler, B. L., & Cottler, L. B. (1999). Childhood victimization and drug abuse: A comparison of prospective and retrospective findings. *Journal of Consulting and Clinical Psychology, 67*, 867-880.

Widom, C. S., & Maxfield, M. G. (2001). *An update on the "cycle of violence"*. Washington, DC: National Institute of Justice, Research in Brief.

Widom, C. S., & Hiller-Sturmhöfel, S. (2001). Alcohol abuse as a risk factor for and consequence of child abuse. *Alcohol Research and Health, 25*, 52-57.

Widom, C. S., & Brzustowicz, L. M. (2006). MAOA and the "Cycle of violence:" childhood abuse and neglect, MAOA genotype, and risk for violent and antisocial behavior. *Biological Psychiatry, 60*(7), 684-689.

Widom, C. S., Schuck, A. M., & White, H. R. (2006). An examination of pathways from childhood victimization to violence: The role of early aggression and problematic alcohol use. *Violence and Victims, 21*(6), 675-690.

Wierzbicki, M. (1989). Twins' responses to pleasant, unpleasant, and life events. *The Journal of Genetic Psychology, 150*(2), 135-145.

Wilhelm, K., Mitchell, P. B., Niven, H., Finch, A., Wedgwood, L., Scimone, A.,...Schofield, P. R. (2006). Life events, first depression onset and the serotonin transporter gene. *The British Journal of Psychiatry, 188*(3), 210-215.

Wilhelm, K., Siegel, J. E., Finch, A. W., Hadzi-Pavlovic, D., Mitchell, P. B., Parker, G.,...Schofield, P. R. (2007). The long and the short of it: Associations between 5-HTT genotypes and coping with stress. *Psychosomatic Medicine, 69*(7), 614-620.

Williams, R. B., Marchuk, D. A., Gadde, K. M., Barefoot, J. C., Grichnik, K., Helms, M. J.,...Siegler, I. C. (2001). Central nervous system serotonin function and cardiovascular responses to stress. *Psychosomatic Medicine, 63*(2), 300-305.

Wilsnack, S. C., Vogeltanz, N. D., Klassen, A. D., & Harris, T. R. (1997). Childhood sexual abuse and women's substance abuse: National survey findings. *Journal of Studies on Alcohol, 58*, 264-271.

Wilson, H. W., & Widom, C. S. (2010). The role of youth problem behaviors in the path from child abuse and neglect to prostitution: A prospective examination. *Journal of Research on Adolescence, 20*, 210-236.

Wolfgang, M. F. (1957). Victim precipitated criminal homicide. *Journal of Criminal Law and Criminology, 48*, 1-11.

Wolock, I., & Magura, S. (1996). Parental substance abuse as a predictor of child maltreatment re-reports. *Child Abuse & Neglect, 20*, 1183-1193.

Wright, J. P., Tibbetts, S. G., & Daigle, L. E. (2008). *Criminals in the making: Criminality across the life course.* Thousand Oaks, CA: Sage Publications.

Xu, J., Burgoyne, P. S., & Arnold, A. P. (2002). Sex differences in sex chromosome gene expression in mouse brain. *Human Molecular Genetics, 11*(12), 1409-1419.

Xu, J., & Disteche, C. M. (2006). Sex differences in brain expression of X- and Y-linked genes. *Brain Research, 1126*, 50-55.

Yang, X., Schadt, E. E., Wang, S., Wang, H., Arnold, A. P., Ingram-Drake, L.,...Lusis, A. J. (2006). Tissue-specific expression and regulation of sexually dimorphic genes in mice. *Genome Research, 16*(8), 995-1005.

Young, E. A., Korszun, A., Figueiredo, H. F., Banks-Solomon, M., & Herman, J. P. (2007). Sex differences in HPA axis regulation. In Becker et al.'s,

Sex differences in the brain: From genes to behavior (p. 95-105). New York: Oxford University Press.

Young, S. E., Smolen, A., Corley, R. P., Krauter, K. S., DeFries, J. C., Crowley, T. J.,...Hewitt, J. K. (2002). Rapid publication dopamine transporter polymorphism associated with externalizing behavior problems in children. *American Journal of Medical Genetics (Neuropsychiatric Genetics), 114*, 144-149.

Young, S. E., Smolen, A., Hewitt, J. K., Haberstick, B. C., Stallings, M. C., Corley, R. P.,...Crowley, T. J. (2006). Interaction between MAO-A genotype and maltreatment in the risk for conduct disorder: Failure to confirm in adolescent patients. *American Journal of Psychiatry, 163*(6), 1019-1025.

Zalsman, G., Frisch, A., Lewis, R., Michaelovsky, E., Hermesh, H., Sher, L.,...Weizman, A. (2004). DRD4 receptor gene exon III polymorphism in inpatient suicidal adolescents. *Journal of Neural Transmission, 111*(12), 1593-1603.

Zalsman, G., Huang, Y., Harkavy-Friedman, J. M., Oquendo, M. A., Ellis, S. P., & Mann, J. J. (2005). Relationship of MAO-A promoter(u-VNTR) and COMT(V 158 M) gene polymorphisms to CSF monoamine metabolites levels in a psychiatric sample of caucasians: A preliminary report. *American Journal of Medical Genetics Part B Neuropsychiatric Genetics, 132*(1), 100-103.

Zalsman, G., Huang, Y., Oquendo, M. A., Burke, A. K., Hu, X., Brent, D. A.,...Mann, J. J. (2006). Association of a triallelic serotonin transporter gene promoter region (5-HTTLPR) polymorphism with stressful life events and severity of depression. *American Journal of Psychiatry, 163*(9), 1588-1593.

Zhang, K., Grady, C.J., Tsapakis, E.M., Andersen, S.L., Tarazi, F.I., & Baldessarini, R.J. (2004a). Regulation of working memory by dopamine D4 receptor in rats. *Neuropsychopharmacology, 29*, 1648-1655.

Zhang, T.Y., Parent, C., Weaver, I., & Meaney, M.J. (2004b). Maternal programming of individual differences in defensive responses in the rat. *Annual New York Academy of Sciences, 1032*, 85-103.

Zingraff, M. T., Leiter, J., Myers, K. A., & Johnsen, M. C. (1993). Child maltreatment and youthful problem behavior. *Criminology, 31*(2), 173-202.

Index

DATE DUE	RETURNED
JUN 1 4 2012	JUL 1 2 2012